THE
APOCALYPSE SEVEN

ALSO BY GENE DOUCETTE

❦

The Spaceship Next Door
The Frequency of Aliens
Unfiction
Fixer
Fixer Redux

TANDEMSTAR: THE OUTCAST CYCLE
Two Suns at Sunset
The Madness of Kings
The Ocean in the Sky

THE IMMORTAL SERIES
Immortal
Hellenic Immortal
Immortal at the Edge of the World
Immortal and the Island of Impossible Things
Immortal from Hell
Immortal: Last Call
Immortal Stories: Eve
The Immortal Chronicles

THE
APOCALYPSE
SEVEN

GENE DOUCETTE

A JOHN JOSEPH ADAMS BOOK
Mariner Books
Houghton Mifflin Harcourt
Boston • New York
2021

For information about permission to reproduce selections from this book, write
to trade.permissions@hmhco.com or to Permissions, Houghton Mifflin Harcourt
Publishing Company, 3 Park Avenue, 19th Floor, New York, New York 10016.

hmhbooks.com

Library of Congress Cataloging-in-Publication Data
Names: Doucette, Gene, 1968– author.
Title: The apocalypse seven / Gene Doucette.
Description: Boston : Mariner Books, Houghton Mifflin Harcourt, 2021. |
"A John Joseph Adams Book."
Identifiers: LCCN 2020023911 (print) | LCCN 2020023912 (ebook) |
ISBN 9780358418948 (trade paperback) | ISBN 9780358450290 |
ISBN 9780358450481 | ISBN 9780358419471 (ebook)
Classification: LCC PS3604.O89446 A86 2021 (print) | LCC PS3604.O89446 (ebook) |
DDC 813/.6 — dc23
LC record available at https://lccn.loc.gov/2020023911
LC ebook record available at https://lccn.loc.gov/2020023912

Book design & photographs by Emily Snyder

Printed in the United States of America
1 2021
4500824287

PART ONE

WHATEVERPOCALYPSE

ONE

Robbie

1

ROBBIE WASN'T SURE HOW HE ENDED UP BACK IN HIS OWN bed.

Not that this was an unwelcome discovery. He'd gone to his first bona fide collegiate keg party the night before—a staggeringly bad idea given it fell just before his first full day of classes—and drank . . . well, a lot. He wasn't sure how much; potentially enough to warrant measurements in gallons, but not enough to convince him he liked beer.

The party was in an off-campus apartment roughly six blocks from the dorm, so his being able to drunkenly stagger back to the room and then pass out on his own bed made plenty of sense. He just didn't remember doing it.

He rolled onto his back and noted that he was still fully clothed. His shoes were still on. He still had his wallet. All good things.

Then he took a look at the alarm clock. It had no display.

"Hey, what time is it?" he said—to nobody, apparently, as he was alone in the dorm room.

He had two roommates. He barely knew them, because everyone was a freshman, and it had only been four days since they had come together for orientation.

There was Nguyen, about whom Robbie knew only two facts: He was Vietnamese, and he groomed his own eyebrows with tweezers every morning, for no good reason. The other roommate was Taylor, who folded his underwear.

That was the extent of what he knew about them, up until he discovered there'd been some kind of power failure during the night. Now he could add "won't wake up their roommate even though he has an early class the next day" to the list.

He dug his cell phone out.

It was dead.

"Aw, come on."

He got out of bed, ignored the rush of blood that made him a little dizzy, and pulled open the dorm room door.

The hallway had no lights. It was daytime, clearly, but the only windows in the hall were at the ends, which didn't do much to help illuminate the middle.

"Hey, does anyone know what time it is?" he shouted.

No answer. He stepped back into the room.

"Well, this is crazy," he said.

It was a weird moral quandary. The sun was up, so it was evidently morning. Probably *early* morning, but maybe not. Could be, he'd missed his first Intro to Macroeconomics class already and was now well on his way to missing Freshman English. He should be grabbing his bookbag—which he'd packed the night before, after memorizing the locations and optimal paths for all his classes—and running out.

Brushing his teeth and getting a proper shower would have to wait, and he probably smelled a little funky in the same clothes as the night before, so when he got to class, he'd have to hide in the back or avoid talking to women until that situation was rectified, but it was all manageable; he just had to leave right away. The quandary was, he should probably be knocking on doors and letting everyone know the dorm had lost power.

Unless they had all gotten up and left already, in which case they didn't do for him what he was thinking he should do for them, and anyway, why was it *his* problem?

He walked around the side of the bed to grab his bag.

It was gone.

"Great."

Maybe the problem is that I'm in the wrong room, he thought.

The beds all had the same bedsheets, which not incidentally smelled like mildew. He didn't notice that the first few nights, but thanks to all the alcohol, his nose was going out of its way to call to his attention every smell that would trigger bad behavior from his digestive system. Likewise, the dressers were all basically the same, and the layout was a standard arrangement. This could be any room in the building; it didn't have to be his.

He opened a drawer, and no, those weren't his clothes.

"All right, Robbie, buddy, when you tell this story tonight it's going to be *hilarious.* Get it together."

He pulled open the door and checked the number: 315. Unless he was remembering it wrong—and he liked to think he had a very good memory—his room number had been 315 all week.

"Right room number, wrong building?"

He was in a section of Harvard called the Radcliffe Quadrangle. Robbie had only been inside one of the buildings—his own —but he could imagine a scenario where (1) all of the room designs in the quad had the same square footage and initial state, (2) he walked into the wrong building the night before but went to the right room, and (3) somehow gained admittance to that room and passed out on someone else's bed.

He decided what would make this *really* funny was if the owner of the bed he'd crashed on had also gone to the same party and later made the exact same mistake Robbie did and was now waking up in Robbie's bed, wondering where all his stuff was.

Yes, that would be funny, but this was not the time for funny.

There were few things in his life Robbie dreaded more than being late. This was likely due to some deep-seated anxiety going back to childhood, although he couldn't point to any trauma in particular. One of his first memories was being upset that he'd missed a television show in which he was deeply invested, because he and his mother were traveling and they didn't make it home until halfway through the show. He couldn't remember the name of the show, and he couldn't remember why they were traveling, so he always took that memory as evidence that he'd spent his *entire* existence fretting over being late and missing something.

Sleeping through his first class, then, pushed all the wrong buttons.

"Maybe it's a closed building," he said. He was talking to himself out of an instinctive need to fill up what was becoming an eerie silence. "That's it, they haven't put anyone in this dorm yet, because freshmen check in early. You've solved it, hero. Now let's get to class."

Except someone else's clothes were in the drawer. It couldn't be a closed building where someone also lived.

As preoccupied as he was with the death of the closed building theory, it didn't register right away that the place was no longer silent.

Someone was shouting. No, not shouting: *screaming*.

It was a woman, and she was screaming "HELLO??" over and over.

It didn't sound like they were on the same floor, but probably they were in the same building. Even then, he wouldn't have heard it at all if the place wasn't so quiet already.

Then he realized it wasn't just the noise in the building he wasn't hearing. There was no traffic outside, either.

Robbie grew up in rural Connecticut, surrounded by farms, a lot of open sky, and a surplus of quiet. He hated it. His joke when giving people directions there was *We live ten miles past the point where you're sure you'll never see civilization again.* When he got into Harvard, he was just as excited for a chance to live in a *city* as he was to go to the school in the first place.

Cambridge wasn't even that loud normally, but the sound of traffic going past his window was more exciting for him than it should have been.

Now that sound was entirely absent. So was all the other ambient noise the neighborhood was supposed to be making.

All except the woman.

Screaming.

He stepped all the way into the hallway, cupped his hands around his mouth, and answered back.

"HELLO?"

The screaming stopped.

Then: "Hello? Someone? Is someone there?"

"Yes," he said. "I'm here."

He had to shout, but a full-throated roar wasn't necessary. She must be on the first or second floor, he thought, just below him.

"Have you seen my dog?" she asked.

This question was just strange enough for Robbie to wonder if she was speaking in code.

"No?"

"You don't see a dog?"

"No, I don't see a dog."

"I'm missing my dog," she said.

"I'm getting that. My name is Robbie."

Introducing himself made little sense in the context of canine retrieval, but he felt it was time to move ahead, because he had stuff to do.

"And I'm late for class," he added. "Do you need, um, do you need help?"

"Yes," she said. "If you are not just a voice in my head, or a ghost, then I need your help."

The notion that he might be a ghost haunting a dormitory at Harvard University suddenly struck him as theoretically feasible.

"I'm not a ghost. Why would you even say that?"

"I'm sorry. I'm very worried about my dog, that's all. My name is Carol. Please come find me and we'll go to class together. I think I'm on the second floor."

He headed for the stairwell at the end of the corridor, wondering as he went how Carol could not *know* what floor she was on. He thought about suggesting she just look at one of the doors and tell him what room number to go toward, but it was only one flight.

By the time he reached the door's crash bar, he was convinced they were in an unused building. It had a certain not-lived-in feel to it, and there was a lot more dust than there probably should have been. Yes, there were clothes in the dresser drawer, but he was willing to excuse that if all the other available evidence supported his theory.

Maybe it was shipped with clothing in it, he thought. *Like the fake televisions in furniture stores.*

The second floor was no more notable than the third. The walls were brick, the doors were wood, the lights were out, and the hallway was empty.

"Carol?" he shouted. "You're not on the second floor."

"I'm not? Okay. Do you see a dog?"

"No dogs."

"Maybe the first floor, then."

"Is this some kind of joke, Carol? Because I already told you I'm late for class."

"No, it is not a joke. I must be on the first floor."

"Can't you just look at a door?"

"No, I can't."

"Are you trapped under something?"

"Your voice is getting louder, you must be getting closer."

He sighed, and went back to the stairwell, and down one more flight.

Carol was standing in the middle of the hallway. She was a short, thin Asian woman, with dark glasses and a cane.

"Hello?" she said when she heard the door open.

"It's me," he said. "Robbie, I mean. It's Robbie."

Sorry, I didn't know you were blind, he nearly said. He didn't say that, because somehow that seemed more awkward than any of the awkwardness that had preceded this moment.

"Nice to meet you, Robbie. I've been shouting for an hour and you're the only one who's come."

"You have a dog?" he asked. *Still awkward.*

"Yes, his name is Burton, and I don't know where he is. He should have been with me when I woke up. I'm worried something bad happened. Not just to him. Maybe we should go outside so you can tell me what I'm not seeing."

2

Robbie took her by the arm and walked her out of the dorm and into the quad.

Everything outside looked wrong. The grass was suddenly too tall, and it wasn't exactly grass. Rather, it wasn't entirely grass: There was crabgrass, moss, dandelions, and some other growths he couldn't readily identify. All of it had become so overgrown, the walkways were essentially gone. Then there were the trees. The ones that were still alive seemed taller somehow, although he'd only been in the quad a couple of times and couldn't speak with authority as to how *much* taller. Two dead trees also took up space on the lawn. One was upright, but clearly dead, as moss had overtaken it completely. The other looked like it had collapsed very recently.

Other than the strange overgrowth, it was a warm, sunny, breezy-but-pleasant September day, with exactly no human beings.

"So?" Carol asked. "What's happened? Where is everyone?"

"I don't know. Not here. Beyond that, I'm not sure. And it looks like whoever does landscaping for the university is on strike."

"What do you mean, 'not here'?"

"I mean, the entire quad has nobody in it except for you and me."

"Oh. Well. That's good, I guess. I think if they were here, they would all be dead, because they aren't making any noise."

She sniffed the air.

"It smells different," she said. "Not corpse-like."

"Honestly, I would tell you if there was a pile of bodies here. It'd be the first thing."

"*Earthy* I think is the word. Like a garden. Did the quadrangle become a garden overnight?"

"Yeah, I think it must have rained," he said. "It's like all the plants went nuts."

He turned around to get a better look at the dormitory they just exited, and realized, first, it *was* the right building, which meant ... well, he didn't know what that meant yet; second, the ivy on the outside wall had an overnight growth spurt, just like the rest of the plants. It covered the entire wall now, and half of the windows.

"Hey, did you wake up in your own room?" he asked.

"What an odd question. Did you?"

"I don't know anymore. The building's the right one, but the clothes in the drawer weren't mine and my stuff was gone. I have no idea what to make of that."

"That's interesting. You were at a party last night, I take it?"

"I, um . . ."

"Your clothes."

All at once, everything that was wrong with the morning disappeared from Robbie's brain, replaced by the embarrassing prospect that his body odor was intolerably bad.

"I'm sorry," he said. "I fell asleep in them, and I didn't have a chance to take a shower."

"It's all right. The truth is, I don't know if I woke up in the correct room. I do know I went to bed in the correct room. When I got up, Burton was missing, my electronics were dead, and my roommate was gone; I didn't stop to check the clothing in my drawers. But we can go back and find out, if you think it's important."

"No, it's probably not. Let's ... let's sit down and see if we can work this out."

He led her to a bench in the middle of the quad. Two rabbits ran past them on the way, and a large squirrel on a tree nearby decided to chirp angrily.

They sat on the bench in silence. Robbie tried to come up with a simple explanation. When that didn't work, he tried a complicated one.

"I've got nothing," he admitted. "This doesn't make any sense at all. Maybe they all . . . *went* somewhere. I mean, they had to, right? They're not *here*."

"All at once? With my dog?"

"I'm not saying it's reasonable, that everyone left at the same time, with your dog," he said. "I'm saying that's the only conclusion we have to go with right now."

Carol turned her head and listened.

"I want you to be honest with me, Robbie," she said. "You asked earlier if I was a part of some sort of joke, or prank, and now I have to ask you the same question."

"No, of course it isn't."

"It's only that . . . your perspective on this scenario is profoundly different from mine. You understand? Someone took my dog, and now you tell me there's nobody here aside from you. I don't think you were a party to the circumstances that took Burton from me, because that is a truly awful thing to do and you don't seem like an awful person. But just the same, the logical conclusion for *me* is that there are other people here, hiding, out of earshot. This is irrational, because I can't imagine a single situation in which it would be . . . *funny* for an entire campus to orchestrate a practical joke on a blind person. I choose to believe people are not this terrible. The second option is that they are all dead. But again, I don't smell death out here."

"That would be terrible," he agreed. "I don't even know how anybody would pull that off. There are no cars, either, right? It's not just the campus; this whole part of town is completely deserted."

"You're right; I haven't heard a car all morning."

"Well, the answer is, I swear, I'm just as in the dark about this as you are."

She smiled.

"In the dark," she said.

"Sorry, no pun intended."

"It's all right."

They fell silent again, waiting, perhaps, for someone to run up and explain it all so that they could get on with their day.

Robbie was stuck between the usual niceties one went through when meeting someone new—where are you from, what's your major, and so on—and the patent absurdity of their circumstance. He didn't entirely know how to proceed.

He pulled his phone out again, just in case it had recovered since the last time he checked. It had not.

"You don't have the time, do you?" he asked.

She laughed.

"Because you're late for class? It's only seven-thirty; you aren't late."

She held up her free arm to show off the featureless disk on her wrist.

"It's blank," he said.

"It's in Braille."

"But it says it's seven-thirty?"

"I checked it when you said you were late, so I could tell you when you arrived that you were not. And then I forgot to do that. But it was seven-fifteen then, so now it's about . . ."

She ran her finger across the surface of the disk.

"Oh," she said, "never mind."

"What do you mean, 'never mind'?"

"It still says seven-fifteen. My watch has stopped."

"I *could* be late, then."

"Yes, I'm sorry. But I don't think you're late."

Robbie could feel a vein pulsing in his forehead.

"You have no way of knowing," he said.

"You can't be late if the class is not happening. It appears we're the only people here, and I promise, I am not your professor. Ergo, you are not late."

"Hey, hey, wait: What if we're in a quarantine zone?"

She raised an eyebrow.

"What is your major, Robbie?"

"Economics. Not sure what kind yet. I was thinking of . . . Anyway, economics. You?"

"Bio. This is not how quarantines work."

"Wrong word, then. Some kind of . . . emergency, where they evacuated this whole area and they forgot us. Or maybe we're radioactive right now."

"What about Burton? They evacuated my dog, but not me?"

"I'm not saying it explains everything. It doesn't explain how someone else's clothes were in my dresser either. Hey, did you wake up dressed too?"

"Yes. I did."

"Do you remember going to sleep that way?"

She thought about it.

"I don't recall. It isn't something I ever do, yet . . . yes, I was already clothed. I didn't even think about it once . . ." She sighed. "I miss my dog, Robbie. I want to find him."

"I'm sure Burton's out here somewhere," he said.

Just then, he saw movement at the other end of the quad and wondered if he'd just managed to conjure Carol's dog into existence by uttering his name.

But it wasn't a dog.

"What is it?" Carol asked. "You stopped breathing. What do you see?"

There was a deer walking through the open field. It looked nervous, as deer tended to, but this was not the behavior of a wild animal who'd wandered into a metropolis by mistake.

"Carol, we have *got* to figure out what's happening," he said.

3

The walk from the quadrangle to the middle of Harvard Yard was barely a mile, which Robbie had already worked out. The way in could either avoid Harvard Square entirely—by cutting through Cambridge Common—or it could skip across the side of the Square, which required taking Garden Street straight down. Both routes involved concerning oneself with some measure of auto traffic, bike traffic, and foot traffic, which grew increasingly heavy and complex the closer one got to the center of the Square.

He'd expected cars, and knew to look for them. Conversely, he'd nearly been killed by a bike at least twice so far. They occupied the boundary space between pedestrian traffic and car traffic, they were silent, and they moved entirely too fast. After the second close call, he learned to check, even when he didn't hear or see any cars around.

He was still doing that as they headed toward Harvard Square, even though there was no evidence of human life in any direction. There were parked cars here and there, but they all looked abandoned: Even with the keys, he was pretty sure none of them was going to start.

Given all the traffic lights were out, that was probably not the worst thing.

Three blocks away from the quadrangle, they still hadn't encountered a single person, or heard an anthropogenic noise. But there were plenty of birds, and the deer he saw was evidently one of many.

Carol was walking in silence, with one hand under the crook of his elbow and the other holding her cane. It was odd enough for him, actually *seeing* all of this; he couldn't imagine what it was like for her.

"Maybe all the people were turned into animals," he said, as three squirrels ran past.

"You suppose Cambridge is under a witch's curse?" she asked. "If it works both ways, this could mean *you* are Burton."

He laughed.

"I should be terrified that this isn't the craziest idea we've come up with," he said.

"That's definitely the craziest idea. The quarantine sounded reasonable."

"I didn't mean that. I meant the one where you asked if I was a ghost."

"Oh. I thought that was also reasonable, because we had not yet met. Now that I can confirm your corporeality, it seems much more absurd, but context is everything."

"Unless we're *both* ghosts."

"Yes, that's still on the table."

He didn't think it was *really* still on the table, but decided that was largely because he didn't think he believed in ghosts. It wasn't something he spent a lot of time considering, notwithstanding when he was eight years old. Back then, ghosts were a major feature of his existence, and so were UFOs, dragons, and Egyptian mummy curses.

"Well then," Carol said, "let's find some people to haunt, shall we?"

4

There was a hotel a couple of blocks from the center of Harvard Square. It was situated across from the leading edge of the Cambridge Common, and was where Robbie and his parents had stayed when visiting the school during the application process. The stay wasn't necessary—the drive from their Connecticut home was under three hours—but his mom wanted to go sightseeing and his dad had a powerful aversion to night driving. Also, they could afford it.

It was a nice hotel; Robbie had thought it an interesting combination of quaintly old-fashioned and situationally modernized: oak desks and WiFi, rotary phones and giant flatscreens, tin ceilings and in-room coffee machines. He enjoyed the experience of the place, and thought about popping in again on the three or four times he'd gone past it during orientation. *Remember me?* he'd say, *I was in room 454 last summer. Just wanted to say hi.*

It looked completely empty now. The front doors were locked, and the awning leading to the street looked frayed. The restaurant attached to it was also empty, and likewise locked up. Both places looked abandoned, as if everyone decided to get out of town all at once, but in an orderly fashion. The chairs in the restaurant were still up on the tables, waiting for the morning shift to arrive.

There was a church next to the hotel. A placard out front listed the upcoming homily subjects. It hadn't been changed for a while—the dates were off—which seemed more like a lazy-pastor problem. Or they lost the key to the lock on the underside of the sign or something.

The place looked just as closed as the hotel, anyway, which was sort of a shame. The upcoming homily was called "Feeling Alone in the Modern World."

"Where are we?" Carol asked.

"In front of the church."

"The church. Which church? It's so quiet, I can't tell."

Robbie was suffering from a failure of imagination, descriptively.

"We're not in the Square yet, but . . . I dunno. The church. The church next to the hotel."

"There are three churches!"

"Are there?"

"Yes."

Carol let go of Robbie's arm and put her hand on the railing that defined the church lawn. She was getting upset, and he couldn't tell why.

"Okay," he said. "If there are three churches, we're in front of one of them. It's across from the common. Um. I don't know what to give you, for landmarks. Name one and . . ."

Carol started crying, so he decided to shut up. It was only a little gasp at first, but then it came on hard, in body-shaking convulsions that dropped her to her knees.

"Hey," he said, quietly. Maybe too quietly for her to hear. "Hey, it'll be okay."

She let go of her cane and rolled over until she was sitting on the pavement, clutching her knees.

Robbie was torn, because when someone you know is falling apart in front of you, you're supposed to hold them until they feel better. But he'd met Carol maybe a half an hour earlier, under perhaps the most ridiculous set of circumstances in history. It was not the best situation in which to gauge whether they had, in their brief time together, developed *that* kind of friendship.

He did not, in short, want to make it any worse in a misguided effort to make it better. Also, *misreading signals from women* was basically his major in high school.

He decided that sitting down next to her and waiting—for her to stop crying, or to run out of water, depending—was the best recourse.

Briefly, he considered whether he should be crying as well, and if not, whether there was something wrong with him. But the situation was so absurd, he couldn't fathom any resolution beyond *it's all a big misunderstanding*. He was sure his parents were just fine because the house was three hours away and therefore well outside of the sphere of influence that resulted in whatever this was. If anything, they were probably worried about *him*. Likewise, Gertie, his younger sister, would be enjoying her first week at prep school in Groton. That was *much* less than three hours away.

The situation didn't seem hopeless; it just seemed ridiculous.

"I'm sorry," Carol said, quietly. She'd taken off her dark glasses to wipe her eyes and was now staring at the space just to his right. "I need you to understand how hard this is for me."

"I do understand," he said.

"No, I don't think you do. I thrive on sound. I need to hear the cars going by, and the chirps of the walk signals, and the chatter of other people. Today was my first day of classes. Burton and I were supposed to be paired with a sophomore volunteer, for long enough until I could count the steps to my classes and Burton could learn the route. The volunteer's name was Derek; I first met him two days ago. Derek didn't show up this morning, and Burton is missing, and now I'm in an auditory bubble. All I hear is birds, and whatever's making that sound in the trees. I can't navigate using birds. I feel . . . *really* blind now. And I miss my dog."

"It's a squirrel. In the trees."

"That's what a squirrel sounds like?"

"I guess. Look, we just have to keep going," Robbie said, standing. "This isn't a big deal; we'll work it out. Meanwhile, I don't think you have to worry about not hearing things."

He took three steps into the street. Pointing out to a worried blind woman that on the bright side she wasn't going to get run over by a car probably wasn't the best approach, but he had no better ideas.

"It's too quiet," he continued. "I get it, but at least if there isn't anyone around, there's less to worry about, right? We can stand in the street if we want."

"Robbie . . ."

"You can try it too. We don't have to stick to the sidewalks and you don't need walk signals to let you know it's safe. Let's just walk right down the middle."

"No, be quiet—I hear something now."

"Not birds?"

"Not just birds, and not the loud squirrel. Something from that direction."

She pointed toward the corner, where Garden Street met Mason Street. Robbie turned in that direction, just in time to see the bike before it ran him down. He and the guy riding it both adjusted, thankfully in opposite directions.

"Whoa!" the cyclist said, nearly losing control before circling around to a stop a few yards away.

He did not look like the sort of person one might expect to see on a racing bike. He had on cargo shorts and sneakers with no socks, and a large black T-shirt that read MY IMAGINARY FRIEND SAYS HI. He looked like he'd be more at home with a game controller in his hand.

"Hey, guys!" he said, genially. "Did you sleep through the apocalypse too?"

Touré

1

Touré screwed up huge this time around: He'd promised delivery on code that was gonna take a solid thirty-six hours to hammer down . . . and then he left himself only eighteen hours to do it.

It was his own fault. It was *always* his own fault, but this particular assignment of blame underscored a larger character flaw, to wit: Whenever he saw all the steps needed to get from point A to point B, he got the time commitment wrong. He was *great* when asked to do something impossible, because then he came in early —usually earlier than everyone else—but the stuff that was right there in front of him? Not so much.

As his second-to-last ex-girlfriend once said, if you asked him how long it would take to cook a three-minute egg, he'd say, *About a minute.*

The screwup here was on a big job, with a firm deadline. It was super easy, and it paid well: the best of all possible combinations not involving a winning lottery ticket.

But because it was super easy, around when he should have been coding, he was down the road at the Science Fiction Interdiction, a bookstore with a too-clever name and a gaming dungeon. The dungeon was a gamer Xanadu, packed on most nights to a fire-code-threatening headcount, with a you-name-it collection of role-playing games.

It was fair to say his *real* screwup was going to the dungeon in the first place.

He didn't escape the Science Fiction Interdiction due to superior willpower and natural charisma, much as he wanted to believe that; in truth, he only left because they had to close the place down for the night. Then he raced home and got to work on the project he was supposed to have been halfway through already.

And yet, all of that was just the penultimate screwup.

He was about six hours into some fine work when he realized he was entirely out of stimulants. There was no coffee, soda, caffeine tabs, or energy drinks to be found in the place.

He tried to push through using sugar packets and toothpaste, but that really didn't give him the necessary boost, so after the third time he caught himself falling asleep at the keyboard, he bolted for the all-night spot on the corner.

That was the last thing he remembered doing before he woke up on the couch in his building's lobby.

Clearly, he significantly underestimated how tired he was.

2

Even without checking his watch, as soon as the sunlight hit him in the face, he knew he'd really stepped in it this time.

"Seriously, nobody could've woken me up?" he said loudly, for anyone in earshot. There wasn't anyone obviously around, but he liked to think they heard him from behind their doors, at least on the first floor.

He started working out stories that could justify how late his code was going to be as he took the stairs. The excuse he'd come up with was good enough—by the time he made it to his door—to buy him at least another day, and probably get him a sympathy card.

He just had to get back into his apartment . . . which he couldn't do, because the door was locked.

That should have been fine. When he ran out in the middle of the night, he sometimes relied on the door to the street to protect his belongings, thinking his neighbors—a harmless combination of grad students and retirees—wouldn't be awake, or if awake, not inclined to steal anything. But this time he'd locked it, which was cool; he had the key.

Except the key wasn't working. He tried it every way he knew how, including shouting at it and banging on the door. Briefly, he wondered if he was capable of knocking the door down entirely, but decided even if he was, it should be the *last* thing he tried.

He went back down to the first floor, around the corner of the staircase, and to the doorway of the building's super. His name was Mr. Elonzo, he was terrifying, and there was some evidence that he was actually a goblin. Touré never saw the man smile, but was positive if he did, he'd have pointed teeth.

He didn't like Mr. Elonzo, was basically the problem. Mr. Elonzo didn't like Touré back, and they were both cool with that arrangement. But now Touré needed Mr. Elonzo in order to get back into his apartment, and so he knocked.

When this didn't work, he knocked harder. Then he tried saying Mr. Elonzo's name loudly.

A lot.

By then, someone else in the place should have, at minimum, poked their head out to see what all the ruckus was. Nobody had, so it was possibly even later in the morning than he thought: Everyone could be at work, and/or wherever old people go during the day.

He checked his watch and quickly decided either it was two in the afternoon or his watch had stopped during the night. The third possibility was that it was two in the morning and a seriously unusual cosmic event was going on outside.

There was a spare key not involving Mr. Elonzo. Ducks had it, and he was only a mile away. Touré didn't know if Ducks was home, and the telephonic device necessary to find that out was sitting on the desk, next to his computer, on the other side of the door.

"To Ducks's it is," he declared, to all the sleeping, dead, or absent cohabitants of the building.

3

Outside was exactly the right kind of wrong to paralyze him temporarily.

He lived one side quest from the middle of Central Square, a place where the traffic was so bad that the only rational response to it was to move to the country and raise animals. But he was used to it, in part because he had no car, and had no real interest in driving one in the future, especially given the aforementioned traffic.

What was interesting was that everyone else apparently decided moving to the country was a good plan, overnight. They left behind the animals, though.

It was dead quiet, except for birds, and he never heard birds before in the middle of the city, regardless of the time of day. What movement existed was non-automotive in nature: squirrels, mostly, plus a few rats, and something that looked a lot like a bobcat.

No people.

He ran to the corner and found more of the same. A family of raccoons was walking down the median strip of Mass Ave., evidently going shopping. Ahead, a hawk swooped down to nab a chipmunk. Up a side street, there was a four-point buck just staring at Touré like the two of them were in the middle of an insurance company commercial. He was chewing grass from a patch in the middle of the road where there shouldn't have been any grass.

Likewise, there were climbing plants all over the sides of the buildings, and the sidewalks were riddled with cracks from an eruption of tree roots.

Nature had exploded.

And still, there were no people. Even the panhandle corridor—where all the homeless congregated to see who had any smokes left—was empty. Those dudes didn't have the money to get out of town, never mind head to a farm or whatever. It made no sense.

Touré kept running, from block to block, looking up and down every street for some explanation. A sign, maybe, like HIDE-AND-SEEK DAY STARTS NOW. TOURÉ IS IT.

He didn't stop until he reached the front of the twenty-four-hour store he should have been hitting the night before. It was a point of pride for the owner, Stefan, that this place never closed, for any reason, ever. Nor'easters, hurricanes, police actions, it didn't matter. Unless it was the end of the world, Stefan said, he'd have the place open.

It was closed. The conclusion was inescapable.

"Touré, my man, the world ended and you survived it," he said, to nobody. Because there *was* nobody. He was the last man left on Earth.

He sat down on a bench, and started laughing.

4

When he was a kid, Touré's parents made him see a psychiatrist to figure out why he hated them. (That wasn't, probably, how they'd pitched it to the doctor.) He didn't remember much about the guy, other than that he liked to play chess with Touré and ask leading questions. It was maybe three sessions before the guy decided Touré was just bored with everything, and then they got on okay.

The psychiatrist came to mind once Touré stopped laughing, which took approximately half an hour. He figured the doctor would call this a minor psychotic break, if there was such a thing as a minor one.

The doctor wasn't there, because he was dead now. Touré's parents had to be dead too, a fact he found a little sobering. It didn't have the sort of impact it was supposed to, though, for a well-adjusted adult human. Touré *wanted* this to be because he was a survivor who had no time for grief, but that wasn't right. The problem was that the idea was so new, and so enormous, that he was probably experiencing something like shock.

Maybe that was what the doctor would say instead, if he were able. The other option was that there was something deeply wrong with Touré, and he didn't want to go down that particular rabbit hole.

The next person he thought of was Ducks, because he and Ducks used to get in arguments about which of them would survive an apocalypse. It got really involved, and included flow charts and props. The great news was that Touré was right all along. It was a little anticlimactic, though, because he couldn't very well gloat about this to Ducks.

Touré decided then that he was jumping to conclusions. He

didn't know for *sure* that Ducks hadn't survived, and he didn't know for *sure* that he was really the last man on Earth. He was the last man on his *block*: anything more than that was prematurely hyperbolic.

So, he knew what was quest number one: Get off the bench and get to Ducks's apartment to see if Touré really *had* won the apocalypse challenge.

He did this—it wasn't far—and discovered a new problem, immediately.

The building was gone.

Admittedly, it had been a while since he and Ducks had hung out, but not *that* long. Not so long that receiving a quick *Hey, I had to move because they're demolishing my building* was an unreasonable expectation.

There was a sign out front saying the place had been torn down to make room for new condos, and that didn't make any sense either. Not because the old building wasn't a rat trap in need of demolition—it was—but because the sign said the new building wouldn't be ready for thirty years.

Touré decided this was a successful completion of the first quest anyway, because he had *arrived* at Ducks's apartment; it was only that the apartment failed to continue existing.

Quest number two: Widen his search parameters for signs of life.

There was a high-end bike shop across the street from Ducks's hole in the ground. Touré was not an athletically inclined person, but he liked riding bikes okay, and he knew how, and this place had a bike in its window that cost more than a small car. He used to go by it all the time wondering what made that bike so amazingly awesome that it cost that much.

This seemed like an excellent time to find out.

5

The super-expensive bike in the window he had to break to get inside was a different one than he remembered, but he tried it anyway, more for the price tag than the utility of it.

This ended up being an instructive error. He learned that most of the price corresponded to the lightness of the bike — it felt like it weighed less than his shoes — rather than the kinds of features he might personally value much more highly. Comfort, for example.

In addition to the lightweight frame, it came with razor-thin, puncture-proof tires. The puncture-proof part was an excellent idea, but the razor-thin component turned out to be a great feature only as long as the pavement was relatively level.

That was not the case anywhere around the shop. The roadway had developed potholes all over the place, apparently overnight. Likewise, the ground under the sidewalk erupted at random intervals, revealing soil and newly grown grass. Touré couldn't remember Mass Ave. ever looking quite this bad, in so many places at once.

After a block of travel in which he nearly fell over three times, he turned around and walked back to the store, in search of a more sensible option. He found a bike with fat tires — still puncture-proof — and a lot of springs. It felt as heavy as a small car, and that was fine.

Then he had to figure out where to go, to accomplish his current quest.

The largest nearby concentration of people would either be Newbury Street in Boston, or Harvard Square. From the bike shop, he figured it was about the same distance to either place; it was just a matter of going left or going right.

He went right, toward the Square, both because he was intimately familiar with the layout already and because there was a bridge between him and Boston. He didn't want to discover that the instantly crumbling infrastructure problem he was seeing on the Central Square streets extended to the Mass Ave. bridge. Certainly not while he was *on* that bridge.

The thing about being on a bike was that, at first, that was all he could think about: watching where he was going and making sure he didn't fall over and so on. This was especially true since the last time he rode one was when he was fifteen—a solid decade ago.

Having something so specific to concentrate on actually helped him deal with the fact that clearly he really *was* all alone, and this really *was* the end of the world.

That was always the fun part of planning for the apocalypse: It was hypothetical, which made it easy to ignore all the dead people and focus on the ones who hadn't died instead. But if he and Ducks ever took any of it seriously, they would have moved to a cabin somewhere and prepped.

Touré came to a stop just past the halfway point to the Square, in the no-man's-land part of Mass Ave. between Central and Harvard, to reassess.

Where he stopped fell between a closed bike shop (another one, because Cambridge) and an office building with a spin class gym on the ground floor. He used to find the fact that these two places of business were across from one another really funny. Today, it was mostly just sad, because the shop was locked and there was nobody on the spin bikes across the street.

The traffic light directly over his head wasn't working, which wasn't notable, because none of them was.

"You haven't seen *any* lights," he told himself. "The power grid is down. What causes the power grid to go down and all the people to vanish at the same time?"

There were no apocalypse scenarios in his mental playlist that included everyone dying without leaving behind a body. The power failure could be an EMP, but unless everyone else in town other than Touré had been a computer-generated hologram, that didn't help resolve the central mystery of the missing people.

He should have been considering a zombie version of the apocalypse, probably. That would mean everyone died, and then got up and went somewhere, which was why there were no bodies. It *nearly* fit the available info.

In that hypothetical, an entire city of zombies was only a couple of blocks away—he just hadn't stumbled upon them yet.

He didn't think that was going to happen, primarily because of the birds. There was no birdsong during a zombie apocalypse. That seemed obvious, although he couldn't come up with a reason why. Didn't make it untrue.

Probably not a neutron bomb, he thought. He knew almost nothing about them, except they were supposed to kill the people and leave the buildings. So that didn't explain the bodies vanishing, or how he neither died nor vanished—unless he was immune to radiation—and it didn't explain the birds . . . or the squirrels, or the deer, or any of the other animals running around all over the city.

Radiation killed wildlife, too, and there was a lot of wildlife about, so unless he fundamentally misunderstood what a neutron bomb was, that wasn't the answer.

As he climbed back onto the bike, he wondered how many more blocks it would take before he considered it proven that he was truly alone.

6

A few minutes later, Touré nearly ran someone over.

The dude was standing practically in the middle of the street, so it wasn't like the near-collision was Touré's fault. If there were still cops and traffic laws, he would definitely be in the right. Fortunately, there was no collision, because there was no ambulance to call, and the phone to call it on probably wouldn't work anyway. They also didn't have to deal with the irony of the last man on Earth accidentally killing the second-to-last man on Earth.

The guy looked like he was new in town. Every year, the colleges brought in a bunch of newbies who didn't know how to get around, dress, or just generally comport themselves in public. Touré dealt with them on the regular, because Central Square fell right between the Harvard and MIT campuses.

He was a Black kid wearing khakis and loafers, a collared shirt and a denim jacket. All he was missing was the too-heavy knapsack on a hunched back and he would've been Every Freshman on His Way to Class. A guy like this was not on Touré's mental shortlist of likely apocalypse survivors. More like *second zombie from the left*.

The Asian woman on the sidewalk, wearing some kind of pantsuit, was a bit harder to peg. They both looked younger than Touré, but for her, this didn't mean she actually was. Part of that was because she was a girl, and he was historically bad at figuring out the ages of women between puberty and thirty.

Basically, she could have been the same age as the kid she was with, or she could have been his teacher. He would have believed either one.

The woman didn't look right at Touré, which was weird up until

he figured out she was blind. That definitely put her off the apocalypse survivor shortlist.

"Hey, guys!" Touré said. "Did you sleep through the apocalypse
too?"

"The apocalypse?" the kid repeated. "Is that what you're calling
this?"

"Sure," Touré said.

"What's happened to everyone?" the woman asked. "Do you
know?"

"Are there other people?" the kid asked.

"Have you seen a dog?" she asked.

"One at a time, guys," Touré said. "But for real, I have the same
questions. Oh."

He turned to the blind woman.

"A dog, huh?" he said. "You're missing your dog?"

"Yes, did you see one?"

"No, I'm sorry. That must super suck."

"Thank you, yes, it does . . . super suck."

"But, look, I've been riding all over the place, and whatever happened, the animals all look okay. Better than okay, actually . . . like
there was . . . an overnight population explosion or something. I
mean . . . what I mean is, I bet your dog's just fine. If he's around
here, like, maybe we can call for him."

She responded silently, with a resigned nod, before slipping her
dark glasses back on and trying to get back up to her feet.

Touré got the sense that he'd interrupted an argument.

"So what happened?" the kid asked. "We were thinking everyone just left town and forgot to tell us, or . . ."

"Or a quarantine," the woman said. "That's what he was thinking. You're the first person we've come across, so perhaps there are
others and we're not alone after all."

"I don't know," Touré said. "You're the first people I've seen too. But yeah, solid reasoning. I'm not the last one alive now, and neither are you two, so we can scratch that off the list and work from there. Definitely we have to find some more people. But hey, maybe we should find someplace to sit down and eat first, huh? I'm starved. Who wants breakfast?"

7

Once it was established that both of his new friends—the guy's name was Robbie and the blind woman was Carol—were indeed new in town, Touré felt an obligation to take charge and pick a place to eat. This was stupid, of course, because it didn't matter how good the brunch was at one place versus another if both places were locked and abandoned.

Yet that was what he tried. He brought them the rest of the way into the Square, past the closed bookstore, the closed banks, the closed pizza place, and the closed convenience store, to the closest thing the area had to a proper greasy spoon.

It was closed too, but more than that: It didn't exist anymore.

"Damn, when did this happen?" he asked.

"It looks like a clothing store," Robbie said.

"Yeah, I know, but it was a restaurant, like, last week. Maybe. I can't remember the last time I came here, but it wasn't that long ago. Crazy."

"This seems very far down the list of our current concerns," Carol said.

"Yeah, but I loved this place."

There were a dozen other restaurants to consider breaking in to, but after the surprise of seeing his favorite one shut down, Touré began to appreciate that the hunt for proper food was going to end up being more involved than he'd thought. Even if they broke into a restaurant, they had no means by which to, for instance, cook an egg, because there was no electrical power. Maybe a gas stove would still work, but he didn't know enough about gas stoves to be positive that this was so.

"C'mon," Touré said. "I need some food in my stomach or I can't think straight."

They crossed over to the pharmacy across the street. Like everything else, it was locked, but thanks to the sudden deterioration of the sidewalk, a loose brick was easy enough to find.

"Are you sure that's a good idea?" Robbie asked. "I mean . . . Actually, never mind. It's a great idea. Let's get the police down here."

"No private property after an apocalypse," Touré said. "It's a rule."

Touré shattered the glass door and stepped through. Robbie and Carol followed, with Robbie guiding her carefully, over the glass.

We're going to have to find a safe place for her to camp out, Touré thought, seeing how much trouble Robbie was having just to get Carol past the glass. *We can't move very fast otherwise.*

It was the first time he considered their situation from a Darwinian perspective, and he hated that it had even occurred to him. He shoved it into the back of his mind, to be dealt with at a future point.

"Whoa," Robbie said, on his first look around.

"What is it?" Carol asked.

"The shelves are kinda empty," Touré said.

This was an understatement. The place had been cleaned out, from top to bottom, by someone in a hurry. Had it not been for the locked doors, Touré would have assumed this was the consequence of looting.

"I'm not certain I understand your concern," Carol said.

"I'm just adjusting the parameters of our apocalypse," Touré said. "This looks like what happens in an evacuation."

"Right, an evacuation," Robbie said. "That's what I've been saying."

"I think you need to stop saying that word," Carol said.

"Evacuation?" Robbie asked.

"Not you."

"She means *apocalypse*," Touré said.

"Yes," she said. "Something clearly transpired to which we weren't privy, for some reason, but I am far from ready to declare everyone dead simply because this one area has been abandoned."

"Quarantined," Robbie said.

"Maybe you're right," Touré said. "But until I . . . Ah-ha!"

Past the aisles, there was a second set of checkout registers, in front of which were a half-dozen candy bars.

Touré scooped them all up and shoved them into his pockets.

"Quest completed," he said. "Let's restore health and then work out what's next."

8

They settled on a bench near a shuttered newsstand, in the dead center of Harvard Square. The owners had pulled down all of the magazines in the windows and taken in the racks. The university bookstore across the street—the Coop—was similarly emptied out, with no books in the windows.

Touré began to get the unsettling idea that maybe he was in a hyperrealistic video game that they hadn't finished rendering yet.

"Here's what I'm thinking," he said, between bites. He was on his second Snickers already, while the other two were still just thinking about eating their firsts. The candy bar was incredibly stale, but he had generous standards of edibility. "The three of us must have something in common that can explain why we're still here and nobody else is. What were you guys doing last night?"

This didn't end up being a fruitful line of pursuit. Robbie was at an off-campus party the night before, near Porter Square, and Carol had gone to a reception at a Chinese restaurant on Mass Ave. She was in bed by nine, Robbie at some indeterminate time past midnight. And Touré had crashed on a couch around three in the morning. None of that left enough time for the entire city to evacuate.

But they already knew that.

Their extended life stories weren't any more helpful. Robbie was an African American from Connecticut, Carol emigrated from China as a child and was raised in Florida, and Touré was a second-generation Mexican American who grew up in nearby Jamaica Plain.

"Maybe we're all sick and we don't know it," Robbie suggested. He seemed preoccupied with a quarantine theory, at which Carol shook her head whenever he brought it up.

"Maybe," Touré said. "Seems sketchy. I don't feel sick."

"We could be, or we could not be," Carol said. "This is a waste of time. We have to stop speculating and find someone who knows what happened. Why don't we get a car and drive to where the people are?"

"We don't know where they are," Robbie said. "That's the point."

"We know where they aren't," she said, "which is a start. How far could they have gotten? I assume one of you knows how to drive."

"I can drive," Robbie said, "but I don't know how to start a car without a key."

"Neither do I," Touré said. "All the cars around here look like crap anyway. Not sure they would even start."

"You're holding out for a nicer car?" Carol asked.

"That's not what I mean. They look ... junky. Not up to the task."

"Then we'll find another way to contact the outside world," she said. "You boys are so interested in solving this mystery yourselves when there's no need. We'll ask someone who was awake when it happened."

Touré thought this was overly optimistic of Carol, but didn't say so. It was self-evident that the world ended and forgot to take the three of them, and that was that. She also wasn't wrong, though, for the same reason he'd taken the bike to go out and look for additional survivors in the first place. He wondered if it made sense to do this again: leave Robbie and Carol to make do where they were, and head further out. Not to discover the entire city of Cambridge was now hiding in Arlington, necessarily, but to see if he could nearly run over another survivor or two.

"We could find a radio," Robbie said. "One using batteries, since the power's out."

"I think we got hit by an EMP," Touré said. "I don't know what that does to radios. Killed my watch, and your phone."

"We'll know when we find someone who knows," Carol said. She turned to Touré. "You need to stop sounding so excited about all this and think about what our real situation is, especially if the three of us are the extent of who we can rely upon, for the near future. Until we find someone else, we're in a circumstance where we have no food, water, or shelter. It's pleasant out right now, but it will be colder at night, and we have no heat. Unless one of you was a Boy Scout, I expect we don't have the knowledge necessary to make a fire. Surviving this apocalypse you keep talking about isn't going to be so remarkable if we can't figure out how to last on our own beyond a week, whether we're the only ones left or not."

"I keep expecting someone to pop up and tell me this is all a joke," Robbie said. "Or I *was* thinking that, until we met you. If it's a joke, you aren't in on it."

"Nope," Touré said.

"But I agree with her; it's a big jump to go from nobody's here to nobody's alive. But for now, we should deal with what's in front of us."

"Yeah, okay," Touré said. "Food, water, shelter. Once we're settled down, we'll work out where to check for more survivors. You're both right; we need a camp. But we have a little . . . Hang on."

Touré stood up, turned around a couple of times to make sure he had his orientation right, and then started laughing.

"What is it?" Robbie asked.

"I think I found some more time in the day for everyone to have gotten out of town," Touré said.

"What do you mean?" Carol asked.

"It's supposed to be morning, right?" he said. "We agree on that?"

"We don't know *what* time it is," Robbie said. He said it like this was the worst thing ever.

"Yeah, but morning. Because we all woke up and it was morning, because that's when you wake up, right?"

"You're going in circles," Carol said.

"The sun's in the wrong place."

He pointed to the sun's current position in the sky.

"That's west," Touré said. "It's not climbing. It's setting."

Robbie stood and did some of the same calculations, albeit with different mental east–west markers.

"I think he's right," he said, to Carol. "I guess we're both *really* late for class."

Just then, they heard something that may have been a howl,

from hopefully a great distance away. It started off high, and then lowered into a more canine register.

"I don't suppose that was your dog?" Touré asked.

"No," Carol said.

The sound had an impressive impact on the local wildlife. Two deer ran past them, then up JFK Street, unconcerned about the nearby humans, but clearly alarmed about the animal howling in the distance. Likewise, an abundance of smaller creatures scampered across the open area in search of shelter. Touré was stunned by how many there were; it was like seeing a nest of spider eggs hatching. Squirrels, raccoons, rats, wild cats as small as housecats and as large as bobcats, chipmunks, possums, a couple of foxes, and a possible badger.

"What's happening?" Carol asked as a tabby cat darted past her leg.

"Um, not sure," Touré said as another howl sounded, from a slightly different direction.

"I think it's safe to say that everyone's afraid of whatever's making that noise," Robbie said.

"It sounds like a wolf," Carol said.

"It sounds like a *lot* of wolves," Touré said.

"Maybe we should step up our plans to find food and shelter," Robbie said. "Where's the nearest supermarket?"

Touré had to think about it.

"If we go that way," he said, pointing up JFK in the same direction the deer ran, "and dogleg left at the river, there's one a couple of miles further."

"Fresh water," Carol said.

"It's a river, so yeah, I'm pretty sure."

"I know, I wasn't asking. Access to a viable source of drinking water is of great value."

"Can we make it?" Robbie asked.

"Shouldn't be that tough," Touré said. "It's just down there."

9

They only got a few blocks before it became obvious that Carol's blindness was going to be a problem.

Touré had his bike still, which he was walking down the middle of the street at the same pace Robbie and Carol were moving. It wasn't fast, but she either couldn't run or Robbie wasn't willing to push her to go any faster.

"I can try jogging," Carol said, aware of the tension in the moment. It had less to do with any immediate, in-their-face threat than with the general atmosphere of panic surrounding them. Even the birds sounded tense. And the baying of the wolves was now coming from at least three directions, and seemed to be getting closer. On top of that, it was as if someone had shot the sun out of the sky, given how fast it was going down. This part Carol probably didn't know.

"Can you?" Robbie asked.

"Yes, if the surface is even. I used to run with Burton."

"No, there are potholes everywhere," Robbie said. "But we're fine. Hey, Touré, why don't you go on ahead?"

Touré stopped where he was. They'd made it as far as a parking garage he considered the symbolic end of the Square. He could see the bridge that spanned the narrow end of the Charles up ahead. He was pleased to see that the bridge was still there.

"You want to split up?" Touré asked.

"It's just down to the river and then left, isn't it?" Robbie asked. "I can find it."

"Yeah, it's hard to miss, if you keep the river on your right. It's still a good distance off, though."

"That's fine. We'll be fine. You go on ahead on the bike. It'll give you a few minutes to figure out a way inside without breaking a window."

Robbie had a point. The brick-through-the-glass approach worked great if you didn't mind who else got inside with you. But now that a predator had been introduced to the dynamic, it was hard to understate the value of an intact window and a closed door.

"Okay," Touré said, "but ... I mean, you've seen at least one movie in your life, right? Splitting up is, like, a textbook mistake."

"For goodness' sake, this isn't a movie," Carol said. "We'll catch up to you there."

"All right, all right."

He kicked his leg over the bike.

"Be safe, guys."

Touré took off.

It was actually sort of a great feeling, getting on the move, even though he was about ninety percent sure he'd never see Robbie and Carol again as soon as he made it around the corner, and he was probably not going to like the way that would play out. An unscientific survey of every movie he could think of led him to the conclusion that if anyone was about to be eaten, it was him. The lone character sent ahead as a scout almost never makes it back unless he's the hero. Touré liked to think he *was* the hero, but it was too early to tell.

Fortunately, as Carol took pains to underline, this was not a movie.

The air near the river was much cooler, although this could have been partly due to the impending sunset. The edge of the Charles was an absolute menagerie of waterfowl and land animals in need of water. Touré was thirsty himself, but—as good as Carol's point about needing a water source was—he would kill for a coffee or an energy drink. If he thought he was dying, he'd have some water. Otherwise, something with caffeine would be really nice.

He was a couple of blocks from the supermarket when a large cat—he decided on the spot that it was a cougar, but had no history with cougars to support the theory—charged across Memorial Drive (which he was biking down) and attacked a crowd of Canadian geese near the waterline.

A standoff ensued between the largest goose and the cat, and if there had been some sort of glass partition Touré could stand behind, he'd have stopped to watch. There wasn't, so he kept going.

He soon reached the supermarket parking lot, at the edge of which was a coffee shop that was just as closed as everything else in the city. It taunted him; he ignored it, and kept on the move, until reaching the main entrance to the market.

He hopped off the bike. The sun was in its full glory now, a simply gorgeous and very red sunset. Touré had to hurry if he wanted to find a way in without breaking any glass, but he became transfixed, temporarily, by the red sun.

Portent of doom? he wondered. *Or does that just work for comets?*

"Never mind, man," he said, forcing himself to turn away.

He checked the front door, which was locked. He'd have to find another way, and was about to when he wondered if it was even worth the trouble. The pharmacy had been looted clean. Why would it be any different here?

Leaning up against the window, he cupped his hands against the glass to block out the glare and peered inside.

What shelves he could see looked empty, all right, but there *was* something else in there. Something weird.

It looked like little cubes sitting on a pallet in the middle of an aisle. The cubes were unevenly stacked, and there was a sign in front of them that he couldn't read.

He had no idea what he was looking at.

"I should just break in," he said. "We'll find another place to camp out in the morning."

Then someone walked in front of the stack of cubes.

"Hey!" Touré shouted. "HEY!"

He banged on the window. The figure jumped at the sound, and turned. It was a teenage girl. He guessed she was no more than fourteen, but again, this was something he was bad at, and looking at her in the dying light through a tinted glass window did not help.

She walked closer. White girl, short black hair, tiny stature. He thought this was what an elf would look like, if elves were real.

"We're closed," she said.

"What?" he asked.

"I said, we're closed."

"Come on, you don't even work here."

She looked around.

"Says who?" she asked.

There was a loud howl from an entirely new direction: up the river, opposite from the way he had come, and very close.

We're surrounded, he thought.

The girl on the other side of the glass heard the sound, too, and looked approximately as alarmed, even though she appeared to be in a safe place.

"Come on," he said. "Let me in."

She stared at him for a few seconds, evidently making her own Darwinian-perspective choice. He tried to look harmless and trustworthy.

"Go around," she said, pointing to his right. "The side door."

He ran past the main entrance and around the corner, to a windowless metal door next to a dumpster.

It was locked. He tried to open it a dozen times, but it continued to be locked no matter what. It was beginning to look as if his entire day was going to be defined by locked doors when it swung open from the inside.

"Come on," she said.

He thanked her and stepped into the near-total darkness of the grocery store.

"I'm Touré," he said, holding out his hand. "Thanks."

"Bethany, and you're welcome," she said, without returning the handshake. She walked past him and back to the front of the store. The sunset lit up the front window; the red made it look like the river was on fire.

"How'd you get in?" he asked.

"I picked the lock. Figured you were here to tell me I was trespassing, but that's dumb, huh? The world ended or something."

"I've got two friends on their way here; we'll have to let them in too."

"Close friends?" she asked.

There was something pacing around at the far end of the lot. It was on all fours, and moved somewhat like a dog would be expected to move, except it wasn't a dog. It looked to him like it was the size of a horse, although there was nothing for scale.

It howled.

"I just met them a couple of hours ago," he said.

"Okay, because between you and me, I don't think they're gonna make it."

Carol

1

It sounded as if she was in the middle of a stampede of ruminants, fleeing the predatory equivalent of a forest fire. There was no fire, and there was no forest, but there was something just as bad out there.

A wolf, surely. It almost howled like one. Carol's prior experience with howling canines involved listening to the nature channel on weeknights. According to Touré's theory regarding their current predicament, this would make her the world's leading expert in howling, if only by process of elimination. Her own expert opinion was that the sound came in too high to be a wolf. A hyena was a little closer, but also wrong.

Wolf*like*, then.

She also couldn't imagine wolves hunting in the middle of a city, but since deer running about in the city *also* made no sense, essentially nothing about this met the minimum rational vigor, and yet appeared to be true nonetheless.

"Careful," Robbie said, without telling her what she was supposed to be careful about. They were walking alarmingly fast, but the frequency with which he stopped in order to lead her around an obstacle was so high that she had begun to question the wisdom of his chosen pace.

But there was a lot he wasn't telling her, either because there was no time to describe it all or because he didn't want her to become unnecessarily concerned. She could feel his pulse, though, through the wrist she was holding on to, and it was elevated.

"You're worried," she said. "We can't have much farther to go."

"I don't think we do, but the sun is going down," he said. "It's happening fast; I can't believe we didn't notice sooner."

"It has been a day of alarming things. The directionality of the sun wasn't near the top of the list of concerns."

"Yeah, but . . . I just don't understand. Whoops, hang on."

They stopped. She heard a creature with hooves walking ahead of them, left to right. A little further up the road, she heard the low growl of a cat. Above, a squirrel scampered among the branches. To their right, something made a sound like a trumpet.

"Deer crossing," he whispered.

"I gathered. Just one?"

"Just one. I don't think it'll attack, but I also don't want to be wrong. Okay, we can go again."

"What is it you don't understand?" she asked.

He chose a pace that was just short of a jog.

"The clock in my head shouldn't have been this off," he said. "I mean, I've been known to oversleep after drinking, but not past noon. I've *never* slept past noon, not *once*. I'm the guy who wakes up before the alarm during the week, and at the same time without the alarm on the weekend. My mental clock's all messed up."

There was a new barrage of wolf howls coming from behind them. It sounded like a call-and-response, as if they were talking to one another. It remained quite distant, but spurred Robbie to up their pace nonetheless.

"Is there a tiger to our right?" Carol asked. Whatever was purring a moment earlier had begun to walk alongside them.

"No," he said. "Mountain lion, maybe."

"There are no mountains here."

"Yeah, I know. It's a cat, and it's big. I don't think it wants to be our friend."

"Perhaps you should find a place to hide me, and then run ahead," she said. "To protect yourself. You can come back in the morning."

"Don't be ridiculous."

Just then, there was a new almost-wolf howl, only louder, and in front of them.

"Crap," Robbie said.

"What is it?"

"Um. Carol, I don't know how to . . . Is it all right if I picked you up?"

"Do you think you're strong enough to carry me?"

"Fireman's carry. I'll throw you over my shoulder."

"If you feel that's necessary . . ."

"I do."

"Then do it."

He grabbed her cane with one hand, then wrapped his arm around her waist and dug his shoulder into her stomach, tilted and lifted. It wasn't at all comfortable for her, and probably was no more so for him, largely because he didn't seem to have broad enough shoulders to accomplish this maneuver. However, once he started running it became clear that this would be a faster approach, provided his strength held out.

They weren't heading down the road, however. She was having a tremendously difficult time keeping track of where anything was, but it seemed like he'd changed course. This was confirmed a few seconds later when she heard a gate open and close. Then he was putting her down again. He pulled both of them into a crouch.

"What—"

"Shhh," he said. "Something's coming."

She reached out and touched the metal bars of the gate he'd taken them through. Wrought iron, flecked paint—cold and sturdy. She felt her way along the bars until she reached the hinge, and then the brick on the other side. It was a walled-in courtyard.

There was an eruption of activity near the river. She heard birds take flight, the cat's purr turn into an enraged roar, and the scampering of hundreds of little feet. There was the clip-clop of hooves on the pavement, as at least one deer successfully fled. Another was not so lucky.

The sound of the deer dying was terrible. It emitted a grunt that turned into a shriek while its legs and feet clapped out of rhythm on the tarmac, a frightened tap dancer stuck in a closet.

What was killing it made hardly any noise at all, which was perhaps the most frightening element of the whole horrible scenario. She heard jaws close on flesh, heavy breathing, and bass-tone growls of at least two, maybe three animals.

They hunt in packs, she thought, *but kill in silence.*

She found Robbie's hand, and squeezed it tightly.

"How many?" she whispered.

"Three," he said. "I think. Two of them came out of nowhere."

"What are they?"

"It's hard to see them; the sun's gone down. Wolves, or close enough. Big ones."

"All the people are gone and the streets are overrun by packs of wolf-monsters. Is that what we're saying now?"

"Shhh."

He squeezed her hand tight, and she heard him stop breathing —voluntarily; he was holding it. There was a slight rustle of movement from Robbie, and then his hand was on her shoulder and he was gently pushing her backwards.

Then she understood why.

There was a noise Burton used to make when he sniffed an odor that displeased him in some way, a sharp exhale through his nose that sounded a little like *humph*.

She heard that same sound, just as Robbie was making an effort to move her away from the fence. She felt the hot breath of the animal on her free hand.

There was a wolf on the other side of the gate.

She wrapped an arm around Robbie's neck and put her lips up to his ear.

"Can it jump over?" she asked.

"I don't know. Maybe."

The beast dug at the ground, sniffed the air some more, and paced along the fence.

It felt large. Carol's interaction with the world didn't include sight, but her other senses were usually pretty good about assembling a loose approximation. Air displacement, perhaps, coupled with the smell of its breath and the sound of its heavy footfall, or the fur rubbing against the bars of the gate. The aggregation of what her other senses told her was that there was a massive hellbeast just a few feet away.

The rational side of her brain—which still had a voice, albeit a quiet one—suggested perhaps her imagination was acting as an extra sense in this case.

It's just a large puppy, she thought. *Think of it as just a large puppy.*

"Okay," Robbie said, after they sat there, as still as possible, taking turns holding their breath, for about a hundred years. "I think it's gone."

They were sitting on grass. The ground was cool and damp from a recent rain she couldn't recall. Her pants might be muddy now, and she had no way to get to a change of clothing for possibly the remainder of her life. They were her good slacks, too.

She couldn't decide what was more frustrating: that she hadn't chosen more sensible clothes for the end of the world, or that she cared.

She heard Robbie get to his feet, so she held out her hand and let him pull her up as well. He handed back her cane.

"Sorry about all that," he said. "That was close."

"Don't apologize. Thank you. Where are we?"

"One of the Harvard buildings fronting the river. It has a walled-off yard. I went by this place during orientation, but the gate had an electronic lock. I took a chance that whatever killed the rest of the power around here also killed the lock. Good thing I was right, huh?"

"Yes. I think we should stay here for the evening. Unless you think it's safe to push forward."

"No, I can barely see my hand in front of my face right now, and those wolves are still out there," he said. "There's no moon tonight, and the stars aren't doing much. Maybe *you* should be leading *me*."

There was more howling at the river, which could mean more wolf-monsters on their way, to share the kill. Carol wondered how long it would be before one of them tried to jump over the brick wall for fresh meat.

Waiting for that to happen would be a horrible way to spend the night.

"It's a building courtyard," she said. "Let's see about getting into the building."

2

The lock at the gate wasn't the only thing to have been disabled by the power outage. All it took to get into the building was a twist of a knob.

It was a musty place. That was Carol's entire experience with it, initially.

"What do you see?" she asked.

"Nothing," Robbie said. "There's no lighting in here. I can almost make out a table in the middle. I really can't believe how dark it is without electricity. We're going to have to find power or make a fire."

"I have a wall on my right," she said. "Why don't I make my way around in this direction and you go the other way, and we'll work out together what kind of room this is?"

"That hardly seems fair; I don't have a cane."

She laughed.

"You're right, that's not fair at all."

She headed to the right, slowly, feeling her way around. The room sounded high-ceilinged, which automatically excluded a number of options: They weren't in a classroom, or a dorm room, or a kitchen.

The wood trim on the wall was finished, but covered in a thin layer of dust. She found a table against a wall, which was similarly covered in dust.

There was a loud noise on the other side of the room that made her jump: a metallic clatter, and then a thud of someone falling over.

"I'm okay," Robbie said. "I tripped."

"What did you trip on?"

"I don't know. I didn't see it, and I still don't."

"Feel your way back to it—that sounded interesting."

"Okay."

He shuffled around on the floor for a few seconds.

"Nope, not interesting," he said. "It's a freestanding light. I'm surprised I didn't knock it over. How are you doing over there?"

"I'm wondering if this building was in use. There's so much dust."

"That's what I thought about the dorm," he said. "Maybe Harvard's just dusty. It's old enough."

She came upon a glass display case. It was shaped like a dome, covering something she would have needed eyesight to discern.

"I think we're in a museum," she said.

"What do you have?"

"A case. I think I'd have to break it to find what's inside."

"Oh, I bet we're in one of the common rooms. Whoops."

"What happened?" she asked.

"Yep, common room. I found a couch."

He coughed.

"You're right, there's a lot of dust," he said. "What are we looking for?"

"I don't actually know," she said. "Something useful."

"Yes, but like what?"

She sighed.

"Robbie, we have such a long list of needs, almost anything would qualify. Food, water, shelter, communication with the outside world, a rational explanation for all of this . . ."

"A toilet."

"Yes, a toilet, and a shower, and a change of clothes, and my dog."

"I can get you a wolf."

She didn't answer that.

"I'm sorry," he said. "That was insensitive; it's been a really long day, and it feels like it's only supposed to be half over."

"It's okay. Yes, we slept in, didn't we?" She felt along the edge of the glass for a latch or a hinge, but if there was one, she was checking the wrong place for it. "When I mentioned this case," she said, "why did that make you think we were in a common room?"

"On my tour, I saw a couple of the nicer dorms. They had stuff under glass in some of the common areas. I think they were just showing off. I figured they took it all back to the museum, or wherever they came from, during the year, but maybe not. I bet there's a pool table around here somewhere."

"Do you think this dorm has a cafeteria?" she asked.

"Don't know. You want to stumble around in the dark where there are knives? Maybe we should wait until morning."

"Water. Food."

"Yes. Right. Water and food. Sorry. You know, I keep expecting to wake up from all of this. Like maybe I can force it if I just lie down right here. Tomorrow will be a nice normal day, and I can go for a bagel and a coffee and forget this ever happened."

"In the morning, you'll just be more dehydrated," she said. "Which will make it even more difficult to function."

"Ah, but in the morning, I will be gifted with the power of sight."

"And I will not."

"Yeah, I know."

She found her way to the couch and sat down next to him. A puff of dust signaled her arrival.

"It was a joke," he said.

"Yes, I didn't take it personally. I'm just not feeling amused right now. What if you aren't *here* in the morning? I would like to know my way around enough to locate water. We can survive for days without food, but not water."

"Why wouldn't I be here in the morning? Of course I'll be here."

"Burton wasn't," she said. "Please, Robbie."

"Yeah, okay."

He stood up. She reached out and found the hand he was offering.

"I'm not tired yet anyway," he said. "Let's go break some shins
and find some water."

3

If the building had a full cafeteria, they never found it. What they
did find, after about an hour of searching, was a public restroom.

There were two, but only one had running water. It tasted clean
enough to drink, which was miraculous. The toilets flushed too. It
was the first sign that the infrastructure collapse they'd spent the
whole day witnessing wasn't actually complete and total.

They didn't find any food, which their bodies started craving
just as soon as they got some water down. But between them they
had one and three quarters candy bars from Touré's haul, and that
would have to do until morning.

"Protein," Carol said. "We are going to need a long-term source
for protein."

"Think we should learn how to hunt?" Robbie asked between
bites of his seven-eighths of a candy bar.

"Barring other viable options, yes."

He laughed. "That's why I suggested the supermarket earlier.
I know the pharmacy was stripped down, but there's got to be a
meat locker or something. It can't *all* be gone."

"There's no power for this proposed meat locker."

"Yeah, one problem at a time," Robbie said. "I'm saying we don't
need to go full native right off the bat, here. Not sure any of us is
equipped with the know-how to assemble a bow and arrow, or
whatever, but we don't have to be. We'll figure out where everyone
went and work this out."

The functional bathroom was on a corridor off of the common room. On the other end of that corridor they discovered a private office with a couch and an easy chair, along with a desk/chair combo. It came with a nonfunctioning telephone and a nonfunctioning laptop. Robbie was clearly sobered by the laptop, as it represented his lack of access to the outside world. Carol was more struck by the lack of dial tone on the telephone.

Once Robbie discovered two blankets neatly folded underneath the couch, the decision to spend the evening in this office was obvious: It was warmer than the common room, had only one door and two windows—thus was easily defensible—and it could be paced from end to end in the dark without any surprises. It was also twenty steps from the nearest toilet and fresh water source.

It was no Ritz-Carlton, but in a city without power, neither was the Ritz-Carlton.

4

They talked for a little while, to sift through the unbelievable occurrences of the day and to get to know one another slightly better. Carol appreciated how normal that felt, going through the details of her life and Robbie's in a time before the world ended (or whatever it was that had happened).

Robbie had a younger sister about whom he was reasonably optimistic. Likewise, his parents. He didn't have to say this out loud, as it was obvious: He thought they were all still alive. It was clear in the stories he told, which were fond, and funny, and not tinged with the kind of sadness one was accustomed to during eulogies and the like.

Carol was an only child. Her parents lived in Miami. She felt comfortable referring to them in the past tense, even though applying the same geographical assumptions as Robbie meant they were far more likely to be alive than anyone in his family. Losing Burton had pushed her in the direction of worst-case scenarios already.

Robbie eventually dozed off. She thought she probably did too, but only for a little while. Her bladder was what woke her. Having gone the day without water, she had drunk her fill and now she was paying for it. But this was why she mapped out the location of the restroom in relation to the couch.

She made it to the toilet okay, performed the task without incident, washed her hands, and then cupped some water from the tap into her now-clean hands and drank.

It was when she returned to the hallway that she heard the noise. It was coming from her left, the opposite direction of the office, where Robbie slept.

It was the same kind of clatter she'd heard when Robbie had tripped on the light stanchion. She nearly called out just then, thinking it was him—thinking he must have gotten up during her brief visit to the bathroom, walked down the hall, and committed the same error he had a few hours prior. But she'd left the door open to the office, and she could hear his breathing from where she stood.

Someone *else* was there.

She walked to the edge of the common room and listened. Unless she'd slept to sunrise, it was unlikely anyone lurking about would have any better luck seeing their way around than Robbie had—so provided she made only a little noise, whoever it was wouldn't even know she was there.

She picked up the sounds of breathing, at her one o'clock. If her orientation was correct, the door through which she and Robbie came in earlier was at her nine. She held up her left hand and felt for . . . yes: a breeze. The door was ajar now, and they hadn't left it that way. Whoever'd joined them had come from the outside and not from another part of the building.

"Hello?" she said, quietly.

No answer.

"My name is Carol. Do you need help? Are you injured?"

She realized the enormity of her error in two ways, almost simultaneously. First, there was the smell. Either the breeze in the room shifted or the creature moved and kicked up some dander —it hardly mattered.

Wet dog. That was the smell.

Second, there was the low growl.

One of the wolf-monsters was in the common room.

I should run, she thought. It was a good thought that nonetheless wasn't communicated to her legs.

She heard sniffling, then more growling. Its vision was clearly better than Robbie's, as it seemed capable of moving about the room almost silently.

It's just a dog, she thought. *Just a big dog.*

She got down on one knee and slowly lowered her cane to the floor. She held out her hand.

"Hello, puppy," she said. "Hi, puppy, hello."

Don't be afraid, don't be afraid . . .

It moved closer. The growl shifted in tone, to something more quizzical. She'd confused it.

"Who's a good boy?" she asked, deciding on the spot that this was a male wolf-monster.

He sniffed her hand, and then licked the tips of her fingers.

"Please don't be tasting me," she said, more to herself.

She leaned forward and touched the top of his snout. The nose was wet and cold, and felt entirely doglike. If her imagination was indeed another sense on which she could rely, right now it was telling her that this was a Great Dane.

He moved his head under her outstretched hand and let her scratch behind his ear. It was upright, not floppy. It twitched as she scratched. He grumbled, and whined, but seemed to be enjoying this. That was apparent in both the way he kept nudging her hand with his forehead and the fact that he had not yet tried to eat her.

The head was enormous. She was trying very hard to ignore that.

"My dog's name was Burton," she said. "What shall we call you?"

He licked her face, and for a few seconds she actually did forget that this was a feral wolf-beast rather than a dog.

Then the wolf-beast heard something. Her fear was that Robbie had awoken and was about to stumble into the room and get both of them killed. But the noise had come from outside.

The animal shook away from her and ran to the doorway, growling once more—not at her, but at whatever was outside. After a moment, she could hear it too: He was picking up the distant call of his brethren.

He whined. His toenails tapped along the cold stone floor, impatient; the dog that doesn't want to do something.

"It's okay, puppy," she said.

He whined some more, but then a second and third howl sounded and he ran off through the open door.

The moment Carol was most afraid was between the puppy's exit and the time it took for her to cross the room to the door. There was nothing in that agonizingly long stretch—that in reality was no more than thirty seconds—to prevent the dog that had been in there with her from returning as the wolf she'd imagined it to be . . . or for some other nightmarish megafauna to find its way inside.

But then she had the door closed. She fumbled around near the knob until she found the deadbolt they hadn't considered checking for previously, and latched it.

She sagged to the floor, exhaled seemingly for the first time in her life, and wondered precisely what had just happened.

TWO

Paul

1

PASTOR PAUL DIDN'T KNOW ANYTHING WAS WRONG UNTIL Sunday, when nobody showed up for the service.

Already it had been a pretty unusual week for Paul, as weeks went, beginning with the morning he woke up to a pink sunrise over the mountains. He didn't know what that meant, but considered working into his sermon a joke about the Lord and breast cancer awareness. He'd chickened out at the last minute, because after fifty-one years on this Earth he'd worked out that he was not gifted with a comic sensibility, and there was nothing worse than telling a joke that didn't get laughs, especially when he was the only one talking.

That same morning, he found the chapel in some inexplicable disarray. Best he could figure, a storm had ridden through, broken a window, and dropped a bunch of forest dirt and whatnot on the interior. It also busted a side door on its way out, suggesting that this was a manifestly malevolent storm that disliked Paul and his mission specifically.

It was a mess, whatever the explanation.

The small room in the back of the chapel where Paul lived was largely untouched, but that was probably because it was better built. He'd reinforced it after a particularly bad winter so that he didn't freeze to death if all those climate change warnings he'd been reading about trended toward an even colder winter in his future.

Kids, he thought, when he saw the chapel. *Coulda been kids.*

That was what his pop used to say whenever property was damaged by means other than the weather or the direct hand of God. When Paul was himself a kid, he used to imagine a roving band of juveniles ravaging the country in the dead of night. These kids—who definitely existed only in his head—became young Paul's first understanding of the devil.

The devil hadn't mucked up his church either, but he was an easier sell than *kids.*

What had happened to Paul's chickens, on the other hand—that might've been the devil, all right.

After he saw the damage, Paul figured the best thing to do—before spending the day cleaning the chapel, which was *not* on the schedule—was to make himself a proper breakfast. Problem was, the storm had also knocked out all the power in his little corner of the White Mountains. (It was all one big circuit in this section; if he lost power, so did all the neighbors.) Power or no, his refrigerator was near empty as it was. No more meat, aside from some old jerky, and the milk had . . . Well, it was impossible to understand what had happened to the milk. He'd seen milk turn, but this was something else. It had turned, evaporated, gained spirit form, and waited for Paul to open the door so it could be released into the world, maybe to go haunt Jed's cows down the road.

Likewise, the bread was beyond bad. It was a rock.

But the morning could still be salvaged with a coffee and a couple of eggs. Later, he would add a visit to Jed for more milk, and maybe with some sweet-talking, a loaf of bread or two from Veronica, so he didn't have to spend the day baking it from scratch himself. Then maybe he'd see about hunting down some meat.

The chickens weren't going to be providing any eggs on this day, though; they were a combination of dead and missing that was difficult to piece together without involving a crime scene specialist. The side of the coop had been torn open, and there was dried blood on the wall, and a few scattered feathers. It also looked like whatever dropped dirt in his chapel had stopped over in the coop for a spell.

The well still had water, though, and there was still vacuum-sealed coffee in the pantry, and a kettle. The pilot on the stove was out, but he had matches, and the gas tank was still half full; no act of the devil had changed that.

And so, there was coffee to be had, and that made most everything a little bit better.

He spent the rest of that morning chewing on the jerky and cleaning the church. Then he unlocked the shed and fetched one of the rifles and set out to hunt.

That ended up being the easiest part of the day, by far. He usually had to climb halfway down the mountain to score a buck, but this time he found one no more than a hundred yards from his back door. The deer let him get close, too, like it didn't know better. In his fifty-one years, he couldn't quite recall a deer being so accommodating.

By nightfall, he'd built up the fire pit, skinned the deer, and set about cooking the meat. He'd have to seal and refrigerate most of it, and he had no power for refrigeration, but usually outages lasted only a couple of days.

There was time.

2

The power still wasn't back the next day. He decided then to place a call to Stewie, who ought to know what was up. But, like the electricity, the line was dead.

He'd lost power before, and he'd lost his landline before, but only a couple of times had he lost both. Those were occasioned by severe winter storms. That was not the case here, unless the storm that mucked his church counted. Hardly seemed likely, if Paul slept through it all.

Still, he didn't worry. He had food, water, and shelter. Stewie, meanwhile, had citizens in *real* peril to attend to; he didn't need the crazy hillside preacher in his business if it wasn't an emergency. The call could wait.

Then came Sunday.

Nobody showing up was the second thing he thought was pretty strange on that day, and was ultimately the linchpin to his realizing just how much had gone wrong.

But the first thing was still downright alarming.

He'd cleaned out the church through the busted side door, not even bothering to go around front until Sunday, when it came time to greet the congregation as they drove up. That was when he noticed the wreath.

It'd been nailed to the door. Just about all that was left was a ring of old aluminum wire, tangled up with dead roots and withered pine branches. There were some climbing vines in there too, which had somehow taken root in the last week and spread across to the other door. The effect was something like a rudimentary mandala, or an eyeball.

He found it deeply unsettling, and tore it down immediately. The vines had taken some of the finish from his doors, but he could repaint. Better that than have the eye of the devil looking out at his congregants.

Not that it ended up mattering at all, since nobody showed.

Paul was a man who lived a life of ritual, so on finding himself without a congregation, the first thing he did was conduct a mental review of his week. Monday through Wednesday was community outreach, when applicable, and repairs on the church, where needed. Thursdays and Fridays were for reading the Bible and choosing his gospel. Saturdays were for polishing the sermon. Except for the power loss and the need to hunt for food, the week had gone more or less exactly as planned.

It was definitely Sunday. It had to be. This wasn't about him; the town hadn't suddenly decided he was a pariah.

Something was very wrong.

3

Coming down off the mountain took up the rest of Paul's Sunday, beginning as soon as he checked on his pickup.

Somehow, just sitting in the garage and minding its own business, the truck had lost pressure in all four tires. He examined them for signs kids had slashed his tires, but they looked fine. Just didn't have enough air in them anymore.

He couldn't even begin to come up with an explanation, so instead he just pumped them up, and then tried turning over the engine.

There were three things about which Pastor Paul could be considered a genuine expert, at least regionally. They were, in no particular order: guns, cars, and the Bible. (Old Henry used to say Paul was the only man in New Hampshire who could shoot you down, pray for your soul, and then give the ambulance an oil change while they were working to save your life. It was a joke that sounded better with alcohol.) So when the pickup wouldn't turn over, Paul knew what he was about.

He popped the hood, and then wondered who'd switched his truck with this old junker.

Everything had to be changed: the battery, the starter, the hoses, the spark plugs . . . just about all but the engine itself. Probably that needed a replacement too, but he didn't have a spare, or a block and tackle, so it would have to hold out at least until he made it to town.

He had a spare for all the other parts, both for himself and for the occasional good neighbor repair work. It was all in his shed, the only thing he owned that was better reinforced than his living quarters. Winter came, folks on the mountain were isolated a lot, and had to rely on each other, so: He was good if you needed a gun, or needed your car or soul fixed. Jed was good for milk, bread, and news. Old Henry had a still, tobacco, and — Paul had been told — some decent marijuana. And so on.

Paul spent the rest of the morning swapping out all he could under the hood and still couldn't get the truck to start. The problem was the spare battery, which was just as dead as the one he took out of the truck, even though it was bought new only a few months earlier.

I could just walk it, he thought. It wasn't far to town. But the problem, as he saw it, was that this wasn't going to be a quick trip down to figure out if his entire congregation had the flu. It was time to consider whether a more serious thing was going on. It was, in other words, time for the slightly paranoid survivalist version of Pastor Paul to take up some space in his head.

He couldn't just head down on foot with no supplies. He needed the truck, even if he couldn't figure out just yet how to get power to it.

One thing at a time.

He packed the flatbed with all the unspoiled food he had—the vacuum-sealed coffee, the rest of the deer, and the jerky—five jugs of water (he only owned five jugs) and an irrationally large number of guns.

That last part wasn't entirely accurate. He had ten guns to choose from. Three of them were hunting rifles, and while he surely didn't need to bring the Marlin 336, the Remington Sendero, *and* the old Winchester 70, he liked each of them for a different reason, and so he took all three. Likewise, for the two shotguns: a Winchester double-barreled, and a short-barrel Mossberg. As for the four handguns . . . he had no excuse to take more than two, but once he decided to bring three rifles and two shotguns, he was pretty much all in. He likely had no use for the five-shot Smith & Wesson or the old Heritage .22, not as long as he had the Glock 40 and the Ruger.

That left the BB gun he used to scare off foxes from the coop. The BB stayed, because for some reason, in his mind—both the paranoid and non-paranoid parts—taking it with him was going one step too far.

It was, therefore, an entirely rational number of guns.

He also threw in a couple of changes of clothing, an extra pair of boots, an overcoat, and both of his Bibles. Then he was ready to go.

By the time he finished packing, he'd come up with the basics of a plan, if not to start the truck, then at least to get it moving.

Getting something with wheels off the side of a mountain wasn't inherently tough. Getting it *up* would be a challenge, but going down just meant accepting the gift of gravity and all it can bring. He also didn't need to get all the way down the mountain in one go; just to Jed's place to start with. He knew for a fact that he could coast there in neutral, because he did it all the time to conserve fuel.

Jed had more power options, so that was a better place to start working out a solution to the larger problem of getting Paul to the town . . . and to figure out what was going on. Better yet: He might not have to go any farther, since Jed's was a news hub.

Before he left, Paul said a quick blessing over the church he'd built with his hands some fifteen years prior, then shifted the truck into neutral, gave it a little shove, and hopped in.

4

Twenty white-knuckle minutes later—following two stops where the road leveled off more than he remembered, four times when the overgrowth meant he lost sight of the road completely, six near collisions with deer, and three Hail Marys—Paul reached Jed's farm. It was late afternoon by then.

Jed and Veronica kept a small homestead: just a few dairy cows, pigs, chickens, and so on. They grew enough vegetables to feed them and the folks at the farmers' market six months out of the year, and made do otherwise by selling homemade butter and cheese. Their biggest crop was pumpkins; every October they cleared enough to cover the finances for the winter.

The pumpkin patch was the first sight to see on crossing the property line, and unless Paul's calendar was off, his friends were in for a problem this year, because the field looked overgrown in a bad way.

Jed always said the way to grow pumpkins was to let the plants find their own bliss—just spread out and take what they wanted. Maybe rein them in if they got fresh with the other vegetables, prune them now and then, but otherwise leave 'em alone.

Paul didn't have to stop to get a hard look—and couldn't, since momentum was his fuel—to know something was up with the patch. Jed would have to go to market soon, but it didn't look like he had much of anything to bring.

The other fields didn't look like they were doing any better. He rolled past the vegetable patches with no vegetables, to the edge of the grazing land near the barn, to a stop a hundred feet from the farmhouse.

He shifted the car back into park and stepped out for a better look around.

The place felt abandoned. Paul kept expecting someone to give a shout from the house or one of the fields, or the barn, but nobody did. Jed employed two part-time hands, and his son, Dave, was a fixture most days, as was Jed himself, and Veronica. A couple of times a month their daughter, Stacy, and her girls would be up for a weekend, too. There should have been *someone* there.

"Hello?" he shouted.

Nobody was around to answer.

The barn door was open, the livestock was gone, and Jed's truck was missing. Possibly, Jed had gone into town with all the animals, except Jed had no reason to do that, and also, the truck wasn't nearly big enough to carry them all.

Paul headed into the barn to see if there were any better explanations inside.

What was in there was an answer, but not a better explanation. He found the remnants of a carcass: mostly just bones. Judging from the size, it belonged to one of the cows.

It looked as if something large and terrible had torn it apart and then picked the bones clean. There was hardly even any odor; the phantom remains of Paul's milk smelled worse.

"Kids," he said out loud. "Running around, slaughtering livestock. What's this world coming to, I tell you."

Out the other side of the barn, around near the pig trough, he found what was left of a pig, and the chicken coop looked a lot like his own.

Whatever had struck Paul's home also hit here.

Aliens, he thought. *Not kids, not the devil. Aliens blew through town, ate all the animals, and got out again.*

Paul wasn't a New Hampshire native. He was raised in Iowa, ending up in the Granite State only due to a comedy of circumstances that included an ex-wife, two failed business ventures, and a stay in the county prison. He'd found God somewhere in the middle of all that, almost by accident. God wasn't why he moved to a shack on the side of the mountain, but He was why Paul decided to build a chapel on the land once he got there.

Iowa farmland was a good area to grow up in if you wanted to meet someone who not only believed in aliens but could tell you about the time he met one. It seemed like every farm town had one or two locals who would swear on their mother's Bible that they'd been abducted, sometimes more than once. There was also the occasional extraterrestrial cattle mutilation that Paul's dad of course attributed to *kids.*

Paul believed in all of it when he was younger, even if he didn't take it all that seriously. Now it seemed like a solid explanation. He'd have to find Jed and Veronica first, to see what their take on it was. Maybe they had a better story.

He left the barnyard, meaning to head to the farmhouse next, when he saw movement around the back of his truck.

"Hey!" he shouted, happy to finally discover a living human that wasn't in the mirror. He ran over, so eager to get on with the part where all this began to make some sense that he was only about ten feet from the black bear before recognizing what he was getting ready to shake hands with.

There was a large plastic tub in the back of the truck, inside of which was all of Paul's food, and the bear wanted a taste.

It was an adult male. Paul had seen his share, up in the hills. Most of them were maybe six feet when on their hind legs. This one had to be seven or eight.

If the truck could run, Paul would have just jumped in, started it, and driven it away. That wasn't an option. Not that there were a lot of better choices. You don't try to kill bears unless you really, really have to. They were endangered, but that wasn't the reason. The reason was, killing one was extremely, almost impossibly difficult.

Paul had a handgun on his hip and a shotgun in his hand, neither of which would do more than annoy the bear, and he sure as heck couldn't outrun it.

His rifle might do the job, if he put the bullet in the right place. But it just so happened the rifle was lying next to the tub of food.

Paul picked up a handful of rocks and threw it at the bear's belly.

"Ha!" he shouted. "Get out of here!"

The bear took his front paws off the car's tailgate and turned to the matter of the crazy man throwing rocks.

"Go on!" Paul said.

The thing to do was to continue facing him up, because running wasn't feasible. Jumping into the truck's cab might get Paul out of immediate danger, but then he'd be stuck in there until the danger had passed. The bear might eat his whole truck before it came to that; it was sure big enough.

The bear roared. Paul shouted some more, and chucked another rock at its stomach. That made the bear bark and growl, but it also backed up, which was a really good sign. Paul took another step forward.

"Get outta here," Paul said. "It's not worth a fight."

Grumbling, the bear decided Paul was right. It went back down on all fours, snorted at Paul, then turned and walked off.

Paul waited until the bear made it as far as the pumpkin patch before grabbing the tub of food from the flatbed and hightailing it for the farmhouse.

5

The back door to the house was unlocked, as usual. It led right to Veronica's kitchen. The kitchen didn't look as if it had been used in a *while*, which made as little sense as everything else he'd seen up to that point, so Paul just added it to the list.

It was already clear that the Wilsons weren't home, but so far he'd also found no explanation for *why*, and how long they'd been away. He added that to the list too.

Paul couldn't remember when they'd last spoken. Maybe on the prior Sunday, but maybe not; Jed didn't stop by every Sabbath. He liked to go between Paul's nondenominational wayside chapel and the Catholic church in town. Paul didn't take it personally; he figured Jed was just spreading the odds on his getting into heaven.

But maybe it *had* been a while. The milk in Paul's fridge had come from one of Jed's cows, and that milk was *old*. Was it long enough for his friend to have left town without telling him? All except for the part where they didn't tell him, it fit the available evidence. Didn't explain the gigantic black bear camping out in the yard, but sometimes nature happened, and it didn't always need an explanation.

Paul thought of most of the folks on the mountain as a part of his family. They knew one another's sins and embraced each other just the same, and it didn't much matter how long it had been or how little they'd seen one another.

They didn't just disappear like this on each other. There had to be another explanation.

The next thought he had was that Jed and Veronica *were* there somewhere … but tied up in the bedroom or dead in the basement. Somehow that seemed even less likely than the two of 'em up and taking off on him without a word, but he had to confirm it anyway.

He did, and they weren't.

After about an hour in the farmhouse, it had become pretty clear he wasn't going to find the answers he was looking for there. What he needed was to reach someone from outside the area.

Jed had a ham radio in his office for just such a purpose. It was the news hub for the mountainside. Paul didn't have one himself — he was trying to stay off the grid, which meant no ham license for him — but he knew how to use it.

The dials were marked with the shared local frequencies, and there was a logbook at the desk with the less common ones. Jed liked to see how far he could reach. Paul liked the idea of it himself — skipping a signal across the ionosphere instead of using the government satellites, and talking to someone halfway around the world. It appealed to the rebel Paul used to be.

He turned the radio on, but of course that wasn't going to do anything because this place had no power either.

Jed and Veronica kept two portable emergency generators in the basement, though. Paul hauled both of them upstairs, left one near the door — no telling how valuable a portable generator was going to be in the coming days—and took the other one into the study.

It didn't start up. He double-checked to confirm that it had fuel —it ran on gasoline—and tried again. Still no good. He swapped it with the one near the door and got the same result.

It was the battery. They used a 12-volt for a spark to get the generator started, and the battery handling that responsibility was dead. *Both* of them were, which was downright strange.

Paul popped the battery out of the generator he was working with, and stared at it for a few seconds to see if it felt like explaining itself. It did not, but did call both of Paul's dead car batteries as character witnesses.

He didn't even know what could cause all the batteries to die at the same time.

"Add it to the list," he said.

The good thing about Jed's generators was that they had a secondary trigger in the form of a hand crank. It took about five minutes, which was roughly three minutes past the point when Paul thought it was broken and he was going to die in the farmhouse because of a couple of burned-out 12-volt batteries, but it worked.

He got the radio plugged into it, and finally, for the first time in a week, Pastor Paul had a way to make contact with the rest of the world.

He turned it to the local frequency first and, using Jed's call sign, asked if anyone had their ears on.

All static. He put the headphones on in case they were there but the signal was faint, and tried again.

"Anyone out there? Over."

Nobody was.

Well, except the mountain had no power. He already knew that. If it was only locals on that channel and they were all short of a charge, this wasn't a surprise. He then switched to one of the channels usually used by law enforcement and was alarmed by the discovery that it was *also* quiet.

Did they lose power down there too?

Feeling some panic now, Paul began combing through all the channels, from the lowest to the highest, spending a few minutes on each one. The world was a big place, and while the ham radio wasn't as common as it used to be, the airwaves should still be full of chatter. Tune it right, and it'd pick up AM/FM signals too. Heck, with the right atmospheric conditions it could connect him with someone on the other side of the world. Eventually, he'd find someone—in another state, or another country, or another hemisphere—who could look up northern New Hampshire on the Internet and tell Paul what in the name of the Lord was going on around here.

It wasn't happening. Every channel was nothing but pure static. That could mean—and probably did mean—that the problem was with Jed's ham radio and not with the entire world, but after all Paul had been through this past week just to make it this far, he was leaning toward the more drastic explanation.

An hour into it, Paul realized what must have happened.

He stepped away from the radio, dropped down to his knees, and began to pray.

6

Paul didn't give up on the radio, mainly because he couldn't figure out what else to do with himself. And that was good, because there *was* another human voice out there, broadcasting on the emergency channel. He'd listened to that channel at least five times already, so maybe conditions hadn't been favorable the other times. He was discounting divine providence on the grounds that the Lord was clearly displeased with him.

". . . recording. If anyone hears this message," the voice on the radio said, "turn to channel eighteen at sunset. I am on the East Coast. This is a recording. If anyone . . ."

It was a woman's voice. Bit of an accent: Indian, he thought. He wondered for a moment if she meant the East Coast of *India,* but no, this was a local frequency.

Paul dropped the headset and ran to the west-facing back porch. The sunset was nearly done; another two minutes at most.

He ran back in and spun the dial to eighteen. He didn't even bother with the call sign.

"Hello, hello, is anyone there?" he asked.

Silence.

"Hello, I turned to eighteen like you said. This is Paul from New Hampshire. Please be there, I can't wait another day. Over."

"Hello?"

Same woman's voice.

"Yes! Yes, hi! This is . . . this is Paul. Who's this?"

"I'm Ananda. Did you say you were in New Hampshire? Over."

"Yes, but . . . Well, I don't know what happened, or what's going on. I can't find anyone else. It's just me, so far. Do you know what's going on up here? On the news, maybe?"

"There isn't any news," she said. "Whatever happened up there happened here too. We're both in the dark."

"Where's here, for you?"

"Massachusetts."

"You're not far at all," he said. "I was gonna try driving into town tomorrow. Might be, there are some answers there. Over."

Her being so close meant this could still be a local event. His inability to raise another soul on the radio argued against that, but he wasn't a hundred percent ruling out other people. Even if he was right about what this was, there'd still have to be more than just the two of them. The world was *full* of sinners.

"You have a car?" she asked.

"Yes, ma'am, a truck. It's not running; battery's dead. Everything else is tuned to go, and I've got my hands on a generator. I figure I can rig something to get a spark under the hood. I'm handy —I'll work it out. After I check out the town, I can come to you if you need help. Over."

"I think we all need help, Paul. You're the only . . . I think everyone else is dead. Um, over."

"They've been called, ma'am. That's my take."

"Called?"

"The Rapture. They've moved on. Over."

Ananda didn't respond to this suggestion right away.

"I don't think we can agree on that," she said.

"I understand. It'll do for me. I'll be talking to the Lord tonight about what I could have done better in my life, but it's out of my hands. Out of your hands too. Over."

"Okay."

"But, look, there'll be more of us. We just have to find them."

He felt as though he should be consoling Ananda for having been equally damned, but he was too happy to find another person to worry so much about her soul in that moment.

Outside, the sun had gone down. Jed's study, which was poorly lit even on a good day, got so much worse that Paul decided to plug a lamp into the generator.

"Exactly where in Massachusetts are you?" he asked, while fiddling with the lamp. "You don't know how good it feels to talk to another person. Like I said, we should connect, and do this face to face. Over."

"I feel the same, Paul. All right. Do you know where MIT is? Over."

"In Cambridge? Sure. And I'll take the radio with me, and check in when I can. Don't know how long before I can get there, but we'll keep in touch—how's that?"

"I'd like that."

"I mean, hell, I'll walk if I have to. Can't be that far. Over."

"I wouldn't recommend that," she said.

Some kind of background noise came in loud.

"Over," Ananda said.

"Ananda, what was that?"

"It's the wolves," she said. "They hunt starting at twilight. I'm safe. But you should find shelter before sundown. I don't know what it's like out of the city, but it's bad here at night."

"I'm pretty well armed, Ananda. Over."

"Well, they're pretty big, and there are a lot of them. God knows what else is out there. Just be careful. Over."

"I'll do that."

"I have to sign off, Paul. The sound bothers them. Be well. We'll talk tomorrow, same time?"

"Same time. Signing off."

He shut down the radio and started laughing. The Lord may have forsaken him, but he wasn't the only one.

His eyes landed on Jed's bulletin board on the wall next to the desk. The lamp was showing off everything tacked onto it. The board was mostly used for market schedules and coupons, so that's just about all that was there to see. Honestly, Paul couldn't remember spending any time looking it over in the past.

Something caught his eye.

Obscured in one corner was a black-and-white image on a piece of paper. Only the top quarter of it was visible, and the only thing in that part of the photo was someone's forehead.

Paul's problem was that it was *his* forehead.

He unburied it and pulled it down.

It was indeed a picture of Paul. Decent one, too, from maybe four or five years ago. Made no sense that Jed would have a copy of it on his wall, but nothing else about it made sense either, most especially the legend underneath the picture.

It was Jed's home phone number. Beneath that, in magic-markered capital letters, was a question: HAVE YOU SEEN THIS MAN?

THREE

Win

1

WIN WASN'T EVEN SUPPOSED TO BE HOME.

That was what bugged her more than anything. Not the horses running off. Not her mom disappearing with the car sometime in the middle of the night. Not the empty cupboard or the lack of power or the dead cell phone. Not even the part where Mother clearly stopped giving a damn, given the terrible condition of the family homestead.

No, it was that Win should never have been home in the first place. She lived in Providence now, an actual city where hardly anyone smelled like manure, and sleeping past sunrise wasn't a sign of laziness. She lived there to have a real job, away from a horse ranch in the middle of farmland that was itself in the middle of nothing in particular.

It was, likewise, away from the dream of an Olympics she never managed to qualify for. That was a childhood ambition, and she was twenty-four.

In hindsight, she thought the mistake might have been in picking a city within driving distance. She should have cut the cord entirely—New York City, maybe, or Los Angeles.

Don't lie, said the voice in Win's head that did a decent impression of her mother. *You couldn't have tolerated living in either of those places. You can barely stand Providence.*

You're probably right, she told the voice. *But let me have this for a little while.*

Not being home when "all this" happened would have been much easier. Cities have certain amenities, food within walking distance being a personal favorite. One didn't need to hunt in order to eat, which is what you resort to when you wake up alone in a house in the woods, fifty miles from the nearest highway on-ramp.

There was a rustling to Win's left. She leaned forward, looking down over the edge of the old hunting blind, one hand on her bow. It was getting dark, and she didn't have anything for night vision. Hunting by moonlight was an iffy proposition. All the same, she was hungry, and didn't have a ton of other options.

She held her breath, nocked an arrow, and was rewarded with the sight of a wild boar.

She loosed the arrow on the exhale. It struck home in the boar's eye. The beast dropped with a satisfying finality.

"First alternate, my ass," she said.

2

The pretext of her mother's call was that Bluebell was sick and Win should come home in case she didn't last the weekend. Bluebell was a horse, and she was okay as far as horses go, but wasn't by any stretch Win's favorite. Win's horse was Max, and he was doing just fine.

Bluebell was *Mother's* favorite, though, so the coded message was *Your mother misses you. Can you please come home and spend time with her?*

It was the kind of exchange that happened between them so frequently that Win was fully prepared not to engage whatsoever. She'd just claim she didn't get the message until the weekend was over, complain about her service provider for a few minutes, and then ask how Bluebell was doing. Inevitably, the horse would turn out to be *so much better,* and then they'd talk for a few minutes about Win's job, Win would say she really had to go but it was nice talking, and that would be that. No trip necessary.

Except for this time. This time, she'd listened to the message in front of Ted from the office, and she must have made a face because he asked what was the matter. She explained it to him in the best way she knew how without coming off like a horrible person. Then *he* said well of course Win had to go, and hey, he was heading up to Boston on Friday anyway, and wasn't the ranch on the way?

It wasn't *really* on the way, but it was close enough, and it was also a superb excuse to get to know Ted better. Since Win was nursing a mild crush on him, the trade-off seemed perfectly reasonable.

The mild crush didn't even last all the way to the ranch, though, because Ted was possibly the worst driver she'd ever shared a car with. She spent the entire trip convinced they were moments away from dying horribly, either because his hatchback, which kept shrieking at him to stop running the engine so hard, was about to explode, or because one of the two dozen cars he tailgated along the way might brake at the same time he happened to be gesturing and looking Win in the eye while speaking, which was often.

Perhaps if this was a side of him she saw after they'd developed a more involved relationship, she would have been able to forgive it, but they weren't there yet. Win was happy to write it off as an irre-deemable character flaw and move on.

Because of this, Ted didn't even make it past the gate. She had him drop her off at the edge of the property—claiming her mom would already be in bed anyway—so that the weekend didn't turn into Mother dropping little hints about how nice Ted seemed.

It actually *was* very late by the time they'd arrived. Win went straight to bed. She undoubtedly engaged with her mom briefly before then, but as it was the usual—they had fifteen ways to have the same conversation—it wasn't memorable. That was, in hind-sight, a shame, as it may have been the last time Win would speak to her mother.

The next morning, Mother was gone and she'd taken the pickup with her. No note. Optimistically, her mom was out getting food, since there wasn't any in the house. So Win waited, and while wait-ing went out back to see Bluebell and Max, and Dusty, and Ginger, and Lido. She did like horses, and it had been a while since she'd visited with the gang, and Mother's guilt trips notwithstanding, she was overdue for a ride around the woods with Max.

Win was alarmed, then, that the horses were gone too. There were six pens for the five horses, yet three didn't even look like they were lived in. The other three, all along the same wall, looked like they'd contained horses . . . before they had *broken out* through the back wall.

On closer inspection, that seemed to be exactly what transpired. One of the horses—maybe all of them—had kicked out the wall.

"What the hell went on here?" she asked.

The other discoveries about precisely how amiss things were came gradually over the course of the day. Win tried calling her mom as soon as she saw the conditions in the stable, but her cell phone was dead and the landline had no tone.

The nearest farm was twenty minutes on foot, so she headed there next to ask about borrowing their phone and to see if they knew about a psychotic break involving her mom. But they weren't home either. Their back door was unlocked, so she checked the place thoroughly enough to confirm that there were no bodies inside, which wasn't a thing that would have even occurred to her a few hours earlier.

Turned out their phone was dead too.

She returned to the ranch then rather than continue on to the next neighbor. She didn't know how much farther that would take her from home, and it was getting dark. Mother had to come back eventually.

Nightfall arrived with no sign of life from anybody human. *Animal* life, however, was thriving locally in a way she'd never seen before. Deer, a howling pack of wolves, a family of badgers, and a couple of wild boars. No horses, though.

By the second morning, Win began to formulate a plan to hike out on her own.

It was hard to know for sure what the prime motivating factor in this decision was: hunger, or fear that something really serious had transpired out there in the world, about which she was somehow neither aware of nor susceptible to personally.

It was probably hunger. At the time she'd struck out, it had been over twenty-four hours since her last bite of food. The well wasn't dry, so water was no problem, but there weren't any calories in water. She needed *more*.

Foraging and hunting for food wasn't entirely outside the realm of her capabilities. Her dad, when he'd been around, used to take her on his hunts, and even taught her about poisonous versus non-poisonous berries and whatnot. It'd been a really long time since those lessons, but she thought she could manage to gather some and not kill herself. (Again, that was probably the hunger talking as much as anything.) Unfortunately, when he left, his guns left with him, and Mother didn't like to keep a gun in the house.

In ninety-nine out of a hundred situations, Win agreed with that stance. This one time, a rifle would've been really useful.

The weapons available in the house were a hunting knife, a hammer, and Win's compound bow with a quiver of steel-tipped arrows.

She also dug out one of her old hiking bags and filled it with water bottles, threw a few yards of rope scrounged from the barn and two books of matches in a second bag, and then took off.

That was five days ago.

3

Win had known she was in legal hunting territory when she saw the hunting blind up in the tree. It was basically just a treehouse floor. Simple, but surprisingly sturdy. It hadn't been used in a long while, and the surface was one-quarter tree and one-third ant farm, but it didn't creak much and didn't feel like it was going to drop her twenty feet to the forest floor with no warning. That was much appreciated. If the boar hadn't come by, she probably would have slept up there rather than taking shelter in an empty homestead.

After taking her fatal shot, she climbed down the rickety ladder to claim her kill.

Or rather, her *near* kill; the boar was still twitching.

Kneeling down next to it, she patted the animal on the head, and then cut its throat. Then she stood back and waited for as much blood to drain out as possible — a lot easier when the beast's heart was still pumping. (This was a lesson she'd learned the hard way after an earlier kill: a goat that bled all over her.)

While waiting for the blood to drain, she pulled an apple from her bag and snacked.

Thank God for the orchards, she thought.

She'd been walking only a few hours on the first day when she'd come across the first orchard. The apples there may have saved her life, because she was seriously dizzy from hunger by then. She would still need meat—and found it when she killed a rabbit the next morning—but the apples were her salvation.

"Come on—you done yet?" she asked the now definitely dead boar. She was still wearing the clothes soaked in the goat's blood and didn't relish replenishing it with fresh blood any more than she had to, but since the boar was going over her shoulders, it seemed inevitable.

The odor of a fresh kill—which she'd mostly gotten over—was bound to draw attention from some of the larger animals, and it was already late in the day. There was a house she hadn't visited yet at the end of the trail, so relative safety was near, but hauling the boar all that way was going to take a while, and the weight would seriously slow her down.

And of course, as soon as the concern sprang to mind, she heard a rustling in the forest behind her. Not from the ground—something *large* was in the trees. She turned, looked up.

It was a cougar. Big one, too.

Tiger in the zoo big.

"Hey, kitty-kitty," she said.

It purred menacingly. She wiped the blood from the knife on her pant leg and slid it back into the sheath tied to her thigh, to free up her hands.

The cat looked uncertain. It wanted the animal behind her, but didn't know what to make of Win. She took advantage of the hesitation its confusion had caused by kneeling down to retrieve the compound bow and an arrow.

"Do you want to play, kitty?" she asked, in a tone of voice so far from the marketing executive she'd been not three weeks ago that it sounded alien to her own ears.

She nocked the arrow, aimed, and waited for the cat to make the next move.

Win thought she could probably drop it where it was before it decided to pounce. It wasn't a bad idea, because pouncing would definitely be unfortunate, no matter what. She could put an arrow in its heart while it was in flight, but she'd still have to worry about a hundred-pound cougar landing on top of her from thirty feet up.

She didn't want to kill it if she didn't have to, though. This wasn't out of altruism as much as it was concern over possibly losing an arrow.

The cat roared, and growled, and paced along the branch. This was to see if it could get her to back away, which wasn't happening.

"Come on, *shoo!*" she muttered. "Sun's going down. You don't like the wolves any more than I do. *Git!*"

It roared and hissed, and then turned and jumped to the next tree over.

She waited until she was reasonably certain it didn't double back, and finally exhaled.

"That's what I *thought*," she said quietly.

4

After she broke into her sixth house, a part of her wished that one of these times, she'd be interrupted by the family whose home she was squatting in, if only so they could see the horrible *mess* she was making.

The gutting and cleaning of the boar carcass was by far the messiest gutting—messier than the goat, and that had been pretty bad. It was also easily the smelliest. If this were anything like normal circumstances, she would have gutted it in the yard and then brought it in. But that would just attract the wrong kind of attention to her location, and she was only staying one night anyway.

Part of the problem, frankly, was that she was self-taught. She got almost no meat from the rabbit, and she ended up wasting half the goat meat because cleaning it became more trouble than it was worth: She got enough to last a couple of days, but probably threw away more of it than she should have.

It was perilous work. She hadn't been getting a lot of sleep, despite being exhausted from all the running and hunting, and that led to moments when her hands shook at particularly inopportune times. When she was using a large hunting knife on a heavy carcass, for example. Even one cut in this land without other people could end up being fatal if she wasn't careful, and she wanted to survive at least long enough to understand what the hell had happened.

It was an odd cycle to be stuck in. She was more confident in her ability to hunt without getting hurt than she was in cutting the meat off the bones of the kill, which meant she had to hunt more often.

So far, it was working out, but it probably wasn't a sustainable existence.

The one thing she hadn't been able to bring herself to do was eat the meat uncooked. This seemed like a bridge too far, as long as she knew how to make fire.

It helped that a lot of the houses had fireplaces. Not all of them, though; two days before, with the goat, she'd picked a house with a chimney—usually a good sign—but its fireplace was bricked up. It was already dark by then, and she didn't know how far the next nearest house was. So she built a fire pit on the terrace instead, and crossed her fingers that the smell wouldn't draw any predators. It took forever, because everything was wet, including her: There had been torrential rains the prior day. But it worked. The meat got cooked and she didn't have to eat anything raw. It turned out she did not care for goat meat, but it was far too late by then to do anything about it.

This new house had a working fireplace. She opened the flue and got the fire going—hoping the smoke had a clear path up the chimney, or she'd have to abandon the house altogether before carbon monoxide did her in—and went about cooking the boar meat.

About halfway through the night—after eating and a small nap, but before the bulk of the meat was finished cooking—Win ended up at the back of the house, looking out on the yard through a picture window. Safe, not hungry, and not tired. That was when her mind went back to wondering just what in the deep blue hell was going on. It was also when she tended to get emotional.

"That's it, girl," she said, wiping her eyes, "budget your time. No room for this tomorrow."

It must have been a trick the firelight played on her, or maybe that she was just bone-tired from all of this, but for barely a blink of an eye she caught a reflection of someone standing behind her. A neon ghost.

She spun around, but there was nobody there.

Obviously.

Glow-in-the-dark phantoms?

"I would have gotten away with it, too, if it wasn't for you med-dling kids," she said. Then she laughed entirely too hard, and won-dered what it would take to find just one house with some alcohol still on the shelf.

She turned back to the window in time to see something large emerge from the edge of the woods below the property. By now, she thought she'd seen every animal that shared this neighborhood with her, at least once. She was wrong.

It was a horse.

5

Win was up and out of the house by first light. The tracks in the yard were still fresh, and she knew well enough what a horse's tracks looked like, so following them wasn't all that hard.

The question was whether it would do any good. It looked like it was just wandering around the area, but if the horse decided to run, she'd never catch it. And if she *did* catch up, she had no idea what to do next.

She didn't know whose horse it was, but there was no saddle, and from the way it looked out the window, the animal didn't think it was lost. It seemed just beyond the realm of the possible that she'd witnessed a feral horse from the picture window—this wasn't the Old West, and packs of mustangs didn't roam New England—but that didn't mean it was tame, either.

Win knew a lot about horses, but she'd never broken one. Given this horse wasn't standing in a corral, she didn't have a lot of room to get it wrong.

She followed the tracks for most of the morning. They circled back toward the house a couple of times, inspiring an optimistic—

and irrational—notion that maybe the horse was out looking for her while she was looking for it.

The sun was high in the sky by the time she tracked it down in a meadow, dining alone on the thick grass.

Win stepped out of the tree line and into the sun, at the far end of the meadow. The horse raised its head and gave her one look, and then went back to eating. That was, she decided, a good sign. It didn't see her as a threat. So far.

"Hi," she said, as she got closer. "I'm Win."

The horse snorted, looked at her again, and resumed eating.

"I was just wondering . . . I could use a ride. Just to go out, to . . . well, somewhere. I haven't worked out where exactly yet. Someplace where there are people. I'm going to run out of arrows, see, and I don't know how to make more. Not soon, but . . . it's not a lifetime supply. Unless I die soon. Then I guess it is. You could take me to a weapons depot, maybe. Really, anywhere. I've been out here for like a week, and look at me. I'm rambling, sorry. So anyway, that's me. Probably sound crazy, huh? Oh, hey, do you like apples?"

She pulled an apple out of her bag and held it up for the horse. When it didn't show any particular interest, she stepped closer until she couldn't be ignored any longer.

The horse sniffed the apple, then looked at her, then took it from her and started eating. While it was eating, she scratched the hair behind its ear. Max always liked that.

When the horse finished with the apple, it turned and silently asked for another, which she provided. Then she pulled out a few yards of rope.

"There's a stable, back where you and I met last night. I haven't checked inside, but I bet we can find a proper brush in there somewhere. You'd like that, wouldn't you?"

She looped the rope around its neck and knotted it up.

"What do you say? Friends?"

She took two steps ahead of the horse, until the rope was taut. Then she gave it a gentle tug.

The horse looked confused. She gave a second gentle tug. It snorted, but then began to follow.

"Awesome," she said. "Now we have to come up with a name for you."

6

They debated names all the way back to the stable, before finally settling on Elton. It was her tenth choice, so it was possible the horse was just sick of her asking which one he liked by then and agreed if only to get her to shut up about it.

She'd come up with the theme—in which he was a knight, coming to her rescue—early on, and then just went through all the names of knights she could think of. She ran out of the standard Arthurian monikers pretty early, as she evidently didn't know as much about English knighthood as she thought. Elton was what she came up with after remembering that Elton John was knighted.

The knight theme was really just to convince Elton to be chivalrous enough to let her sit on his back. It was hard to tell if this was sinking in.

He seemed even-tempered enough. She wondered if he was alone in the woods or if there was a team of horses out there somewhere. He was on the young side, a little thin but otherwise healthy. Possibly, there were few grazing opportunities in the area he was familiar with. Or he spent as much time as she had, over the past week, evading predators. That can wear you down. Not that there were a lot of things in the world eager to challenge an adult horse.

He didn't look happy about entering the stable, but he did it with the offer of another apple. She tied him up inside, gave him a little hay, and looked around until she found a stiff-bristle brush and a saddle.

The brush was no surprise. She figured just about every stable had at least one. It was next to a pile of torn clothes, in a corner. The clothing was a little odd, but only a little; it wasn't the first time she discovered bits of clothing in her wanderings. There was never anything useful about these discoveries, clue-wise.

The saddle, however, *was* a surprise, and a welcome one. She really didn't expect that she'd be so lucky, and in fact had already been parsing the logistics of trying to ride bareback while keeping all the gear she expected to need. It wouldn't have been easy.

She put the saddle down next to Elton, showed him the brush —he sniffed it, then looked at her to determine if she was expecting him to taste it next—and then started brushing him down.

It was clear immediately that (1) he had never been brushed down before, and (2) he liked it enormously. Win was pretty sure this was a universal truth for horses.

She spent a good hour on him, cleaning out the nettles in his mane and checking for any cuts or irritation from bugs. There was an old bite mark on his leg, but it was scarred over; it was definitely a wound incurred more than a week ago, meaning before all the madness happened. This contributed to the theory that he was indeed a horse who had been roaming wild for a while. The theory's counterpoint was that this was entirely ridiculous, which was admittedly also a good argument.

Win talked while she brushed, telling Elton about Max, and her mom, and what she'd had to do to survive. Then she covered what her life was like in Providence, and before that, when she was an Olympic hopeful.

Elton didn't share any of his own history, but that was because he stubbornly remained a horse. He was a very good listener, though.

Once the brush-down was done, she got him a bucket of well water and another apple. Then it was time for The Talk. She pulled up a stool and sat in his line of sight.

"Here's the situation, Elton," she said. "I think everybody else might be dead."

He snorted.

"I know! It sounds crazy, and hey, maybe I'm wrong. I really hope I am, because, you know. Who wants to be right with those kinds of stakes? You get me. But I think I'm right. I've been out and about for a week now, and there's nobody, and okay, this isn't a big area, fine. But I haven't seen any airplanes, either. Not once. And no cars."

Elton stared at her.

"Yeah, I tried driving. I've found a bunch of abandoned cars, with the keys in the house. None of them would start. Just as well, probably, since the tires were mostly flat, like, every time. Your guess is as good as mine why that is. That's why I need your help. I want to figure this out and you don't have any flat tires. We talked about this before, but you probably didn't appreciate what I meant."

She picked up the saddle, and held it out for him to examine. It was old, worn brown leather and suede. It probably smelled like someone else's horse, which Elton surely didn't appreciate.

"What I want to do is, I want to put this on your back. Would that be okay?"

He voiced no objection. He didn't even look particularly concerned, opting to drink more water as his only response.

She lifted the saddle onto his back. He raised his head and twitched his ears, and if he could speak, what he'd probably say was *Hello, what's this?* But he didn't kick her to death, which made this a success automatically. He did glare at her, and snort, two clear expressions of disapproval.

She brushed his neck with her hand.

"It's okay. Let me buckle it down; you won't even know it's there."

He stood still and let her tie down the saddle. So far so good.

"See, it's not so bad," she said. "It's like a big purse . . . that you wear. Okay, not a purse, but . . . Here, I'll show you."

She hung her bags on one side of the saddle and attached her compound bow and quiver to the other side. She kept up the patter as she did this; Elton responded well to the sound of her voice.

"Okay, next is the bridle. Noooo big deal, okay? It goes on your head, like this."

She demonstrated on herself first, then slipped it on him.

This did not go well, but also could have gone worse.

He tried to bite her. He *didn't*, but he tried to. This was an ominous development considering she hadn't even tried to get the bit into his mouth yet.

Max rode without a bit, but Max was older, and was well trained. Elton had either no training or very little. On one hand, he seemed really calm, but on the other, there was no evidence that this horse had been tended to by human hands before meeting Win.

She got the bridle on. He wasn't happy with it, but once she started rubbing the spot between his eyes, he calmed right down.

The bit didn't happen, though. She tried for something like twenty minutes and nearly lost a finger twice. If the world was still normal, she'd probably have gone online before then to look up *how to get a stubborn horse to take the bit,* but that wasn't an option. Her choices were get bitten, or stop trying.

"Okay, we'll try it later," she said. "Let's get used to having a human on your back and we'll see where that leads us."

Win walked him to the meadow behind the stable. It was a fine afternoon, the kind of day the younger version of Win would have used as an excuse to take Max down the trail until nightfall. And when she climbed onto Elton's back, for a full two seconds it felt like that again.

But only for two seconds.

Win kept a shortlist of the very worst ideas she'd had in her life. They included such chestnuts as piercing her own nose, trying to reconnect with her dad, and a wide range of drastic hairstyle choices.

Climbing onto the back of an unfamiliar horse who wouldn't take a bit, and possibly never wore a saddle before, moved to the top of the list pretty fast.

Elton *took off*. It was fortunate that she had one hand wrapped up in the bridle, as otherwise she would have ended up on her back right away. That would have been all sorts of devastating, considering Elton was wearing her weapons, food, and water. He still nearly swung her off in transit; she was able to get her other hand around some rope, and then her arms around his neck.

"It's okay, boy, it's okay," she shouted into his ear. "It's me, Win. It's okay."

It appeared her voice was no longer soothing when she was using it to shout at him. Elton didn't have much to say in return, but she imagined if he could speak, he would say, *Get off get off get offffff.*

Her efforts to rein him in or even steer him in one direction or another proved fruitless, so she opted to just hold on tight and wait until he calmed down. And also until he stopped trying to knock her off with tree limbs.

This didn't happen often, mainly because the speed Elton needed to obtain in order to scrape her off didn't blend well with the available trails. She noticed this when she first set out from home; all the trails in the woods were overgrown. They would have given a competent team—like her and Max—a real problem above anything faster than a trot.

Elton mostly stuck to open fields and roads instead, thankfully not so panicked about having her on his back that he risked harming himself. Although that might have been because there was simply a dearth of cliffs to run off.

It took him about an hour to calm down. By then they were who knows how far from where they started. She didn't know which direction he ran, even. Not until she saw the on-ramp for the highway.

"I had no idea I'd gotten so close," she muttered, patting Elton on the neck.

She climbed down. He huffed in her face, so she gave him another apple and apologized for a few minutes.

"It wasn't so bad, though, right?"

He didn't seem convinced, so she pulled the stiff-bristle brush from her bag and used it on him for a few minutes.

"Are you speaking to me now?" she asked.

He huffed some more, which she decided to interpret as a yes.

They spent a little while in the field behind a vacant gas station, stretching and eating, before she took ahold of his lead again.

"No, it's okay," she said, because he looked concerned. "We're just walking. Come on, let's go see if we can find signs of life."

She led him—not all that reluctantly, so she thought maybe real progress had been made—across the street and up the ramp to the Massachusetts Turnpike.

"Would you look at that," she said.

Elton whinnied.

"That's what I'm saying."

The scene told an interesting story. There were hundreds of

cars on the road, stretching all the way over a hill on one side and around the bend on the other. But they were only on the outbound side. The inbound half was completely empty. Evidently, on the same night Win was climbing into bed in her childhood home after a long day of travel, the entire commonwealth was actively fleeing the Boston area.

Why hardly mattered. She was well beyond putting her experiences against a logical litmus test. Evidence first, understanding later. Maybe. She was also well beyond expecting any of this to make sense. Plus, after a week of this, she wasn't sure if she was even the best judge of what did and didn't make sense anymore.

She walked up to the nearest car: a subcompact with open windows and no apparent occupant. The interior looked about like one would expect the interior to look for a car with windows open during a rainstorm a few days earlier. Just a lot of mud and dirt.

The car behind it had its windows up, so she went to check it out next. The window glass and windshield were both dirty enough — due to something going on *inside* the car, not outside — that they were difficult to see through. She held her hands up to peek in, but it wasn't any help.

She drew her hunting knife. Elton snorted.

"It's okay," she said. "Hang tight. Loud noise coming."

She choked up on the knife handle and smashed the pommel down against the passenger window. It shattered, and a puff of dust escaped the interior.

There was another couple of piles of clothes inside: one in each of the two front seats. They sat amid a lot of dust and . . . shoes.

There were shoes on the floor. That changed the dynamic entirely.

She reached through the broken window and picked up the blouse in the passenger seat.

A jawbone holding a full set of teeth fell out of it.

Win screamed and jumped back, startling Elton.

"It's okay, it's okay," she said, trying to calm him. "It's okay. Oh, my God, it's *not* okay. No, no, it *is* okay. Shhh."

She brushed his neck to calm him down, although really, this time she was the one in need of calming. Her eyes kept drifting up and down the highway at the vast chain of cars stuck in eternal gridlock.

"This is a graveyard," she said.

Wandering the countryside alone, she had imagined that everyone was dead already. But it was one thing to come to that conclusion after looking at circumstantial evidence. It was another to find the bodies.

What were you all running from? she wondered.

She reached back in through the window and grabbed the jawbone, holding it up.

"What *does this* to a person?"

Elton sniffed the bone and looked away. Win shoved it in her bag and looked up the highway again. There were answers to be had, and now she knew which way to go.

"You ever been to Boston?" she asked Elton.

He had not.

"Me neither."

She walked Elton across the median to the inbound side of the turnpike and pointed his nose inbound.

"Well, here's our chance," she said. "If you still want to run when I'm on your back, go ahead. Just do it in that direction."

She climbed onto his back, and held on tight.

FOUR

Robbie

1

IF THERE WAS ONE THING THE TEAM CONSISTING OF A COM-puter programmer, a biology major, a probably econ major, and a thirteen-year-old juvenile delinquent named Bethany could agree on, it was that none of them possessed the survival skills necessary to last for long in a world without stocked supermarkets or the supply chain that stocked them.

It was a harsh discovery, made shortly after Robbie and Carol left the dorm to reunite with Touré and meet Bethany: Between the four of them, nobody had once gone hunting, skinned a rabbit, deboned a fish, or plucked a chicken. The only knives any of them were familiar with were steak knives. And not one member of the party had fired a gun or even picked one up.

On the last point, Touré had at least *some* knowledge, except that it all came from a role-playing game, so what he knew didn't extend beyond familiarity with guns that were used in the Wild West. He likewise knew the difference between a katana and a wakizashi—also from role-playing, albeit from a different game

—which was still useless information, as he could neither use one of them nor get his hands on one.

They couldn't get their hands on any guns either, because nobody sold guns in Cambridge.

The only reason they were still alive after a week was because of the fortuitous discovery of the many, many bricks of "nutrient bars" they'd stumbled upon in the supermarket. They were on a pallet in the middle of the otherwise nearly picked-clean store, which was interesting for a lot of reasons. It implied that nobody wanted the nutrient bars and went for the regular food first. A counterpoint to this observation—made by Carol, who was quickly turning into the closest thing they had to an adult—was the suggestion that the bricks were put out only after the shelves had been stripped, and possibly *because* they were. A supporting point in favor of this argument was that there were three empty pallets next to the one with the nutrient bricks.

The sign in front of the supply was only nominally helpful. It read:

NOOT BARS
MAX 2 PER CUSTOMER

Beneath the message was a company logo—a triangle with an off-center rectangle inside of it—that matched the logo stamped on the bricks.

According to the Noot bar packaging, one brick was the equivalent of six to eight meals for an adult. Doing a little math, this meant the four of them had between sixty and seventy days to figure out how to feed themselves off the land, find someone who could teach them how to survive, find *more* Noot bars, or discover where everyone else in the world was hiding and move there.

The two problems with the Noot bar were (1) none of them had ever heard of it, even though the in-store advertising suggested a ubiquity on par with certain brands of soda, and (2) it tasted kind of blah. Not *awful*, not *great*, just somewhere between sawdust and unseasoned tofu.

They ate the bricks anyway, washed down with water from whatever source was available. Both the dormitory in which Carol and Robbie had hidden on the first night and the grocery store that kept Touré and Bethany safe had tap water that tasted just fine. Whether or not it was actually contaminated with some tasteless and odorless terrible, awful thing was the subject of occasional discussion, but everyone agreed it was preferable to getting water from the Charles.

On this point, they *could* pull water from the river, but they didn't have many receptacles to carry water in, so it would make for a lot of trips. There was also an open question as to whether the Charles River was a better option than tap water. Carol and Robbie seemed to think it had to be, by default, but they weren't raised in the area. Touré had been, and so had Bethany, and they'd both been told that falling in the river meant a tetanus shot. Nobody was sure if this was true or if it was just something people said, but given the evident health of the animals living on and around the river, it seemed the latter was closer to being correct.

The real problem was the same as it had been from day one: If they wanted to know whether the water in the Charles was safe, they had to look up the answer in some kind of online resource, which they couldn't access. They lacked electricity, and because of that they lacked information. To get information, they had to find another way to communicate with the outside world.

They were all staying in the dormitory, because it had plenty of beds, whereas the grocery store had none. Conversely, the store had the pallet of Noot bars, which was too large and heavy to take everywhere, so they wanted to stay close. It wasn't as if one of them had suggested they simply stay put because the dorm was safe and was near their only food source. It was more that nobody offered an alternative and they were already there.

Staying at the dorm contributed to the sense that all of this was temporary. Why find a long-term solution when surely people who knew more about surviving were out there, just waiting to be discovered?

Consequently, every plan they made was a short-term answer to an immediate need. When it was clear their isolation was going to last more than a day or two, Robbie and Touré went out on the bikes and filled up backpacks with clothes for all four of them, but it was clothing meant to last through the next two weeks: T-shirts, jeans, socks and underwear, and a couple of jackets. Toothbrushes, toothpaste, and deodorant took three days to discover, and they were still looking for shampoo.

Soap they had plenty of, because the janitor's closet was well stocked. Likewise, they had lots of towels and toilet paper. Most personal grooming had to involve cold water, so nobody was taking proper showers so much as sponging and toweling off before they froze to death—because the building had no heat. Inevitably, when their rescuers arrived, they would find four living people who smelled awful, had too much hair in too many of the wrong places, with bad breath, and who were suffering from a vitamin C deficiency.

But they would be *alive*.

Making contact with these hypothetical rescuers continued to be Robbie and Touré's primary focus. This manifested both in harmless ways and in less harmless ways—meaning, they could be doing something better with their time.

A harmless example was the day Robbie took another look at

the display case Carol had found back on their first night in the dormitory. Inside the case was a device called a field phone, from the Second World War.

The fact that it was a portable phone wasn't the interesting part. The interesting part was that it had a lever on the side that could be used to charge it before making a call. Maybe, Robbie reasoned, if they hooked it up and charged it, they could make a phone call somewhere. Whose number to try remained an open question.

They broke it out of the case and spent the evening attaching the landline wires to the back of the field phone. (This was some work, because they needed to strip the wires first, which meant finding a knife, and it took them three hours to find a knife.) Then they cranked it, and listened for a dial tone that never came.

The experiment was deemed a partial success, as it seemed as if the lever did manage to create an electrical charge. Since none of them knew how to produce electricity—Touré vaguely recalled magnets being important, but couldn't remember why—having something that gave them a charge was a solid step forward. They just didn't know what to do with it.

Less harmlessly, after getting additional clothes and various sundries for the dorm, Robbie and Touré spent their days roaming the area on bikes. This wasn't inherently harmful—they were gaining a better understanding of how wrecked certain parts of the commonwealth were—but it was a waste of the time at least one member of the party thought they simply didn't have.

Not that looking for other survivors wasn't of value.

They were hoping to find someone with complementary skills. Medical training would be of particular use, everyone agreed, for while nobody had suffered a serious cut, bruise, or break as of yet, it was sure to happen eventually. Better than a doctor would be someone who knew what happened during the whateverpocalypse—Touré's word, which they'd all adopted without entirely meaning to—but they'd all come to some sort of peace with the notion that no explanation would be forthcoming. Or if it did, it wouldn't be soon.

The daily jaunts were something Robbie and Touré decided to do on their own, and as the only people in the group who could ride bikes—Bethany claimed she didn't know how, and Carol obviously couldn't—they didn't seem to think additional input was needed.

Carol disagreed. Her reasoning was solid: It was going to be cold soon, and they needed to be prepared for that.

One of the reasons this point became a subject of debate was that nobody could agree on how soon was soon.

2

"I am saying," Carol said, "that we need to plan for winter, and we need to do it now."

They were sitting in the common room after another day in which the guys returned with little more than stories of wrecked places. On this day, they reported that a mall in Porter Square had been vandalized by animals, a neighborhood near Teele Square had burned down recently, and there still wasn't anyone alive other than them. Also, they saw a bear. This was very exciting.

Carol was pushing them to collect more winter-specific provisions. Robbie and Touré had already picked up spare bits of outerwear on their trips—mostly for themselves, since they could try stuff on as they went—but the problem was, there was only so much they could carry back on the bikes. To do this right, they really needed a car, and that wasn't an option.

"I understand that," Touré said to Carol, "but we have time. We'll pick up things every day, okay? It's no rush. You're from Florida; you probably think winter here is way worse than it is."

"I'm familiar with seasonality," Carol said, "and I'm up to date on the severity of the winters in New England. The climatic changes—"

"Yeah, yeah, but it's *months away*, I'm saying. Maybe we get five feet of snow this year . . . it's still five feet of snow *four or five months* from now."

"It's five feet of snow we won't know is coming until it's here," Carol said. "We have no forecasts, and *meteorologist* isn't on our list of skills. And it isn't just clothing. It's heat. We have none. We'll freeze to death where we're sitting if we don't prepare. It's already chilly in the evenings, and we have only so many blankets."

"Hang on," Robbie said. "Touré, what do you mean, four or five months?"

"Yeah, I was wondering about that too," Bethany said. "What are you talking about? It's like eight or nine months."

"Right," Robbie said. "No, wait, hang on. That isn't right either. It's two or three months. I don't know where eight came from."

"Yes," Carol agreed. "Robbie's right. We're nearing the end of September. The weather is surely about to turn."

"Whoa, what?" Touré said. "It's July."

"It's September," Robbie said. "Maybe second week."

"Closer to the fourth," Carol said.

"No, the first week of classes was the first week of September, and then . . ."

"Classes began the middle of the second week," Carol said. "And I know exactly what time of month it is now."

"How do you . . . Oh. Right."

"I'm . . . quite regular," she said.

"So I guess we can use *that* as a timepiece now," Robbie said.

"But honestly, this is turning into the weirdest conversation I've ever had."

"You're all nuts," Bethany said. "It's not close to September or July. It's the middle of May."

"*May?*" Touré said. "You're off your meds, kid."

None of them knew very much about Bethany. She had a way with locks that implied an extensive history of minor criminal behavior, but that wasn't as illuminating as it probably should have been. Robbie could envision a backstory for her that was built on this particular aspect of her character, but it would have been ripped from *Oliver Twist*, and this wasn't nineteenth-century London. Granted, he never lived in a city before, but he didn't think there were roving packs of street urchins pickpocketing Boston's well-to-do.

Her being an orphan was certainly still a possibility; she never spoke about her family, or about any friends, which could indicate some reticence to discuss painful matters—on the assumption they were all dead—or it could mean she had no parents or friends. Either way, Robbie hadn't figured out how to ask her about herself yet; she tended to get defensive quickly.

One thing he *did* know about her was that she hated to be called a kid. This was probably why Touré always called her that.

"I will cut your throat in your sleep if you don't stop with the *kid* crap," she said to Touré.

"With what?" he asked. "Are you packing a switchblade?"

"I know how to handle myself."

"Sure."

"I should never have let you in!" she said. "I should have let the wolves get you."

Bethany lamented having ever allowed Touré into the supermarket at least once a day.

"Guys, knock it off," Robbie said. "This isn't helping."

"Well, it's *not* May, Robert," Touré said, "and it's not September. It's *July*. You think I don't know what month it is? What's the matter with all of you?"

"Harvard classes don't begin before September," Carol said. "Why would we be here otherwise?"

"That's between you and the school," Touré said. "I know what I know."

"We don't need to rely on what you *think* you know," Robbie said. "There are other ways."

"Yeah, I checked online this morning," Touré said. "It didn't help."

"No, man—*look outside*."

The windows on one side of the common room looked out over the courtyard, beyond which was Memorial Drive and the Charles River. Out of the other windows was a formerly well-groomed lawn with a copse of trees.

Robbie pointed to the windows facing the front of the dorm, and singled out the trees, still visible in the light of the setting sun.

"I've been outside," Touré said. "What's your point?"

"The leaves are turning. You want to tell me that happens in July?"

The leaves weren't just turning; they had already turned. There was no green left, and there hadn't been for at least a week. Everywhere they looked was an explosion of oranges and browns.

"Oh . . . damn," Touré said. "It didn't even register."

"You're right," Bethany said. "He's right."

"But I think we're all wrong, guys," Touré said. "I mean, unless the seasons got messed up along with everything else, it's gotta be October. How's that even possible?"

"How is *any* of this possible?" Carol said. "As I said, we live in a building with no heat, and we have no winter clothes. How long before we're in trouble?"

"Maybe a month," Touré said.

"We'll need firewood," Carol said. "Perhaps tomorrow you could find an axe. Has anyone chopped wood before?"

"I've set a couple of fires," Bethany said.

"*Of course* you have," Touré said.

3

The next day, Robbie and Touré hit up the hardware store on Mass Ave. It was only a mile or so from the dormitory, a few blocks from Touré's apartment, and within sight of the bike shop. Given the store wasn't terribly large, there was a decent chance there *were* no axes, but according to Touré the nearest big chain store was in Watertown and they hadn't even attempted to explore in that direction yet.

They were both very familiar with the neighborhood. That neither of them had tried to tap the contents of the hardware store already only spoke to how unprepared they were to survive the whateverpocalypse. Surely even a half-decent prepper would have started there. A half-decent prepper would have also known what to do with the stuff inside.

Robbie had a passing familiarity with tools. His dad was handy enough, and he'd provided Robbie with plenty of opportunities to watch someone else use tools correctly. He just never did much of it himself. When something broke, he'd tell Dad, and Dad would fix it.

Robbie never used to think much about what his adult life was going to be like, but he imagined a day when he was out on his own, living in a different state with a wife and child, calling up his father because he needed a shelf hung and figured it would end up crooked if he did it himself. He also imagined his father seeing no problem with just driving over to take care of it.

The idea that his father would never be able to do that now had just begun to sink in over the past couple of days. When Robbie was alone, he discovered that he was prone to crying jags without any evident trigger. He wasn't thinking about his father when it happened, or his mom, sister, or friends from home. This was almost worse, because it meant that just being alive was its own trigger.

He kept the crying from the others, as much as that was possible.

"Yeah, man, I don't know what it is," Touré was saying. "She bugs me; I can't explain why."

He was complaining about Bethany, which he did regularly.

"Here's one," Robbie said, kneeling over to pry a brick loose from the sidewalk.

In Cambridge some sidewalks were paved with regular old cement, some sections were brick, and a couple of spots—around the trees—were covered with some sort of breathable rubber. Robbie thought the rubber was sort of cool; it allowed the tree to grow (and must be letting water through a porous surface) without the roots destroying the sidewalk. It was especially noticeable now that the trees had gone mad. There were several cracks in the cement, and the tree roots under brick had managed to work most of the bricks loose, but the rubber held.

They needed bricks to get into stores. It was either that or bring along the resident lock-picker, which Touré considered a last resort.

"I think she's hiding something," Touré said.

"You're the only one picking that up," Robbie said. "She's just private. Next you'll be telling me you think Carol can actually see."

Touré laughed.

"Nah, I tested that," he said.

"How?"

"Never mind how. You gonna throw that, or can I?"

"Have at it," Robbie said, handing over the brick.

It was still early morning. There was a low fog hanging over the street which, in the red sunrise, turned everything pinkish. It looked like it was going to be a clear day, but they had rain a few days back that had come out of nowhere, so he wasn't sure how much he could trust his predictive skills.

Rabbits, squirrels, and chipmunks were scurrying this way and that through the ground fog, not at all certain about what to do with the humans. It was like they thought they probably *should* be afraid but were waiting on confirmation.

Robbie wondered for the umpteenth time what it would take to kill and eat one of the rabbits. It was a thought he never expected to have, certainly, not to mention a skill he never expected to need. On the other hand, his breakfast had been five bites of a Noot bar, which he was quite thoroughly sick of. He was pretty sure if he didn't eat something else soon, the next meat-centric daydream he had was going to involve cannibalism.

Touré chucked the brick through the front window of the hardware store. The glass shattered loudly, disrupting the peaceful morning.

"Boy, that's fun," Touré said. "We should do this more often."

"Probably heard that for miles," Robbie said. "So maybe not."

"So? We're looking for other people, right? Do more of this and they'll find us."

"That's not the kind of attention I'm worried about."

"The wolves only hunt at night. C'mon."

Robbie didn't say so, because Touré already knew it, even if he wasn't willing to acknowledge it, but there were creatures other than the wolf-beasts to worry about. They'd seen—from a distance, thankfully—two bears, on different occasions in different parts of town. They also met an elk who looked downright furious, gotten charged at by a four-point buck, stared down a wild boar, and saw a moose from afar. Nature was terrifying, and it was all over the place.

They stepped into the store, past a cardboard display touting chainsaw technology.

It was dark in the back. Robbie took the bag off his shoulder and extracted a wooden table leg with a torn piece of bedsheet wrapped around the tip, a container of lighter fluid, and a book of matches.

The carton of matches was the big prize of their second day's quest for provisions, and the lighter fluid the big prize of the third day. They had proven to be more useful than just about anything other than the Noot bars. The team still had to learn how to rediscover electricity, but fire remained discovered.

He squirted some lighter fluid on the bedsheet, lit the torch, and headed into the back.

"And another thing," Touré said. "She keeps harping on how she saved my life, like that's a thing."

"But didn't she?"

"We don't know that. You guys made it through the night okay. I mean, all she did was open a door. I bet I could've found a way in on my own."

The store was selectively empty. All the camping gear was gone, which was frustrating but not surprising. They needed sleeping bags, blankets, and winter gear, but this wasn't the place to get those things anyway. Robbie didn't know where *to* go, but that was the next problem after figuring out how to turn a tree into firewood.

"Axes," Touré said, from the other end of the aisle. "I think. Bring the light over."

Not just axes; a *selection* of axes, which just struck Robbie as weird. How many different ways could there be to design an axe?

"Look, I understand," Robbie said, regarding Bethany. "She annoys you. You annoy her just as much, I'm sure. It's normal. I probably annoy all three of you."

Touré laughed.

"Sure, but not so much. And I don't think you and Carol annoy each other at all. How's this?"

He held up one of the four axe options.

"Super. What do you mean, about Carol?"

"You know what. Speaking of, you ever think about . . . ?"

"Think about what?"

"You know. Come springtime, we're going to have to start talking about repopulating, right? Last people on Earth, we have a duty here."

"I am begging you to stop talking right now."

"Fine. We'll take two axes. Unless you want to try a chainsaw? They run on gas, don't they?"

"I don't know. I don't know how to use one and I like having all my limbs."

"Yeah, me too. It's an option, though. Keep it in the back of your mind, in case it turns out chopping down a tree is too hard."

Touré turned around to head back to the street, and Robbie was about to follow when he caught a flash of light at the edge of his vision.

It was coming from the back of the store.

"Hey, Touré?" Robbie said.

"Yeah?"

Touré looked back. Robbie didn't have to add anything, as it was quickly obvious what was bothering him.

There was a collection of fireflies in the back. That wasn't really what it was, but that was what it looked like — a swirl of light spinning in a tight circle, not obviously emanating from or being manipulated by anything nearby.

"What . . . the hell . . . is that?" Touré asked.

"I have no idea."

The lights settled into a stationary orbit: vaguely vertical, about six feet tall and three feet wide.

And then, after a collective shimmer, they re-formed into something with two arms, two legs, a torso, and a head.

Robbie and Touré had just enough time to register this before it blinked out of existence.

Robbie realized he was holding his breath.

"You saw that, right?" Touré asked. "That wasn't just me?"

"I saw it."

Robbie walked to the back of the store, to the spot where the shimmery whatever-it-was had appeared. Nothing was there that could explain what they'd just witnessed, although he couldn't really imagine what a proper explanation would look like.

"What do you think it was?" Robbie asked.

"I have some ideas. A human being trapped in another dimension, trying to tell us what happened to everyone. An alien. A silvery ghost piercing the veil to warn us about something. All sound good to me."

"A hallucination?"

"Both of us?"

"A joint hallucination."

"Sure, if that's possible," Touré said. "I like the other options better. I can probably come up with ten more if you give me a few minutes."

"We should ask Bethany if she's seen anything like that," Robbie said.

Touré shrugged. "Maybe," he said.

"You don't want to ask Bethany."

"I didn't say that."

"I know you don't like her, but she *can* see, so . . ."

"No, I get it," Touré said. "I'm not sure we should even mention it until we have a better idea what just happened. Put that out. Let's get out of here."

Touré headed back to the street while Robbie tried to douse the torch.

They were still working on torch technology. Holding a match up to the end of a table leg didn't accomplish much other than to make the wood smolder, which wasn't entirely resolved by wrapping the cloth around the end of it. They tried this — leg, then match, then cloth — after finding the matches. It caught, but didn't stay that way for long.

What they needed was an accelerant, which was what led to the lighter fluid. (Bethany, who evidently *did* know a lot about setting fires, was the one who worked this out.)

But once the cloth was lit, there was a decent chance that flaming bits of material would fall off, right onto the hand of whoever was holding the torch. They'd nearly lit the dorm on fire three times because of this. Worse, once the wood caught, there was nothing preventing the flame from creeping all the way down and engulfing the entire leg. Holding the torch upright—so the flame would have to go against gravity—sometimes did the trick, but not every time.

Robbie had a couple of painful burns on his hands because of all that. Nothing serious enough to need a doctor, which was great, because, again, they didn't have one. But that day was coming.

He was still trying to extinguish the torch, by waving it around to put the fire out, when Touré began shouting.

"HEY! HEY, NO! DON'T RUN!"

Robbie looked up, half expecting to find that the sparkling man had returned and was now being accosted by Touré.

That wasn't it.

There was a teenage boy a quarter of a mile up Mass Ave. He looked skinny, and scared, and malnourished . . . and disinterested in having a conversation with the guy holding two axes and shouting at him. He turned around and ran up a side street.

"We got a live one," Touré said. "C'mon!"

He dropped the axes and broke into a run.

On any other day, they'd have the bikes, but for the axe-fetching task they'd agreed walking made more sense, because neither of them relished the idea of biking around while carrying axes. Not on these roads.

"Right," Robbie said. He chucked the torch into the middle of the street, where it was less likely to ignite something else, dropped his backpack on the ground, and started running.

He was in better shape than Touré, but in worse shoes. Getting some running shoes and a decent pair of boots was near the top of the list of things he wanted to do before the snows came; he just hadn't gotten around to it yet. Until he'd had to sprint in his penny loafers, it hadn't really seemed urgent.

He caught up with Touré eventually though, about four blocks down Mass Ave.

"He went up there," Touré said, between heavy breaths. He was pointing down a side street. "That road doesn't lead anywhere. It goes right, and right again, and then it hooks back up with Mass Ave. down there. You keep behind him—I'll go straight and try to cut him off."

"Okay."

They broke, doing the one thing Touré was in the habit of insisting they *not* do: split up.

Robbie ran down the middle of the side street, past all variety of scrambling woodland creatures who thought he was running after them.

One of these days, we're going to stumble on the wolf den, he thought. And of course, as soon as he thought it, he became certain he was about to do exactly that.

But instead he turned the corner on nothing in particular. Just more disabled cars in permanent parking spaces, ruptured pavement, trees with the occasional scary-looking furry beastie, and, importantly, no frightened teenage boy.

Robbie slowed to a walk. If the kid wasn't in view, he had either turned the next corner already—in which case Touré was about to meet up with him—or he was hiding somewhere nearby.

"Hey," Robbie said. "If you can hear me, we're friends. We have food and shelter."

No answer. A horny squirrel started chittering, but that was probably not directed at Robbie.

"Come on, you must be hungry," he said.

There was a corporate parking garage to his left, about halfway down the street. He stopped in front of it and started scanning the decks, as this was the sort of place he might hide out if he were on the run. It was open, unlike all the presumably locked buildings in every direction, and it offered a raised vantage point.

His eyes settled on the second level. There was something peculiar about the shadows up there. It wasn't a peculiarity he could pin down, so he just kept staring in case an explanation arrived.

It did, sort of. He became convinced something in the darkness up there was staring back at him. The shadow *itself* was peculiar; the sunrise wasn't hitting the front of the garage yet, but the ambient light of the sun was reducing the bite of the shade everywhere else. The middle of the garage refused to succumb.

Robbie decided that was the problem he had with the second floor; the lack of light was unnatural somehow.

There was probably an excellent explanation that would present itself if he stared at the spot for long enough, he decided. So he continued to stare, as if this was a competition to see who blinked first.

Robbie won when the darkness blinked.

That wasn't right. There was a better description for what just happened. There wasn't anyone up there, and what wasn't up there didn't *blink,* and if it *had* blinked, it was a dark thing in a dark place, *blinking darkly.* He couldn't have *seen* it. This was just the underutilized creative side of his brain, trying out a new and fun hallucination, right after showing him a bunch of fireflies shaped like a person.

Or maybe the Noot bars had hallucinogenic effects that were just now kicking in.

If he really wanted to prove nobody was up there, he could charge up the ramp. It wasn't far; just one flight. But that wasn't happening, because he needed his legs for that and his legs didn't feel like moving.

Robbie was still standing there when Touré ran up. It had probably been just a minute or two, but felt longer.

"Did you see him?" Touré asked.

"Who?" Robbie asked. He broke off from the staring contest with the darkness.

"The kid. Did you see him? He didn't come out the other side."

"No, man," Robbie said. "I didn't see him."

He looked up at the garage again. It looked perfectly normal now.

All in your head, Rob, he told himself.

"Are you sure he came this way?" Robbie asked.

"Pretty sure. You all right?"

"Yeah, I'm fine. I need some rest, is all. Come on, let's head back. The kid's gotta resurface eventually."

Carol

Carol walked along the river, alone. She had her cane, and her ears, and that was enough to get around during the day in a world without cars and only a few predators. Probably.

She needed the air. They'd been living in the dorm for only a week, but the place smelled stale and artificial, like the air had already been used by someone else. She'd explored every floor at least once, in search of . . . well, not really in search of anything so much as just keeping busy.

When it came to looking for stuff that was of use to the team, she was not the person best equipped to be on point. She could hear things better, perhaps — although this wasn't really true; she just *listened* better — but that was only helpful if they wanted to know how many mice were living in the walls. (The answer: quite a few.)

Everyone else wanted her to be safe, so they insisted she stay inside. Carol appreciated their concern, especially since they could just as easily have concluded it would be best for them if she went away and died somewhere. They'd have more food, and they would be more mobile.

It was conceivable that were it not for the burden of the blind woman, Robbie and Touré would have already biked halfway across the state to wherever the people were . . . if there were in fact any people to be found. Like the others, she continued to hold out hope that this was just a temporary existence, even if she was also the one arguing that they needed to plan as if it was permanent. It was an attitude she tried not to push too hard, because without that hope, she didn't know what the others would do.

She stopped on the path to listen to the world around her. Every now and then, she got this sense that Burton was near, but of course he wasn't. It was her mind playing tricks again, twisting what she desperately wanted to be true into an illusion of reality.

Carol had been struggling with the implications of this evident human apocalypse a lot in the last couple of days. It kicked in once she felt safe for the first time since the day she and Robbie awoke in an empty dormitory. The scope was just too vast to absorb all at once, so it rolled in slowly instead, in waves of understanding.

Everyone she ever knew—her parents, her high school classmates, the first boy she ever kissed—was dead. And yet, as she came to grips with that, the one she missed most painfully was her dog.

Something scurried over her foot. She jumped back in surprise, and then laughed.

There were so many animals moving around her now. She found it terrifying at first; a week later, it was fascinating, and somewhat entertaining as long as none of them was trying to eat her. Had all these creatures *always* been there, just biding their time until humanity exited the food chain?

Up ahead, she heard what had to be a Canada goose squawking angrily at . . . well, not at *her*—of this she was fairly certain. A disagreement between the geese and some other creature was heating up to her right, toward the riverbank, and that was enough of a reason not to head in that direction until it was resolved.

She found a tree and sat down under it.

There was a cat of some kind over her head. It didn't sound heavy enough to pose a threat. Of course, it *did* pose a very real threat, because she couldn't see it in order to defend herself properly. But it didn't know that.

Presently, she heard Bethany coming down the path.

"Hey," the girl said, "I don't think you're supposed to be out alone, are you?"

"I'm not alone," Carol said. "You're here."

"I'm here *now*. For real, these animals are whackjobs. *I* don't feel safe, and I can see . . . Shit, sorry. I mean, I know they're coming."

"It's not a secret, my being blind. You can talk about it. It's perhaps a blessing right now, not to see what's around us. They're leaving us alone. As with bees."

"Not sure I know what you mean," Bethany said. "You know, there's a bench right over here. Probably more comfortable. Fewer ants, for sure."

"Is there?" Carol held her hand up. "Help me over."

Bethany was a little thing, not quite finished with puberty. She had to really lean back to counterbalance Carol. Then she helped her to the bench.

"This *is* better, thank you," Carol said.

"You're welcome."

"What I mean is, bees are harmless if you don't try to swat at them. They only attack out of a need to defend themselves."

"Oh, I didn't know that. Cool."

Carol leaned back and enjoyed the breeze coming off the river, while Bethany sat there and struggled to come up with a way to verbalize what was on her mind. She fidgeted, and inhaled as if to speak, but then did not. Carol waited her out.

"That thing you were saying earlier," Bethany said, finally. "About knowing the time of month."

"Oh. Yes. What about it?"

"Do you . . . how do you . . ."

Carol reached out and took Bethany's hand.

"Have you had your first yet?" she asked the girl, wondering if she'd just been elected to have *the talk* with their resident pubescent.

"Oh, yeah. Yeah, yes, I have. But, um, I don't know when it's supposed to happen again. Or if it even will. And, like . . . I don't have any other clothes right now? Underwear, I mean. I was gonna go out and get some, because I don't want to ask . . . I mean, that's the last thing I want to tell Touré, and . . . maybe Robbie would be cool with it, he seems okay. So I was gonna go out and find some on my own, but I don't want to leave you. I've been washing my stuff in the sink, but man."

"You don't want to soil yourself."

"I'm saying."

"I have pads. I made Robbie find some for me on the third day. The poor boy, I think I could hear him blushing."

Bethany laughed. Carol thought it might be the first time she'd heard the girl laugh genuinely. She had a witheringly scornful artificial laugh that was reserved for whatever came out of Touré's mouth, but this was very different.

"What's up with you and Robbie, anyway?" Bethany asked.

"I don't know what you mean."

"I dunno. You guys are like . . . a *team*. Whenever there's a vote, you two always agree on everything. Even what month it is."

"I guess we do," Carol said. "But you seem to always abstain."

"I what?"

"You decline to vote."

"Well, yeah, it doesn't matter. If I agree with you two, there's no point saying so. If I disagree, I'm siding with the asshat."

It was Carol's turn to laugh.

"Touré is a challenge, but he's not so terrible."

"Right, well, anyway, you and Robbie are in charge, so . . ."

"Are we?"

"One of you is. I can't tell which. You're a team, like I said. It doesn't matter anyway."

Bethany pulled her hand away.

"I can give you some pads," Carol said. "And you're right—we should task the boys with fetching some undergarments. But tell me: Why did you say 'if it will'?"

"Why did I say what?"

"Just now, you were talking about your time of the month, and you sounded uncertain as to whether you'll have another. Do you have questions? Biologically?"

"Oh. No, I know it's *supposed* to happen again, you know, if this was normal. I meant because of how things are now."

"I still don't understand."

"Yeah, forget it. Maybe . . ."

Carol reached out to take Bethany's hand again, but the younger girl had stood. She was still there, but out of reach.

"Bethany, what did you want to say?" Carol asked.

Bethany was dragging her toe along the sidewalk. Carol could hear it sliding around; auditory indications of a deep reluctance.

"I figured it was obvious," Bethany said.

"I don't understand," Carol said.

"But either way, if you're still doing it, so will I, so I should prepare for it. Wasn't sure if everything was put on pause, you know?"

"No, I don't know. 'On pause'?"

Bethany sighed.

"I mean," Bethany said, "I can't be the only one who figured it out."

"Bethany, *what?* Tell me."

"We're all dead," she said.

Bethany

1

When Bethany's family first moved into the house on Fayerweather Street — she was eight — they gave her the bedroom with the windows that opened over the roof of the carport. She'd been taking advantage of this ever since.

Sometimes, it served as a makeshift porch, where she'd lie down on a towel placed over the too-hot shingles and roast herself in the sun. Or she'd use it whenever she needed to win a game of hide-and-seek. It was also where she would go to get away from her younger brother, Dustin, who had perfected a kind of annoying designed specifically for her torment.

It wasn't until she turned twelve that it became more than a secret extension of her bedroom. That was when she got her hands on an old wooden ladder.

The ladder lived under the window, where it couldn't be seen from the street, except when she needed it. Then it lived on the back side of the carport.

Late at night, if there was a place to be—or even if there wasn't and she just felt like it—she'd hang the ladder over the side, climb down, and then go do whatever. Later, she'd come back and pull it up after her.

Mom and Dad were either not wise to this, or were indifferent. It was hard to tell with them. Dad was a big deal with a local bank (CFO or CEO or CIO or something else that began with a C) and Mom was . . . Actually, she didn't have a job. Her existence seemed defined by who she was married to and how many charity events she could cram into her schedule. She was always busy, anyway, with whatever. Bethany didn't mind; it freed her up to pursue her own personal interests.

Locks were always her biggest interest, although she couldn't say why.

She figured out how to pick a lock on her own, when she was six, using the underside of a barrette. This was in response to the nanny's decision to punish Bethany by locking her in her room for an hourlong timeout. Bethany didn't remember what she'd done, or much about where they were living then—it wasn't as nice, and it wasn't in Cambridge—but she did remember figuring out how locks worked by trial and error, over the course of that hour.

Half that, actually. She got the lock open in thirty minutes, then tiptoed down the hall and used the house phone to tell her mom that the nanny hit her and locked her up. She *hadn't* hit her, but since the rest was true, how much did it actually matter?

The nanny was fired, and that was cool.

By the time she was twelve, having already figured out how to pick all the locks in the house and in the midst of a crescendo of boredom that only mandatory summer reading lists can engender, she used the ladder to sneak out in the middle of the night in order to start a personal, largely harmless, crime spree.

She picked the neighbor's locks, just for kicks, not even going inside at first. For some reason, she thought it would be funny if there was an argument about who left the back door open the night before. That got boring—and less funny—fast, though, so then she started sneaking through the doors she'd opened.

Then she began taking things. Dumb things, like a garlic press, or all the refrigerator magnets. She'd return them later, but in weird places, like under the couch. Or she'd swap them: put what she took from one house in another house. One time she found a wedding ring on a holder next to the kitchen sink. She took it, broke into a house across the street, and put it next to the sink there.

It was fun. The only downside was almost never being able to appreciate how these little stunts played out. That was true up until the day her mom sat her down to have an Important Talk.

Bethany *thought* it was going to be on a different subject—sex, or the first time she bled, which hadn't happened yet—so she was prepared for all manner of awkward. But it wasn't that.

Instead, Mom began with "I want you to know that you're completely safe," which was a crazy way to go.

"Okay," Bethany said. "That's great, thanks."

Mom then went on about how there had been a series of break-ins in the neighborhood and everyone was worried, but added, "We're all safe here."

This should perhaps have scared Bethany into stopping—Mom used the word "safe" seven times, which got increasingly alarming as the talk went on—but her reaction was more or less the exact opposite: This was the best thing *ever*. Not only did they not know it was her, but they thought some guy was coming into the neighborhood and breaking into their houses in the middle of the night. This was *hilarious.*

Once she knew the whole neighborhood was trying to out-smart her, she was doubly interested in keeping it up.

Because now it was a competition.

Some of the neighbors got dogs, but they were easy to out-smart. All Bethany had to do was go over during the day and ask if she could pet the new dog, and then she was on the canine okay list and every dog on the street thought she was a friend.

They also added burglar alarms, which were harder to charm. Three times, she nearly got caught by an alarm, although it wasn't as close as it could have been. There was usually a *beep-beep* from the house alarm that preceded a full alert. As soon as she heard that, she ran for the back fence.

The cops also rolled up and down the street more often, but that was the easiest to avoid, because they were looking for someone who didn't look like they lived there.

It was all just for kicks. She never took anything of value, except to put it back where it came from or somewhere else, and nobody got hurt. She figured at worst, if she was caught, she'd be grounded, quietly. Nobody was going to want to admit that the terrible neighborhood crime spree was being perpetrated by a thirteen-year-old girl.

Bethany didn't remember *exactly* what happened on that night in May, the last time she snuck out the window. She did recall going down the ladder and heading to one of the big houses on the rich side of Reservoir, and she sort of remembered an alarm going off, and running. She had to take refuge in a tree for a couple of hours that night too, which in hindsight had to mean that the hunt for her was getting more serious. Somehow, in the moment, it still seemed fun and worth pursuing. It was only after the fact that it seemed crazy and stupid.

She fell asleep in the tree, but woke up before sunrise and made it back home before she got busted.

The next morning was when everything stopped making sense.

2

Her room was exactly as she'd left it, so she didn't even think anything was wrong until she tried leaving.

The bedroom door was locked. Her mom had locked it from the outside, which was, at minimum, a little weird. Granted, Bethany had her own bathroom, so it wasn't like any emergency short of a fire would have necessitated her exiting into the hall, but all the same, punishment usually works better on a person if they know they're being punished.

She didn't sweat it. Whatever was going on, she'd figure it out, either after Mom unlocked the door or after she picked the lock.

Since she was still in her clothes from the night before, she thought it best to wash up. There was no hot water for some reason, so she just did a quick rinse and changed clothes. Then, as nobody appeared to be coming to set her free, she let herself out.

The house was quiet. It was a pretty huge place, with an epic staircase leading up to a rotunda of rooms. At the far end, opposite the top of the staircase, was a grandfather clock that always tick-tick-ticked and chimed the hour. It was the job of one of the maids to make sure it was always going. That involved opening up the middle chamber and pulling until a weight was moved from the bottom of the clock to the top. *It's a magic clock that runs on gravity,* the maid told her one time.

The clock wasn't running that morning, though; somebody screwed up.

"Hello?" she shouted. Her words echoed back, trembling in the glass front of the grandfather clock and in the chandelier at the bottom of the stairs.

She headed down, around the staircase, to the kitchen.

It was an old, old house, the kind of old where the kitchen and its staff were hidden in back, away from the presumption of guests in the front of the place. A whole section was separated from the front, accessible only via a staircase from the kitchen. Dustin played on those back steps all the time, thinking it was a secret passageway, with ghosts and all.

Nobody was in the kitchen. Not even a ghost.

"Hello?" she shouted again. More tinny echoing.

It made zero sense. Mom certainly could not be there, and Dad was almost *never* there, because he shuttled between Boston and New York so regularly that he kept a place in Manhattan. But Dustin at least should be there, and someone making breakfast for them should be there, and at least one of the maids should be there.

The power's out, she realized.

To confirm, she crossed the kitchen and pulled open the refrigerator door. The inside was warm, and also empty.

This triggered something like panic in Bethany.

She started running from room to room, for any sign of life, first on the ground floor and then the bedrooms on the second floor. She even rechecked her own room, and the roof of the carport, just in case they were all hiding out there for some reason.

There was one thing of note about the roof, but it didn't involve her missing family: The ladder was gone.

She climbed out and looked over the side in case she forgot to pull it up, but it wasn't against the side of the carport, either.

Something else about the outside gave her pause: She couldn't hear anybody. They lived halfway up Fayerweather and looked down on Brattle, where there was always traffic—but today, there wasn't *any*. It was all weirdly quiet, except the birds, who were weirdly loud.

She climbed back inside, closed and locked the window, then ran back downstairs.

The house phone was in the study. Mom and Dad had adamantly refused to give her a cell phone before she turned sixteen for blah-blah-blah reasons that only made sense to them. *If you want to call someone, young lady, there's a perfectly good telephone right there,* her father said, without even laughing. Then he'd retire to that very study to do bank stuff, ensuring that if Bethany did have someone to call she wouldn't be doing it while her father was home.

The study was past the living room, through two sliding doors. She went inside and picked up the phone.

It was dead. She pushed the little button in the receiver cradle a bunch of times. Still nothing.

She got down on the floor and checked the connection. While she didn't know a lot about telephone maintenance, this one looked like it was hooked up to the wall in all the right ways.

On her knees, beside the desk, she was at the perfect angle to notice the altar.

That's what it was; there was no better way to describe it. It was through the double doors, in the living room, next to the front window. She must have run past it two or three times already and just not seen it, because she wasn't used to anything being there.

She got up and went for a closer look.

It had been set up on what looked like an old vanity. There was an enormous picture of Bethany in the center; a headshot from when she was twelve. In orbit around it were a number of other pictures of Bethany at different ages. In front was a row of candles, and a book.

Wait, am I DEAD? she thought.

She jumped back, her heart trying to pound its way through her throat.

When she was in third grade, a kid in her class drowned. Barney something. She didn't remember him at all, but she remembered his wake because that wasn't the kind of event a third-grader should ever attend.

Barney's parents had a collage on display in the funeral home, with a bunch of photos of Barney playing, and having fun, and smiling for the camera. It looked just like what Bethany was looking at now.

Only now *she* was the one being mourned.

Trembling, she opened the book.

It was a scrapbook. The first page was a copy of her own birth announcement, and her baby-as-a-burrito photo from the hospital. The next page was just pictures of her: in a stroller, in a crib, in a walker. The next had the first time she crawled.

This was a book about her life, beginning with childbirth and ending with ... ?

She flipped to the last page. It was a clipping from the *Boston Globe.*

NO SUSPECTS IN CASE OF MISSING CAMBRIDGE TEEN

Cambridge, MA — Police have no suspects in the case of the missing Cambridge teen, but a local burglar may be the key to the case.

Bethany Jacobs was believed to have been taken by an unknown individual who gained access to her bedroom by way of a ladder and an open window. Police are now saying a series of burglaries in the area may be linked ...

That was as far as she could read before the tears made it impossible to focus.

"I'm not dead!" she shouted. "I'm right here!"

Nobody was around to hear her: not Mom, or Dustin, her father or any of the house staff.

She ran outside to tell the neighbors she was still alive, but there wasn't anyone outside, either. A raccoon heard her testimony, but nobody human.

She kept on running, but there was no life to be found.

Bethany stopped running when she reached the river, which was full of every other kind of life.

Her eventual decision to break into the supermarket was made without a great deal of thought: She was hungry, and that was where the food was. She'd only been inside a short while before Touré showed up.

Up until then, as far as she knew, every human was gone.

3

Bethany didn't tell Carol any of this. She wasn't sure why—it just felt like there would be consequences if she did. She still woke up every morning half expecting Carol, Robbie, and Touré to be gone, just like her family.

"Why do you think we're dead?" Carol asked.

"What?"

"I said, why do you think we're dead? That's a peculiar suggestion. We seem to be the only ones *not* dead."

"I dunno," Bethany said. "Maybe not *dead* dead. Like, in another dimension or whatever. Like in a story. Or, what's that place in between heaven and hell?"

"Purgatory?"

"Yeah, that."

"If I believed in such a place, then . . ." Carol stopped, and sniffed the air.

"What is it?" Bethany asked.

Carol held her hand out.

"Rain is coming," she said. "We should go back inside."

FIVE

Paul

1

PASTOR PAUL SPENT A GOOD PART OF THE NEXT DAY TRYING to get power to the truck.

First, he pushed the vehicle around the side of the house, near the kitchen entrance, just in case he needed to sprint from the truck to the house in less time than it would take a bear to chase him down. Then he went about hooking up the battery to the generator to see about recharging it.

He needed a DC current—the generator had a rectifier, so that was fine—and a lot of prayer. If the Lord was of a mind to blow up Paul, this would be when to do it.

It didn't blow up, but it also didn't work. He got the car started, but as soon as the wires came off the battery, the truck shut down. The battery wouldn't hold a charge.

Still, he did get the engine running, which was a positive development. It just wasn't going to be all that helpful if he wanted the car to drive anywhere.

He scrounged heavy-duty wire, electrical tape, and plastic sheeting by going through Jed's house. Some of the wiring had to be torn out of a wall, which he would definitely apologize to his friend about if he ever saw him again.

When it was all done, the generator got a new home in the passenger seat, with a wire running from it to the hood of the car. It was attached directly to the alternator—if the battery wasn't going to work, there wasn't much of a point in involving it in the transaction.

It worked, but the generator had an exhaust problem, so he had to rig up an exhaust pipe that evacuated through the same window as the wire to the engine.

All that remained now was a fuel problem, which had gotten worse since he'd left the chapel. Whereas before he just had to worry about gassing up the truck; now he needed to make sure the generator had enough gasoline to keep running too.

Out in the barn, Jed had two gas canisters for the tractor. Paul took both, and added them to the haul he was carrying around in the flatbed. The back of the truck now had all his food, water, extra clothes, his guns, a first-aid kit, a couple of knives, twenty feet of rope, the spare generator, and a tarp to cover all of it. If he lost the truck, he'd lose everything.

The ham radio wasn't really meant to be portable, but he took it anyway and put it on the floor below the generator.

He was prepared for anything except rain. That'd muck up the whole endeavor.

"You're not going across the country, friend," he said, either to the truck or to himself. "Boston's just down the road."

2

He'd only made it as far as the middle of town before the sun started to set.

It was just as empty as Jed's farm, but far more ominously so. Most of the cars were gone, but the cars still there were just *stopped* at intersections. Paul saw a couple of indications that something had gone awry—most dramatically, a sedan had driven through the picture window of the coffee shop—but nothing added up to an explanation.

Animals were damn near everywhere. He began to understand why it was so easy to hunt that deer a week prior, seeing as how they'd taken over the area. Them, and the wild pigs, and goats. It was like Maine had a statewide forest fire and everyone ran south.

Paul steered the truck to the police station. Stewie had a garage Paul could use for the night, so he wouldn't have to worry so much about someone getting at his food, and while he was there maybe he could figure out why Jed's family thought Paul was missing. Ideally, he'd get an answer from Stewie himself, but he wasn't holding out much hope on that one.

The garage door was open and both the cruisers were out, so Paul just pulled in, shut down the jerry-rigged truck, and spent the next several minutes unjamming the garage door. By then, sunset was only about ten minutes out, so he grabbed the ham radio and the generator and took both into the police station. He had the radio up in five minutes.

"Ananda, this is Pastor Paul, over."

Static.

What followed was a terrifying delay; the thought that something had befallen the only other human in the world was too awful to contemplate.

"Ananda, come in. This is Paul, over," he repeated, every few seconds. He got silence in return until . . .

"Paul. Hi, it's good to hear from you," Ananda said.

"Hah!" he said. He almost dropped the microphone. "Thank the Lord."

"Sorry, getting to the radio can be a challenge. Were you able to start the truck? Over."

"I was, and I'm heading your way at first light. I only made it to the town. Nobody here. I think it's just you and me. Over."

"Not just us. I saw someone else, a young man. He was near this . . . this object. I don't understand what it is. I don't understand a lot right now. How does the world outside of here look?"

"I'll let you know tomorrow," he said. "In person, if this goes well. Did you talk to this young man?"

"He ran off. I'm still piecing together what happened. Like I said—" There was howling on her end of the connection. "I can't talk long," she said in a whisper.

"Ananda, where are you right now? Are you safe? Over."

"The wolves are in the building," she said. "I can move freely most of the time, but I have to be careful. The radio bothers them. It's worse the closer we get to sundown."

"Then maybe we should talk at sunrise instead."

"You'll be on the road at sunrise. No, it's okay. It sounds worse than it is. Over."

"What kind of wolf are we talking about?" Paul asked. "This doesn't sound like normal behavior for the wolves I know. Storming buildings and the like. Pigs might do it. Over."

"They're bigger than they should be so . . . behaviorally, all bets are off, you know? It's difficult, Paul. I'm used to knowing everything. And there's something wrong with the stars."

"The stars? What do you mean? Over."

More howling. It sounded like an animal was trying to dig through a wall.

"I'm sorry," she said. "I have to go."

"Okay."

"Be safe," she said.

"You too," he said. But she'd already signed off.

He held on to the microphone for a few extra seconds and listened to the static fill up the channel.

He probably didn't hear her right, because otherwise, what she said didn't make any sense.

There's something wrong with the stars.

3

After putting the radio and generator back into the truck, Paul looked around the police station for something to help make sense of it all. This became impossible in about two minutes, because there weren't any lights inside. Power failures were common around these parts, though, so it was with no surprise that he found a store of candles in Stewie's desk. He got a few lit and continued his search.

What he found was that his friend had given up on a long-standing personal oath and had gotten himself a computer. The whole *station* was networked, it looked like, with some classy-looking screens and keyboards, stuff Paul wouldn't know what to do with if the power was up, and which was now about as useful as a paperweight.

There were paper files, too, in locked cabinets. Paul didn't know where he might begin in his search to find evidence pertaining to him being a missing person, but he had a feeling any such files were going to be stored on the computer, especially seeing as how it would've happened very recently. Also, searching by candlelight wasn't working all that well.

By some miracle—and maybe that was exactly what it was—

in the storage room in the back where they kept all the office sup-plies Paul found a case of pork and beans.

The kitchen had a can opener and a spoon. The stove didn't work, but beans were beans. He opened one up and had something other than deer for a meal for the first time in a week. This was an excellent development, especially since the deer wasn't going to last much longer. Were he not in a hurry, he'd use the leftover ven-ison to entice one of the pigs, then maybe spend the week eating that instead. But he'd lose a day just cooking, and without any in-door means to do that other than the candles.

He was up with the sunrise, and the pork and beans were added to the haul in the back of the truck. The engine and the genera-tor argued for a few minutes before agreeing to work together, and then he was on the way to Boston.

4

Getting to 93 wasn't an issue. There were abandoned cars here and there, and local wildlife kept jumping in front of him, as if they'd never seen a car before, but he wasn't driving all that fast, so colli-sions were easily avoided.

The highway itself was a powerful mess. Both sides, although the northbound half was much worse. It seemed there was a greater in-terest in heading up to Maine than down to Massachusetts. Wher-ever everybody was going, they didn't make it, and their vehicles were now permanently in the way, so it was a good thing he didn't want to head to Maine.

Southbound had collections of pileups every couple of miles. He could go around them, most times, by taking the shoulder, but there were parts that had no shoulder: just a drop into a ravine. Once, he was able to go down a hill next to the highway, drive a couple of miles along the side, and then climb up again. The truck didn't care for this, but it didn't stall.

The worst jam he came across was just before the Massachusetts border: a ten-car pileup that looked like it would have been pretty lethal if there had been anybody behind the wheel.

He studied the pileup for a while before working out which car would have to move to create a lane. Then he broke into that car, shoved aside the clothing of the lucky soul who'd left it behind, and put the vehicle into neutral. Then he rolled it into the ravine, and kept going.

"You can't bodily assume everyone without breaking some eggs," he said. He thought it was funny, and wished he could find someone to share it with. That was the problem with Rapture jokes; there was hardly anyone around to hear them.

5

Things were going fine on the Massachusetts side of 93 . . . until they weren't.

A storm was rolling in from the west, and quickly, as if someone was fast-forwarding a movie. In no time, the skies took on an ominous purple hue, heralding the arrival of a bank of clouds that looked like a blanket being pulled over the planet. Lightning arced across the sky, and occasionally dropped to Earth.

Paul watched it all with growing trepidation, thinking at first that it was just a *threat* of rain, no more than that. Then he thought it was definitely going to rain, but he had at least an hour.

By the time he realized he had only minutes, it was too late.

What Paul was about to bear witness to was the wrath of God writ large upon the landscape. He would need shelter to stay out of it, but Route 93 didn't have a lot to offer in that regard.

Something with a roof to put the truck under was the ideal. He'd wrapped the wire and the connection points with plastic, but it still wasn't going to respond well to moisture. He also preferred not unhooking the link between the generator and the car more often than he had to; he had a feeling it was eventually going to stop working, and there was too much to carry on his back.

He passed a sign for a rest stop ahead, with fuel and food. He had no expectation as regards the food, and the fuel pumps were probably electrical — and therefore useless — but gas stations had overhangs to keep the rain off and to store the fire suppression nozzles. That would do, and it was only five miles away. He accelerated.

The hail beat him there. Stones the size of golf balls started pummeling the area, some bouncing off his not-quite-closed hood like it was a trampoline before launching into his windshield.

"I just needed one day without rain, Lord," he said. "I can see that displeased you."

He kept going, now to a steady drumbeat, which he accompanied with a slightly off-tune rendition of "Be Not Afraid."

Still two miles from the exit, he got to witness something new: a wall of rainwater, heading his way, straight up the road. It looked like the last thing the pharaoh's men saw before Moses un-parted the Red Sea.

It was between him and the off-ramp.

"Nope," he said. "We're making our stand right here."

He pulled off the road and jumped out. Immediately, a hailstone clocked him off the top of the head. He almost fell over then. It would have been a dumb way to die, but there were worse.

Yanking his jacket over his head to give the Lord a less welcome target, he stumbled around to the front of the truck, lifted the hood, and tore the wire out. A long spark came with it, because — fool that he was — he'd left the generator running.

He dropped the live wire—it wasn't enough volts to kill a man, but he bet it wouldn't tickle—and stumbled back to the car, jumped in, and shut down the generator.

Then the gates of hell opened: the rain arrived, and the hailstones upped their game to around the size of a baseball.

Paul pulled the wire attached to the generator in through the window, unhooked the makeshift exhaust pipe, and got the window closed before too much water got in.

Behind him, the tarp was flapping madly, but holding. He had no way to reinforce it, so there was no point risking a full concussion to tie it down any better than it was. If the tarp flew off, it flew off. Instead, he sat back in the driver's seat and got a good look at the glory of God.

It was indeed glorious . . . and *terrible*. Thick ropes of water inundated the landscape, electricity cascaded in the atmosphere, winds shrieked an atonal chorus. Were he not in harm's way, he would have been awed by the power and majesty of it. He was still awed, but it was far more bittersweet when it seemed as though all of it was being directed at him personally.

But then—something was *moving* in the air above the hood.

At first, Paul took it to be some kind of localized tornado, with the moisture refracting and reflecting the lightning in the background, but that wasn't the case. It was a collection of lights, like a herd of firebugs, moving in a way that suggested a common guiding force.

They came together into something that looked almost human-shaped, and he gasped because then he knew it without a doubt.

He really was in the presence of the divine.

"*And they sparkled like burnished bronze,*" Pastor Paul shouted over the rain. "*Under their wings on their four sides they had human hands. And the four had their faces and their wings thus.* I am ready for your instructions, Lord."

The angel vanished rather than answering in a more conventional way. His disappearance signaled a redoubling of the hailstones. Paul's hood began to smoke, and a crack formed on the windshield.

The angel of the Lord had come to convey not God's grace but His wrath.

The windshield glass was going to go, unless it was one of the side windows first. Paul was too large to fit on the driver's-side floor, and the passenger side was already full up, so he was out of places to hide from broken glass.

"All right, then," he said. He jumped out of the car right as the passenger-side window shattered inward and just before the windshield followed. He crawled under the truck.

"Whatever I have done, Lord, let me make it right. Let me stay and make it right."

There was a river of water waiting to sweep him away from under the truck and off to parts unknown. He held on to the chassis and restricted himself to deep breaths whenever he could find air.

He was going to drown, right in the middle of Interstate 93. That was also a dumb way to die, but it was all out of his hands now.

The tarp that had been protecting his gear blew away; he saw it as it took flight, on its way to the middle of the Atlantic, no doubt. Everything he owned that couldn't get wet was now getting wet, inside and outside of the vehicle. Not that it mattered.

The truck wasn't going to make it to Boston, and neither was he.

"Sorry, Ananda," he said. "I tried."

SIX

Ananda

1

ON THE FIRST MORNING, ANANDA WOKE UP IN THE OFFICE of the adjunct professor and knew right off that something was amiss. She was at the desk, head down, drooling on her own arm, in her Monday clothes when it was not Monday; it was Tuesday.

The problem—the first problem—was that she had *not* fallen asleep on the desk, or if she had, it wasn't for the entire night.

And yet, it was morning.

She recalled dozing off at the desk on Monday night, briefly, before waking up and deciding there was no way she was going to be getting through the exams she was supposed to be adjudicating without some real rest in a real bed. Then she left for the evening. She remembered doing that quite clearly.

Her office—for she was indeed one of the current adjunct professors for the department of astrophysical research at MIT—was a mere ten blocks from the apartment she was renting on the other side of Kendall Square, and so after her bout with sleep-grading, she left the Kavli Institute through the main Vassar entrance and walked to the apartment. When she got there, she took off her Monday clothes and put them in a pile, put on her Monday nightgown, and crawled into bed.

Of all this she was absolutely certain. Yet the evidence to the contrary was overwhelming.

If, after sleeping for the night, she'd gotten out of bed, showered, put on her Tuesday clothes, walked to the Kavli Institute, went up to the adjunct professor's office, sat at the desk, put her head down and fell back asleep, and then woke up again having forgotten she'd done all of that . . . she would be wearing Tuesday's clothes.

She was not.

Ergo, she either did all that, forgot all of it, *and also* picked up Monday's clothes from the pile and put them back on—the statistical likelihood of this was close to zero—or she only *imagined* leaving the office and instead slept through the night at her desk.

She wiped the drool on her arm onto her pant leg and stretched, then opened the shade over the window for a decent look at a brilliant April morning.

What time is it? she wondered. It looked like the city was still asleep, but the sun's positioning suggested it wasn't early. She pulled out her phone to check and discovered that once again she'd neglected to charge it.

The computer would have the time, though. She tried wiggling the mouse attached to the network computer to make the screen jump to life, but . . . well, evidently someone forgot to charge the mainframe, too.

It was probably a power failure, except the Kavli Institute had redundant systems and Cambridge almost never had blackouts, so that was highly unlikely.

But, again, the contrary evidence was overwhelming.

Ananda probably spent most of that first morning just trying to work out what time of day it was and being strangely confounded in every respect.

She had no watch to consult, but other people owned watches, and had phones with charged batteries; one of them could provide the correct time. Except there wasn't anyone around to ask. There were services she could call whose entire job was to provide information, including the time of day, but she couldn't find a working telephone. Televisions, when tuned to news stations, displayed the current local time in the corner . . . but none of the televisions were working either, as the building had no power.

She considered a theory in which this was actually nighttime and the thing in the sky wasn't the sun. It was an intriguing thought, but suffered from too many successive unlikelihoods to be feasible outside of speculative fiction.

I could open the window and shout for someone to give me the time, she thought. But this, too, wouldn't work, because the windows didn't open enough for her to stick her entire head out.

No, what she was going to have to do was leave the office and find someone.

That was when she stumbled upon the wolf den.

2

She found the den in a lecture hall under the Great Dome, which was a good distance from her office. Far enough, certainly, that she wouldn't have simply stumbled upon it by accident. However, even ten days later, she couldn't figure out how she'd ended up in that part of the campus that afternoon.

When she decided to leave her office, the rational choice would have been to run outside in an attempt to find a pedestrian and ask them what time it was. This is definitely what someone who was otherwise confined exclusively to one building would have done. She wasn't, though; she could go anywhere on campus without once reaching the street.

All of the campus's central buildings were linked internally, such that one could walk from the Kavli Institute on Vassar to the Great Dome without ever experiencing direct sunlight. It made perfect sense in New England winters, but less sense on a nice April day.

Whatever the route, and whatever the reason, she ended up in the Infinite Corridor, desperate to find at least one living human being in a place that should have had hundreds ... and without once checking outside.

When she saw the lecture hall doors open, she arrived at the conclusion—an illogical conclusion she couldn't countenance in hindsight—that there were people in it.

The doors to the lecture hall were being held open. They were pull doors, so the wolves had undoubtedly found them this way. (As she soon learned, they were excellent at pushing open doors, but couldn't pull them open or use a doorknob.) Perhaps she'd heard a noise coming from the inside and mistook it for an anthropogenic sound rather than something inherently canine. More likely, she was just in a blind panic by then.

Regardless of why and how, what she definitely did do next was burst through the doorway, shouting, "DOES ANYONE HAVE THE TIME?"

This would have been an inappropriate way to enter a room midlecture, and would have elicited a profane rebuke from any lecturer worth their salt.

The wolves were not in midlecture; they were sleeping. They knew no profanities, but took it poorly in their own way.

They didn't get her, that day or since. But one of the things she came to learn, very quickly, was that there were many doors in MIT that could be pushed open without turning a knob of any kind.

Also, it wasn't necessarily a great idea to have all the buildings connected to one another.

3

In hindsight, it took surprisingly little time to work out that something immensely terrible had taken place and that Ananda might be the only living witness to the aftermath. Coming to grips with it—the acceptance portion of trauma recovery—would have to come much later, after she figured out what had happened in the first place.

According to her husband, Luke, Ananda tended to let a problem that needed solving consume her so completely that it made her impossible to live with. He emphasized this conviction by moving out. Then Jakob, their son, re-proved the point by electing to live with Luke. It had been three years since Jakob left, on a day that also happened to be Ananda's thirty-seventh birthday. This somehow made his decision feel like much more of a personal attack.

They were probably right. Had there *not* been a problem to solve —if she knew exactly what took the lives of everyone, including (she assumed) Luke and Jakob—she likely would have fallen apart entirely. Luke's idea of an insoluble character flaw was what kept her alive, especially in the first few days.

Once she came to grips with the basic facts of her situation, and after five or six debilitating panic attacks, she made a list of needs. It was short: food, water, power. Water was the easiest and most important of the three, as the pipes in at least some of the buildings still had water in them. (Several did not, and a few had something akin to water, only it was brown.) If that ever failed, the backup plan was the Charles River. It wasn't a great backup; she would need to relocate her base of operations from the Kavli Institute to one of the buildings closer to the water. But the wolves liked that part of the campus in particular. She couldn't just lug buckets back and forth, either. And in winter, the river froze. What she'd need was to find out where the facilities building was, get as many hoses as they had, and run a line to the river. Then she'd have to either find or invent a hand pump to get the water from the river to the building.

It probably wouldn't work, but it was all she had. If she was lucky, the water in the working pipes would remain clean and would continue to flow. That seemed unlikely, if only because surely she must have used up all her luck surviving the extinction of the human race.

She expected food to be a bigger challenge than it was. At first she was existing off of enormous cans of beans, and cans of fruit and vegetables she found in the back of one of the kitchens. She couldn't heat any of it, but it mostly didn't need to be heated, so that was fine. It wasn't much in the way of protein, though.

One of her more poorly considered ideas was to befriend the wolves so they'd share their kills with her. She didn't try this. The difference between success and failure was entirely too extreme, and also (although she didn't learn this until later) they weren't technically wolves, so none of the behavioral books she scrounged from the library was going to be very useful.

They were eastern coyotes, or coywolves. That was according to another book she'd found after determining that the pictures of wolves in another book didn't correspond as well to the actual beasts she was sharing the building with. Coywolves were mixed breeds of coyotes, wolves, and dogs. They hunted at all hours (but preferred night), weren't afraid of people or traffic, were highly intelligent, and "have been seen in urban environments more often of late."

That part of the sentence made her laugh out loud.

You don't say, she thought.

The one problem was that these coywolves were a good deal larger than the ones described in the book. They looked right, though, so that was what she decided they must be. Perhaps the dog they crossed with was a Saint Bernard. Or they'd added bear to their biological soup. That was probably a genetic impossibility, but she was an astrophysicist, not a geneticist, so who was she to say?

This didn't help her to resolve the big questions at all, but because the wolves were the most apparent daily example of the end of the world, she'd taken to calling it the coywolf apocalypse.

She found a less life-threatening source of protein in a pile of something called Noot. There were twenty bricks of it, sitting in the same kitchen where she found the cans. It was almost a week before she realized it was ostensibly edible and not some sort of bulk soap product.

It was surprising to find something like this just lying around when it looked like it had sprung from a food technology that—last she checked—barely existed.

There was almost no documentation on Noot in the kitchen, but what was there implied that it was a famine solution product.

She didn't think Cambridge had been going through a famine, but she wasn't going to question the logistics that landed something this useful in her lap.

Power was an interesting challenge. She learned pretty early on —the first day—that none of the batteries worked. Not just *her* batteries, like for her phone and laptop; all batteries, period. *Why* was a waste of a question, as long as it was true.

After embracing this fact, she worked out her other options. The first idea: Get a powerful magnet and some coils, and build an engine. That got her down to the electronics laboratory, where surely such components were available.

They were, but also available was a stack of unused solar panels.

Solar panels aren't useful by themselves, and they're not useful at *all* when they're just sitting on a shelf in a storage room. These were spares, an indication that somewhere—presumably on a rooftop—there would be more of them. Find that array—and the wires running from it—and she'd have power.

She found a destroyed solar panel array on the roof of the same building. It was impossible to say exactly what destroyed it, but some combination of severe weather and a direct lightning strike could have. So could a sledgehammer, probably. Not a wolf, though; it was likely not a victim of the coywolf apocalypse.

Ananda made the solar panel discovery in the evening, by moonlight. Night was when it was safest to move around, oddly, because while the wolves preferred night hunting, they didn't hunt in the building.

Being on the roof of the electronics laboratory building, at night, proved serendipitous, as the rooftop afforded her a partial view of Main Street.

And something in that part of town was *glowing*.

It could have been a fire, but it didn't look like one. It looked electrical. Besides, even if it *was* a fire, that was worth examining too, because animals didn't typically set fires and there hadn't been any kind of lightning that night.

But it *wasn't* a fire.

She ran down through the building, a seeming eternity in the stairwell, making enough noise to attract the attention of even the wolf cubs, who—while adorable—could probably cause plenty of damage.

Next, she cut through the Compton lab building, then exited to Compton Court. It was sneak-and-creep from there—in the shadows, next to the buildings, listening for an indication that something hungry was nearby. Nighttime in the city of Cambridge when there was no electrical lighting was *dark*, but not impossible to see by, because it was also a night when the moon was waxing gibbous. There were still plenty of onerous shadows, but she felt confident that if an animal charged, she would at least see what was about to kill her *before* it killed her.

She had this theory that if she hung around the coywolves long enough, they'd get used to her smell and think of her as one of their own. The notion went hand in hand with the idea that she might persuade them to feed her someday, and both were probably irrational, but as she tiptoed down a path to the North Court—a wide-open grassy area that was perfect for running down game— she hoped she was right. Even better if the other animals thought she smelled like one of the wolves. Then they'd leave her be too.

Whatever the reason, she made it through unmolested.

North Court dropped her at the corner of Ames and Main, where she realized there was an entire building missing.

It was a big building, too, although she couldn't remember what was in it. Just that it existed. Except now it didn't.

It was hard to tell exactly what had happened to it. Probably it had been demolished on purpose, which she imagined happened as a matter of routine. A new building couldn't be erected if there was an old building in the way and all that.

The demolition looked only partial in this instance, and it further looked as if there was a reason for its interruption not strictly based on construction concerns. The half-collapsed structure spoke to that, certainly, but the perimeter established around it spoke more loudly.

There was a police barrier, then a ring of cement blocks, and then a heavy fence, all screaming some variation of STAY OUT.

A wide variety of apparatuses were pointed through and over the fence. She only recognized a few of the pieces: a spectroscope, and a couple of radiation detectors.

Looking past the police barriers and up the road, it was evidently the case that Main Street had been closed rather recently, and the several army Jeeps littering the street in both directions suggested that whatever was wrong at the site, it had attracted the attention of the federal government.

It was an orgy of evidence pointing toward something important going on in the middle of the construction area. That also happened to be where the glow was coming from.

She ignored the police barrier, climbed over the cement barrier, and pressed her face up against the fence.

On the other side was a trash-can-size white cylinder with a domed cap standing in more or less the center of the excavation site. It looked a little like a venting pipe for a sublevel. Among dirt as it was, it seemed too clean, but was otherwise not terribly remarkable. Not call-up-the-army interesting, certainly.

She thought maybe it had been uncovered when they started leveling the building, and could imagine a scenario where the city had been unable to figure out what it was, then someone from MIT had a look and also didn't know what it was, and up it went. That was a logical chain of events—but there wasn't enough time for all of that to have occurred between Monday and Tuesday.

It did appear to be generating some kind of electrostatic field. The air above and around it was crackling with light and energy, as if a thousand flaming bees were circling their hive.

This was all very curious, but the cylinder and the energy field weren't what grabbed her attention initially. Far more remarkable —to her—was the existence of another living human being.

It was a boy, fourteen at most, which would make him about the same age as her son, Jakob. He was crying, and hitting the cylinder with a piece of rebar.

The buzzing field of lights seemed to be interested in stopping him; they kept passing through and around his body, which just made him attack the cylinder more violently.

"Hey!" she shouted to the kid. "What are you doing?"

He turned at the sound of her voice.

"Not my fault," he said.

"What's not your fault?"

"NOT MY FAULT!" he shouted. Then he tossed down the rebar and ran away, through the rubble on the other side of the construction site.

The flaming bees stopped spinning around the cylinder then, and took off . . .

By flying directly through Ananda.

She didn't feel anything when it happened, but was stunned for long enough to make chasing after the boy not worth the effort.

The cylinder didn't generate that, she thought. *It exists independently of it.*

"If you want to find me," she shouted—to the boy, and perhaps also to the light field. "I'm at the Kavli Institute! On Vassar!"

4

Ananda could have spent the rest of every day studying the odd cylindrical object at the construction site, but now that she'd seen another living human being, she became emboldened by the idea that maybe there were other survivors. To find them—and also to conduct any equipment-based research on the object—she was going to need power.

She got the solar array up by swapping out three broken panels with three good ones from the storage room and patching the wiring where it had gotten severed. It didn't give her a *lot* of power—she couldn't power the whole building, and she couldn't get the university's mainframe running—but all she needed was a little.

The first thing she did was plug in her cell phone. The local memory came right back up, including all her family photos, which broke her heart for the rest of the day. But that was *all* that worked; it couldn't find a cell phone tower to bounce a signal off of. And as soon as she unplugged it, it died again. The battery wasn't holding a charge.

Next, she turned on a television. None of the stations was broadcasting. Then a radio, which was all static.

She didn't consider trying a shortwave radio until the end of the day.

After scanning all of the channels, and adding in the lack of cell, radio, and television signals, she decided it would be a good idea to return to her original hypothesis: Everyone was dead . . . her and the kid down the street notwithstanding.

Discouraged, but not yet willing to give up entirely, she dug up a dictation machine from storage, set it up, and pressed record: "If anyone hears this message," she said, "turn to channel eighteen at sunset. I am on the East Coast. This is a recording." Then she set the dial to the emergency channel and made the message run on a loop.

Then it was time to do more of what she was actually good at.

5

Essentially the only upside to the entire city going completely dark was that there was no longer any light pollution in the atmosphere getting in the way of a decent view of the stars. It brought to mind the first time she'd seen the stars in an unpolluted sky.

It was when she was only seven, on holiday sandwiched between her family's drastic relocation from Mumbai to Chicago. She was on a beach on the Hawaiian island of Moloka'i, at a nighttime show of some kind. A luau, or a performance, or both; she could never remember, because she hardly paid it any attention.

She was looking up the entire time.

Thirty years later, the awe hadn't gone away. She still felt the same way about the sky . . . and couldn't really understand anyone who didn't.

Stargazing was one thing she hadn't done *any* of since the apocalypse. It was enough to know that the stars would be there, in the same place as always, waiting for her to look up again whenever she was ready. But they couldn't feed her, or tell her what happened to the entire human race, or answer any of her multitude of other questions.

She started to rethink those assumptions when she saw the missing building.

The problem was this: Pre-apocalypse, she walked down Main

Street every day, twice. She would have done it when leaving for the night in her Monday clothes for a good night's sleep, to return the following day in her Tuesday clothes.

Somehow, that hadn't happened, and she had no answer as to why. But even if she *had* lost ten hours—even if for ten hours she didn't leave the office at all, and just fell asleep at her desk, as the evidence suggested—entirely *too much* had happened during that stretch of time: (1) the building's demolition, (2) the cordoning of Main, (3) the army's arrival, (4) the local wild animal population exploding, and, yes, (5) the extermination of the human race. Clearly far too much to be feasible in any ten-hour span.

There were other indications that she had something wrong. The leaves were turning. The air was getting colder every day, not warmer. The sunrises and sunsets had a reddish hue, indicating a high level of sulfur dioxide in the upper atmosphere.

The most obvious explanation for the latter was a volcanic eruption, but it would have had to have been truly massive. Another explanation was that someone inserted sulfur dioxide on purpose, as a way to slow climate change. Both of those possibilities were entirely plausible, but incredibly unlikely to have happened without warning, in one night.

All of that was why she should have looked up earlier. She'd spent a whole day, the first day, trying to find someone who could tell her what time it was when all she had to do was check the timepiece over her head. It couldn't give her hours and minutes, but the other evidence strongly indicated that she was missing a lot more than hours and minutes.

Ananda didn't even need the telescope to confirm this first suspicion. The constellations were wrong for early spring. They were right for late autumn. She'd either lost ten hours *plus six months,* or the entire city of Cambridge had been relocated to a different part of the planet.

Losing six months in one night was impossible, but the contrary evidence was overwhelming.

"Worry about how and why later," she said. "Get the *when* right first."

She aimed the telescope at Polaris and started taking measurements.

6

Ananda almost didn't make it back to the room with the ham radio by sunset.

After her night on the roof with the telescope—an activity that made her feel almost normal for the first time in what felt like ages—she nearly forgot she was living in a situation that had life-threatening predators literally around the corner.

She'd had to run for her life several times since the morning she'd encountered the coywolves in the lecture hall. About eighty percent of the time, when she ended up staring down one of the creatures, the animal either decided it wasn't worth trying to catch her or didn't regard her as potential food. She didn't know how to make herself appear unappealing as a food source, but she did try to come off as unaggressive and nonthreatening as possible —which was easy, as she happened to be both of those things already—so that the coywolves wouldn't become defensive, which seemed a big risk in a place where they were raising their young.

The twenty percent of the time, she and a wolf startled each other. She'd turn a corner too fast and end up right in front of a coywolf minding its own business until a human jumped out from nowhere. They'd both be surprised, but the wolf's teeth were bigger than hers, so it got problematic quickly.

On those occasions, she ran until she found a door she could open and close and lock, and then waited for the coywolf to stop barking at the door.

Once, when she couldn't find a door, she had no choice, so she stood her ground and shouted back. This confused the wolf so much, it whined, turned around, and walked away. She had no plans to try that a *second* time, but it was an interesting discovery.

To avoid the twenty-percent-of-the-time problem, she got in the habit of checking corners before rounding them. This usually kept her out of trouble. But not always.

She didn't go back to the ham radio room until it was late in the day, and she didn't check the corner before she turned it, because she was doing math in her head. This was a common problem in the corridors of MIT, but normally one didn't have to worry about bumping into a pack of predators.

There were six coywolves in the hall, right in front of the door. Ananda was standing in their midst before she even realized it.

She thought she was dead.

The coywolves looked just as surprised, though not in a murderous sort of way: They were actually *whining.* The three closest to the door kept scrabbling at it, and at the carpeting in front of it.

The sound of the shortwave was driving them nuts.

"Okay," Ananda said. "I'll take care of it."

She raised her hands above her head and started walking between the wolves while electing not to breathe. All it would take was for one of them to decide she was food instead of a solution to their dilemma, and it would be over.

But she got to the door.

"Excuse me," she said.

The one nearest to the door stepped back. She opened the door and it tried to follow her in.

"No," she said. "Stay. I'll take care of this."

Miraculously, it stayed.

It felt like she had just developed a superpower.

Then she closed the door, and the coywolves started barking and clawing at it immediately, and the feeling went away.

She shut off the radio, and the barking stopped.

"You're welcome," she said.

After about ten minutes, she opened the door to confirm that the wolves were really gone. They were.

That left her with a problem. However remote, the possibility that there might be someone out there who could hear her message wasn't something she was willing to give up on. That meant possibly having to wade through a corridor of enraged wolves every day she left the message running. Her mental risk/reward scales didn't know what to do with this.

She ended up turning the radio back on and resuming the emergency channel broadcast. Then she started looking for ways to insulate the radio and reinforce the door.

An hour later, it was sunset and she was talking to someone named Pastor Paul.

7

Two nights later, she was back at the radio.

The wolves were in the hallway, whining and barking, but she hardly noticed, because her reality was falling apart.

She needed to talk to someone, but Paul wouldn't answer.

"Paul, it's Ananda. Are you there? Over."

She'd been trying for twenty minutes. The sun was already down, and the wolves were going to be late for their evening hunt.

It didn't matter. According to her calculations, the universe no longer made sense.

She'd finished the math, but none of it added up, so checked it again and again. Then twenty more times. When that still didn't change the numbers, she re-proved the equations she was using and tried once more. No change.

"Paul, are you out there? I'm worried."

A big storm had blown through earlier in the day. He might have been caught in it.

The weather is a new kind of violent now, she thought. *He could be dead.*

"Paul, if you can hear me, I'm going to sign off now, but I'll try again tomorrow. Be safe."

She turned off the radio so that the coywolves pawing at the door behind her could go back to their evening schedule.

Hearing Paul's voice had been just about the only thing keeping her going the past couple of days. She was looking forward to his arrival so, so much . . . if only to have someone to share the death of the human race with.

Also, though, she really wanted to ask him what year he thought this was. Because according to her calculations, she hadn't just lost ten hours and six months.

It was much more than that.

That was the thing about the stars. They moved in ways that made sense, would *always* make sense, thanks to a lot of firmly grounded mathematical calculations going back to before Galileo.

When she looked up into the night sky, she realized that not only was she looking at the wrong stars for the time of year, but those wrong stars weren't in exactly the right places, either. They too were off. It was a tiny difference; almost immeasurably so, the problem being that *almost* from her perspective meant light-years for the stars she was looking at. It simply wasn't possible for all of those vast, distant objects to have moved in the way that they clearly had in only six months.

This time, the overwhelming contrary evidence wasn't enough to override that impossibility; not when a more viable (yet still impossible) conclusion existed.

If the observer and the observed change position in respect to one another, either the observed has moved or the observer has moved. But if *she* was the one out of position . . . well, it would take a cataclysmic event on a scale far larger than anything she'd witnessed—way more than a volcanic eruption—to tilt Earth in such a way that would align with her measurements.

Unless the problem wasn't *where* Earth was in respect to the stars, but *when*. The *year* was the variable.

Adjusting to account for Earth's obliquity over time, she worked out what year it would have to be for the measurements she'd taken of Polaris, the pole star, to work.

The conclusion was unequivocal and refused to change no matter how many times she reran the numbers. No matter how many times she stress-tested the formulas. No matter how many times she retook the measurements.

It had *not* been six months since Ananda had put on her Monday clothes and headed to work.

According to the stars, it had been more like a hundred years.

PART TWO

WE HAVE SEEN
THE ENEMY

SEVEN

Touré

1

THE HAILSTORM REALLY DROVE HOME THE POINT THAT they were unprepared for the arrival of inclement weather.

It came on with such suddenness and ferocity that it caught Robbie and Touré out in the open, a few hundred yards from the dorm, at the mercy of hailstones the size of golf balls. They made it inside before the real rain came, and the heavy winds that had them all wondering if their building had a bomb shelter. (It did not.) After the rain came the severe lightning. They began to question if *any* building was safe, then.

But once it was clear the storm wouldn't be taking out any windows, and the lightning strikes were heading away from them, and once the hail stopped (and since they had no power to lose) it was treated as a spectacular thing to witness from their safe remove.

The day was washed out, though, so they couldn't do anything until the next morning. That was when Touré said the words he promised himself he'd never, ever say.

"If we want to get this done fast, and right, I think Robbie and I have to split up," he told the others.

"What are you talking about?" Robbie asked. "We have to stick together."

"No, I've been thinking about this. We have too much to do and maybe Carol's right that there isn't enough time to do all of it. We're going to have to start taking some chances; we can't afford a day where neither of us finds something we can use, and that's gonna keep happening if we're looking in the same place all the time."

"I can go out too," Bethany said. "I know the Square as well as you do."

"And what, carry all of it back in your arms?" Touré asked.

"Dude, the Square is six blocks that way. Don't make it sound like you're on some high crusade. I can make more than one trip."

"We've checked everything six blocks that way. Learn how to ride a bike and we'll talk. Meanwhile—"

"What were you looking for?" Bethany asked.

"When?"

"When you checked everything six blocks away."

"I dunno," Touré said. "Stuff."

"Underwear? Bras?"

Touré looked at Robbie.

"Help me out, man," he said.

"Because we need undergarments," Bethany said. "And some other things."

"Women's things," Carol said.

"Then tell us and we'll get it," Touré said.

"Oh, big hero," Bethany said, "protecting the womenfolk. Aren't you just, like, running from bunnies?"

"Okay, hold on," Robbie said. "Bethany, it actually *is* dangerous out there. You know that. But if you think there's a place you want

to check out? You're right, it's just a couple blocks. I can stay here
with Carol—"

He didn't finish this suggestion, because all three of them wanted
to jump in then. Carol ended up claiming the floor by stamping her
cane on the ground.

"I've told all of you this before," she said, "so I'm beginning to
wonder if you have hearing problems or just comprehension problems. As much as I appreciate it, I *do not need one of you to stay here
with me.* Bethany is right that we need certain sundries that may not
immediately occur to a man as being a necessity. If she wants to go
find some of those things, we are in no position to stop her. Touré
may be right that he and Robbie can cover more ground by heading
in different directions, but it would be wise to work out the exact
parameters of such a plan beforehand."

"That's what I was trying to say," Touré said. "I already have a
plan. Are you guys ready to listen now, or do you wanna argue
some more?"

2

The plan wasn't all that complicated.

The bike shop had lightweight two-wheeler trailers hanging
from the ceiling. The trailers were meant to hook up to the back
of a bicycle so that parent cyclists had a way to drag their spawn
around town without adding to their carbon footprint, or so
child-free climate-conscious locals could go shopping. Or so local
health-conscious serial killers could move a body, probably. They
were multifunction.

Touré figured if both he and Robbie took one of these and
headed off in different directions with a shopping list, if they were
lucky, they might be able to collect all of it in a couple of days.

Then he and Robbie could go back to looking for survivors, an explanation, or whatever, until the weather turned.

"So where do you want to go?" Robbie asked. They were looking at a map of the area, which was probably the fourth most helpful thing they'd discovered after the Noot bars, the matches, and the lighter fluid. They had been using the map to mark the areas they'd already visited.

So far, their exploration focused on Cambridge and parts of Somerville. Touré had been talking a lot about "trying the Paul Revere": going down Mass Ave., through Arlington, into Lexington and Concord. It was as good a trip as any if you were looking for survivors, perhaps to notify them that the British were coming. It was less useful if you were looking for provisions.

"I'll head downtown," Touré said. "You head up the river to Watertown."

"I'd rather see Boston," Robbie said. "It looks like more fun."

"It *is* more fun. Have you ever been there?"

"You know I haven't."

He did, because whenever they planned out their day trips, Robbie asked about going into the city. Touré argued—correctly, he thought—that survivors would head out of the downtown area, not *into* it, for the obvious reason that there was nothing on the other side of Boston but the ocean.

"Then you won't know where anything is," Touré said, "and it'll take longer to find stuff."

"I've also never been to Watertown."

"Yeah, but you've been to a mall, right? Here's what you do: Keep the river on your left, then bang a right on Arsenal, and you're there. Two malls, right across from each other. One with a great big hardware store."

"Well, I don't like it."

"Which part?"

"The part where I don't get to go into Boston."

"If we do this right, you'll get to see the whole town before the snow starts."

Touré was about to wax eloquent about the charms of the city and what it looked like in the winter. The whole "Norman Rockwell with brownstones" deal.

Then he remembered, *Oh yeah, but everyone's dead*, and he couldn't breathe for a couple of seconds.

3

There was a moment, as Touré crossed the Mass Ave. bridge from Cambridge into Boston, when he felt free.

Not *normal*, as in there was no apocalypse and the world was back to the way it was supposed to be. Free—in a way he hadn't ever been before, even back when things were normal.

The center point of the bridge gave him a great view in every direction, and came with a pleasant wind and bright sunlight, clean air, and the whole shebang. And because he was alone, he could ride down the middle of the road without having to worry about becoming a victim of vehicular homicide.

Sure, the sun was still tinted kind of reddish in the early morning—it went away by the middle of the day and came back again at sunset, and they still didn't know what was going on with that —but it was still beautiful. Also, the air was clean enough, though there was this gassy kind of aftertaste to it he'd been trying to ignore for the past two weeks.

The river was over its banks, too. That was different. It was because of the storm; it'd go down again. It never *used* to do that, though, or if it did, not after just one storm.

The Longfellow Bridge was on his left. That was the bridge they always used in movies and what he grew up calling the salt-and-pepper bridge, because of the towers in the middle that looked like saltshakers.

Or rather, it *used* to have towers that looked like that.

Two of them had collapsed, one onto the bridge and the other (he assumed) into the water. Touré stopped the bike to get a better look, which soon turned into a much more thorough review of the panorama than he'd allowed himself previously.

"Sleep through one apocalypse and the whole town goes to hell," he said.

The Hatch Shell, on the Boston side, was in ruins, and parts of Storrow Drive were underwater from what he assumed were more incursions from the river. Several of the buildings that marked the edge of the Back Bay neighborhood looked damaged in ways that insurance companies used to blame on God. And, weirdly, the city had added a skyscraper, to the right of the Prudential.

This last one was probably his fault, for not paying more attention, but for the rest? The only thing that made sense was that the condition affecting the quality of the streets was also affecting some of the buildings. The entire commonwealth had gotten decrepit at the same time.

It did not bode well for the four of them, holing up in a dormitory building that was a couple hundred years old. He made a note to recommend they find someplace newer.

"What about a disease, where everyone gets super old at the same time, including all the buildings?" he said. "Let's add that."

He was walking around with a collection of apocalypse theories in his head. He hadn't shared any of them with the others so far, because they seemed pretty broken up about it right now, but they'd appreciate it later. He planned to write it all down just as soon as they rediscovered computer technology.

Or with a pen and paper, if absolutely necessary. Like a barbarian.

He hopped back on the bike and continued into town.

4

The bottom half of Newbury Street was in ruins.

The shops on Newbury were designed strangely, at least in the context of potential flood concerns. Half of them were below-ground—you had to descend a staircase to reach the front door. The other half were on top, up a flight of stairs. (It was clear that this was a design that predated the legal requirements for handicap accessibility.) All of the below-street-level shops were wrecked from some combination of flood damage and wild animal foraging, but the top-level businesses looked relatively unharmed.

Touré'd had an admittedly immature notion about what he might do as a survivor of an actual apocalypse, back when the entire exercise was still hypothetical. The idea was that he would get to wear the nicest, most expensive clothes available, because price was no longer a problem.

There were plenty of issues with this idea, none of which he'd bothered to explore back then. To begin with, he was in no way a fashion-forward kind of guy, so his even *knowing* what the finest clothes might look like was wishful thinking. Also, there was no reason to think the finest clothes might look good on him, expensive or not. He cosplayed as Batman once, thinking he would look at least a little like Batman. Instead, he looked like a chubby bad idea of Batman ... only worse. Fashionable clothes would probably have the same effect. Admittedly, there were presently only three people in the world who could laugh at him about it — two, really, since Carol couldn't even see what he looked like — but that didn't mean he wouldn't know if he looked ridiculous . . . and judge himself poorly because of it.

He still wanted to at least check out the clothes. And although he was (probably) not capable of picking the very finest of clothing in a mannequin storefront lineup, he knew where that clothing was sold: on Newbury Street.

Except, again, Newbury Street was half destroyed.

He stopped in a couple of shops. One was a clothing store with a front window display consisting entirely of antique sewing machines; there, he tried on some jackets. A couple fit, but by then he felt embarrassed to have even come out this far for such a waste of time. He was supposed to be shopping in bulk for survival reasons, to save everyone, not picking up a good wool topcoat.

Also, all the clothes had these antitheft clips on the sleeves that he couldn't pry off. He hadn't considered that in his post-apocalypse planning.

Another place he stopped was a coffee shop. The one near their supermarket on Memorial Drive had been cleaned out, which continued to be a source of frustration for Touré, so he was excited to find another one and hoped for a more positive outcome.

He got his wish.

Deep in the back of the store was a tiny supply of vacuum-sealed coffee beans and an unused French press. It wasn't pre-ground, so they were going to have to figure out how to grind the beans — and also produce hot water — but it was progress. Until then, he could *chew* the beans. He was pretty sure that was safe.

Other than that, Newbury was a straight-up bust.

The end of the street opened up on the Public Garden. On the other side was Boston Common. Beyond the common, and up a hill, was a shopping area called Downtown Crossing, which had a ton more clothing stores.

If he didn't have any luck there, he could hit the mall at the Prudential on his way back. If he timed it right, he'd return to the dorm well before nightfall.

5

Touré was biking past the edge of the theater district when he realized a pig was following him.

He'd made a conscious decision not to go through the Public Garden, even though that was the fastest way to reach Downtown Crossing. The park was an oasis of plant life that he figured would likely attract all sorts of animals, and he wasn't in any mood to be in the middle of all that wildlife.

Either in spite of or because of that very intelligent decision, there now was a pig running behind him.

He was probably calling it the wrong thing. It was almost certainly a *boar*, but they were scarier when he called them that, so he stuck with *pig*.

The pig wasn't really running very hard in its efforts to keep up. Touré wasn't biking as hard as he could, either, but he got the sense that if he were to pick up the pace, the pig would have no trouble staying close. That was a little disconcerting.

"Should I be scared of you?" he asked the pig. He didn't say it loud enough to expect a response, and also, it was a pig.

He turned the corner on Tremont, going the wrong way down a one-way street, around the bottom corner of the common to climb the hill toward Park Street.

The pig continued to pace him.

They passed the movie theater on the right. Touré was about to turn from there, down one of the side roads that would get him to Washington Street, when he saw a horse.

It was eating grass on the common, all by itself, not looking remotely concerned about the pig, or the human being chased by the pig, or any of the large number of other pigs loitering on the grass. It seemed vaguely interested in a wild turkey ambling along the sidewalk, but that was all.

Touré knew very nearly nothing about horses. This one was brown, and it had a saddle, and if Touré got on its back it could take him places faster than a bike. It probably wouldn't be willing to pull the trailer, but it would be so much better if Touré could find a carriage and somehow hook up the horse to it. He could get all their supplies in one trip, and also he'd have a horse.

Touré had no carriage and didn't have a clue how to hook one up to a horse and didn't know if the horse would be even remotely cool with it, but he was willing to give it a go.

Once he got rid of the damn pig.

He pulled the bike over near another coffee shop — Boston had a *ton* of coffee shops — and stood in the middle of the street.

The last time he'd seen one of these, he just had to stare it down, so he decided to give that a try again. Robbie had been with him then, but it wasn't like Robbie was the intimidating one, of the two of them.

"Go on," he said. "*Git.*"

The pig snorted, or oinked, or whatever that noise was supposed to be called.

"You heard me."

There was a shuffle behind Touré from the side street at his back. He turned and realized his mistake.

This wasn't one lone boar running after him.

It was a gang.

"Oh," he said. "You guys are meat-eaters, aren't you?"

He moved toward the bike, as the fastest nearby means of conveyance, but the animals were smart enough to cut him off.

In the seconds before deciding to run and actually running, Touré had another epiphany about the magnitude of his error. All this time, he just assumed he was the plucky apocalypse survivor, the one you hate to root for but who you know will be there for the end credits.

But that wasn't right at all.

Who he *was* was: the cocky idiot who makes a tragic mistake and dies before the end of the first act.

"I thought for sure that was gonna be Robbie," he said.

Then he ran. Straight up Tremont.

He thought about running for the common but decided he had no advantage in an open, grassy field. His advantage was being able to climb stuff and go through doors, two tasks pigs sucked at. He just needed to find something to climb or a door he could open.

He wasn't nearly fast enough to reach either. He got to a corner in front of a bank, tried to cut it at an angle, and lost the position to a boar coming off the sidewalk. He tripped over the animal and ended up on his back.

"No, no, no, no, no," he muttered, trying to get to his feet before the rest of the pack got to him.

It didn't work out. He made it to his feet, but then the next boar to the scene stabbed a tusk into his right thigh.

Touré screamed, punched the boar in the face, and fell onto his back. That boar staggered away, but one of its friends came up next, teeth out, going for the neck.

Touré was about to die, and he was really, really annoyed about it.

"All right, *come on!*" he shouted.

The boar lunged forward, squealed . . . and then fell over dead on the ground next to Touré.

There was an arrow buried in the back of its skull.

Touré had no time to come to grips with this, because the one he punched in the face was back for more, and another two were flanking him. Touré couldn't stand because of his leg, so he rolled over to the dead boar and tried to yank the arrow from its head. It wouldn't budge.

And once again, he was about to die.

A leaping woman appeared on the scene, directly above the nearest boar, with a knife in her hands and a scream on her lips. She landed on the boar's back and buried the blade in its skull.

Touré fell in love with her immediately.

Leaving the knife behind, she rolled over the dying boar and onto her knees, facing off with the other two, an arrow in each hand.

"Who's next?" she hissed.

The two boars huffed and stamped their hooves.

"Come on, piggy-piggy, *try it*," she said.

They made a show of challenging her, but didn't. They ran off instead.

"Hey, they're gone," she said over her shoulder. "You. You're . . . *real*, right?"

"I was going to ask you the same question," he said, and gallantly blacked out.

6

Touré woke up on the floor of a food court next to a deceased boar and a few feet away from a small fire providing both heat and light to a space that would have otherwise had neither.

"Aaah," he said, in a not-at-all masculine way.

He was on his back, wrapped in a blanket, with a sleeping bag under his head for a pillow. The boar was lying on its side, the arrow still buried in the back of its skull. It was sticking its tongue out at Touré.

"Don't look at me like that," he said. "This is your fault."

He sat up and shouted again—in what was hopefully a slightly more manly scream—from the pain in his right leg. It felt like someone was going under the skin of his thigh with sandpaper.

He pulled the blanket back to have a look.

The pant leg had been cut away and there was a piece of a cotton shirt wrapped tightly around the wound, which he was bleeding through. He wanted to lift the bandage, but he also didn't.

"*This* is your fault too," he said to the boar.

A loud clip-clop echoed through the food court, presaging the arrival of the brown horse he'd seen on the common.

"And yours," he told the horse. "For making me get off the bike. Nice bandage, though, thanks."

He caught a whiff of smoke, and . . . something else.

"Hey!" he shouted. "Hey! Is that bacon?"

The woman who was definitely real came around the corner. Her appearance was so startling, he nearly screamed again.

The knife she'd used to dispatch the second boar was in her hand, dripping with blood, which made perfect sense since the rest of her seemed to be doing the same. She had blood on both arms and across her chest. Her hair—which was either brown or a lighter color, but dirty—was back in a ponytail, revealing a face caked in mud and probably more blood. He thought there was a white woman under all of that, but at this point felt like he needed to see a hand not soaked in blood to be sure.

"It's boar meat," she said. "I'm skinning and cooking it. I don't know how to make bacon. I think I need salt. Right? Curing salts. I don't know how to do that. How is your leg? You shouldn't get up. Elton didn't think you were going to make it. Excuse me a second."

"Elton?" Touré asked. "Is there someone else here?"

She was right; he shouldn't be getting up. The leg was furious with him when he tried, such that he nearly fell over again, both from the pain and the leg's disinterest in supporting him properly.

We have no doctor, he reminded himself, *so don't get hurt.*

Unless they did now. Maybe the woman who was deboning and cooking a wild boar on the other side of the mall was also a doctor. She didn't *look* like a doctor; she looked like an extra from a Viking movie.

He performed some combination of hopping and falling his way down the concourse and around the corner toward the smell of cooked meat. Yes, walking was bad, but this was the greatest smell he'd smelled in his entire life; the leg could be missing and he'd find a way to get closer.

He realized they were in the Corner Mall, in Downtown Crossing. It was only a couple of blocks from where he was nearly gored to death. This woman must have dragged him there, then gone out and fetched the boars she'd killed. Or she collected the boars first and then went and got him. That wouldn't be surprising; in this situation, the pigs were clearly the most valuable.

Touré could only remember being in the Corner Mall twice before this, and both times were to get out of the rain. It was a peculiar throwback to when "mall" meant something far more pedestrian, consisting of wide concourses, a big food court specializing in inexpensive fast food (which was like a delicacy in this part of town, oddly), and three street-level exits.

Even with electricity, it was a shadowy, not altogether welcome place, with stores that somehow reflected this aesthetic.

He found the woman at one end of the mall, near the Winter Street doors, standing over another open fire. The glass doors were open, but she'd pulled down the metal security fencing to block any of the animals who felt like coming in for a bite. It was a good idea; the fencing gave the smoke a place to go.

It was dark out. He was missing dinner with the others. Had they declared him dead yet? Probably.

He got another three steps and then fell over. The leg just wasn't cooperating. What he needed was a crutch.

What he got was a horse. The brown-haired steed walked up next to him and looked down, confused at Touré's inability to get bipedalism right.

Touré got back to his feet, grabbed the side of the saddle with his right hand, and tried walking that way.

"Um, help. Horse. Help?"

This was the closest he'd ever been to a horse. He was probably doing it wrong.

Or not; the horse started walking.

The woman had both hands deep in the boar's rib cage, and kept pulling out soft, mushy internal organs and dropping them on the ground.

Touré was about ready to throw up two days' worth of Noot bar.

"Elton likes you," she said, not even looking up.

"Who's Elton?" he asked.

"The horse. His name is Elton, and he likes you."

"Oh. Hello, Elton. This is your horse?"

"No, he isn't anyone's horse. He lets me ride on him sometimes, but he picks the direction."

She did something to the hide that sounded like a heavy blanket getting torn in half.

"Could you . . . could you please stop doing that for a minute?" he asked.

She looked down at what she was doing, then at him, then at Elton.

"Is this gross?" she asked. "It probably is."

"It's very gross, yes."

"I have to take what I need and toss the rest before the others come. They'll leave us alone if they have all this. Cook it and move. I'm sorry—I haven't talked to anyone for a while who can talk back, and I don't know when I slept last. Do you have a place?"

"What others are coming? Other people?"

"No, no, the pigs, mainly. I've seen bears, too. Wolves. Lots of wolves. Saw a cougar. But not here. It's mostly pigs around here."

"How long have you been here?"

"Just a couple of days, I think. It all runs together. When was the storm? Was that today?"

"That was yesterday."

"Maybe three days. I thought it was just me and Elton from here on out."

She was cutting the meat from the rib cage now. Touré started to see black splotches in his vision, which he was sure was unrelated to the grisly show she was putting on. He felt incredibly lightheaded.

"Whoa, don't fall over there," she said. "Fall over somewhere else. There's blood on the floor right under you."

"I'm trying not to fall over at all."

"That'd be better. You should go back and lie down. We've got a long night ahead of us."

"What do you mean? We're not going anywhere *tonight,* are we? We have to stay where we are until morning."

"I told you, we have to move before the others get here. I can't lock this door, and the gate isn't going to hold. We need another place. Do you have someplace safe?"

"Not here. In Cambridge."

"No, that's no good. May as well be Wisconsin."

She stopped what she was doing to look at his leg.

"You need antibiotics, too," she said. "That pig might've killed you and we just don't know it yet."

"What's your name?"

She hesitated, meaning either she forgot her own name for a second or she was making one up on the spot.

"Win," she said.

"Win? Like, Winnie? Short for Winifred?"

"Nobody calls me Winifred. Or Winnie."

"Well, I'm Touré, and everyone calls me Touré. It's nice to meet you and thanks for saving my life. Please stop saying things like that; it's been a rough day already."

"Like what?"

"Like how I'm already dead from infection that hasn't happened yet."

"But you might be. We won't know until later. I remember this horse we had at the ranch, got bit by a snake—"

"Please."

"Right, okay. I'm usually better with people. It's the lack of sleep. Maybe the diet."

"I'm sure I'm not doing any better. Now I definitely have to pass out again, hopefully after I reach the blankets. Wake me when the food's ready."

7

Touré's first taste of non–Noot bar sustenance since who knows when was perhaps the best thing to ever happen to him.

He was prepared to go so far as to say that it was worth getting his leg gored and also nearly worth what he went through next.

Nearly.

The problem, as stated repeatedly by Win, was that the fresh meat and the cooking of such was going to attract a lot of predators to the Corner Mall. Touré joked that predators were always attracted to the Corner Mall, but Win either didn't think that was funny or lost her sense of humor when she started living off the land.

They had to leave, was the point. After getting her arrow out of the undissected boar's head—which took a lot of work—Win dragged the carcass next to the same entrance where she'd set the fire. Then she scattered the remains of the other boar, including that pile of internal organs, around different parts of the mall: a carnivore scavenger hunt.

She washed up next, thank goodness. There was evidently a functioning sink in the food court somewhere. She didn't get all of the blood off of her, but nothing short of a high-pressure hose was going to do that.

Then came the fun part. Touré couldn't walk, and his hopping skills weren't exactly championship caliber. He also didn't know how to ride a horse and was a risk to faint from the pain. Not certain what to do about this, Win had a long conference with Elton to hash out their options. Touré had neither a vote nor an opportunity to voice an opinion, which was a shame.

"Elton agreed to let me tie you to him," she said, after.

"Like, in the saddle? Okay. I mean, I can probably hold on all right if he doesn't go too fast."

"That isn't what I meant. I'll tie you *to* him. You'll be on the saddle, but not sitting."

"So, basically the most undignified way to get me around town that you could come up with."

"Also the fastest. C'mon."

She helped him onto the saddle, belly first, and then tied him down. He could barely move, which—she explained—was so Elton didn't end up dragging him if he started running. Touré countered that if he couldn't untie himself and something happened to Win, Elton would end up running around with a corpse on his back. She laughed, and shrugged, and made the rope a little tighter.

He could sort of see where they were going by looking up and to his left, but it was exhausting, holding his head up like that. Win positioned herself to the right of Elton, near Touré's head, and half the time she blocked his view anyway, so he gave up on trying to see.

She held a bow in her right hand, with the quiver on her back. He only counted ten arrows.

If this were a video game, he'd tell her to look around for a reload, maybe near the body of a dead archer.

Hyperrealistic video game was actually on his list of apocalypse scenarios. It was the only one he hoped was correct—once they beat the game, they'd be back home again. But they had to figure out what the big quest was first. Thus far, to his extreme annoyance, there didn't appear to *be* a big quest. All he had was a bunch of side quests, necessary only in order to continue to survive.

It wasn't a game; he knew that. But thinking of it that way made all of this much easier, especially when he was lashed to a horse like some expository NPC. Suddenly, saving *him* was a side quest and Win was the player.

"How well do you know your way around here?" she asked.

"Pretty well," he said. "But everything's upside down and I'm looking over a horse's shoulder, so I don't know how helpful I'll be."

"We need someplace with multiple doors so we can break in through the outer door and lock the inner door from the other side. It has to have water and elevation, but Elton needs to come in with us."

"You want maid service too?"

She hesitated. "That was a joke," she said.

"*Yes*, it was a joke," he said. "This might have gone better if we had this conversation before you tied me to the horse."

"Don't call him that."

"What?"

"'The horse.' Don't call him that. He doesn't think he's a horse."

"Right," he said. "Where are we?"

"Shhh." She stopped Elton, then turned to look past his hind-quarters. "They found the meat," she said. "I can hear them arguing."

"What kind of 'they'?"

"Wolves, I think."

"Which kind? We have regular, and supersize around here."

"Regular. The big ones aren't wolves. They're crossbreeds."

"With what?"

"Dunno. Tell me where to go. We have to get off the streets."

He strained his neck more to get a look around. All he could see was the side of a department store, but it was enough. They were on Washington Street.

"Turn me," he said. "Counterclockwise, slowly."

She did. He got a good look at the area, albeit sideways. They were only a couple of blocks from the mall.

"Was that another gang of boars?" he asked, once the full circuit was completed.

"Yeah, or the same one as before. It's really impossible to tell. They don't wear matching outfits. They've been behind us since we left."

"Maybe we should move faster."

"I agree, but a destination would be helpful."

"Okay. Okay, do you see that glass-enclosed staircase up there?"

"Yeah."

"That leads to a third-floor gym. I've been there; it's nice. Big bathrooms, lots of floor space for Elton. If we hurry, maybe the boars won't get to us first."

"Oh, they won't. They're afraid."

"Of you?"

"Of Elton. There aren't enough of them to take him on yet. We need to be off the street before the rest arrive."

8

They had to break in through the doors on the ground floor and then deal with the challenge of persuading a horse to climb two flights of stairs. Win coaxed him up to the first landing with an apple — Touré was never a big fruit eater, but he would have eaten the hell out of that apple himself — and then pointed out to Elton that the stairwell wasn't wide enough for him to turn around, and he'd probably fall if he tried to walk backwards, so he may as well keep going.

Elton wasn't at all happy about being tricked. He expressed this first by pooping on the stairs, and later by refusing to talk to Win for the rest of the evening.

The gym was more or less as Touré remembered it, the one time he visited. He wasn't a visit-a-gym kind of guy, except for the two or three occasions in his life when he tried to *become* that kind of guy. He got a cheap gym membership with a fitness chain that turned into an expensive membership after about three months.

He went to the one in Central Square a couple of times, decided again that exercise wasn't his deal, and never went back. The visit to the Boston location they were now inside of was just to use the bathroom.

Win untied him and helped him onto the rubberized floor, while the aggravated Elton walked over to the other side of the room to see if any of the free weights were edible.

"I was supposed to be collecting all this stuff," Touré said. "For the others. Parkas and more blankets and . . . hats and gloves and all that, for winter. We were prepping for winter."

"You think that's going to happen soon?" Win asked.

She was sitting cross-legged on the other end of the mat, chewing on a piece of meat and holding eye contact for an unsettling length of time.

"Pretty soon, yeah," he said.

"You're probably right. How many are there? Your friends."

"Counting me, there are four. Well, five. We saw this kid running around, but he took off."

Win nodded.

"I was hoping for more," she said.

"Me too. We kept taking the bikes out farther, to find more survivors. Might have to wait until the spring now, but we'll figure it out."

"Figure what out?"

"Where all the people went."

Win started laughing,

"All the people are dead," she said.

"We don't know that."

"I know you're looking in the wrong place if you're heading out of the city to figure that out. Where do you think I came from?"

"I dunno, a Renaissance faire?"

"I saw the dead. They're everywhere. You've probably seen them too."

"Do you . . . see them right now?"

She gave him a sour look, then got up and started pacing around the mat. She still had that big knife on her hip, and was coming off as a little unbalanced. He hoped he was wrong about being the expendable character.

"Piles of dust in stacks of clothes," she said. "That's all they are. Something turned all the people into piles of dust. Even the bones. Most of the bones. All except for you and me. And the others, I guess, if they're real."

"Of course they're real. Why would I make that up?"

"I didn't say you made them up. Sorry. I've been . . . sorry. I'm sure they're real. I don't know when you'll see them again, but sure, they're real."

"We can go see them tomorrow. I just need my bike."

"Tomorrow, you stay right here while I go looking for something to help with that wound. Or you'll die."

"I asked you to stop talking like that."

"I'm just telling you, you're going nowhere right now. The pigs are all over the parts of the city that aren't underwater. You'll never make it."

"Underwater? Literally?"

"Yes, literally. I can't have you limping around behind me or you'll get both of us killed. You know you can't ride a bike on that, right?"

"I can use a crutch."

"No." Win stopped pacing and sat back down. "Maybe you should tell me what happened here," she said.

"What do you mean?"

"I mean, what happened? What did this to everyone? That's why I came into town. Here, maybe this will help."

She reached into her bag and pulled out a bone, tossing it on the mat between them.

"Less than two weeks ago," she said, "the owner of that jawbone was sitting in a car, in traffic, trying to run *away* from Boston. That's all that's left now. Well, and a couple of loose teeth. I didn't take those."

"He was in his car?"

"Her car. I think. Based on the shoes. What does that to a person?"

"Maybe the same thing crumbling all the streets and the buildings," Touré said, as his *everything gets old at the same time* apocalypse scenario gained new prominence on his list. "What makes you say she was trying to get away from *here?*"

"They all were. That's what I'm trying to explain. You said you were heading out of town to work out what happened, but this is the epicenter. I came here to find you so you could tell me why everyone else in the world is dead."

"Oh," he said. "I'm sorry, I don't know. I'm as in the dark as you. I woke up and it was like this. We all did."

She looked him in the eyes for an uncomfortably long time, without saying anything, before breaking off.

"I mean, obviously, right?" he said. "Why would we be riding around looking for answers if we had answers ourselves?"

"Okay," she said, climbing back to her feet again, nodding, and making him nervous. "Okay."

"We're all in the dark here," Touré said.

"I understand. Yeah. I'm going to … I'm going to see about cleaning us up and then maybe get some sleep."

"Yes, sure. I understand."

She disappeared into the bathroom. A minute later, he could hear her crying.

He felt like he should go comfort her somehow, even though he had no real comfort to give.

If she was right about the leg wound becoming infected, he probably wasn't going to survive the winter. Meanwhile, without him to help collect gear, and do whatever else, the others might not make it through the winter either.

If Win was right, they were the last remnants of the entire human race … and they were about to go extinct.

There was nothing comforting about that whatsoever. The longer he thought about it, the more crying in the bathroom seemed like the only sane response. A hug certainly wouldn't make it all better.

So instead of getting up and hopping to the bathroom to see if Win was going to be okay—or to see if he was—he curled up in a ball under the blanket and tried to sleep.

EIGHT

Robbie

1

THE EMOTIONAL CONSEQUENCE OF TOURÉ'S FAILURE TO RE-
turn didn't hit them all at once, because there was precedent for
this already.

Back when they'd first met, Robbie and Carol ended up in the
dormitory, while Touré was at the supermarket, assuming the others were dead. Now *he* was the one who failed to show up when
and where he was supposed to, but they weren't prepared to think
the worst.

Surely all that happened, they reasoned, was that it got dark
early and so he holed up somewhere safe until morning.

It was a perfectly reasonable assumption, especially since the
days were getting noticeably shorter. Robbie almost had to do the
same thing.

Robbie's trip to the malls in Watertown was fruitful enough
that he had to go back and forth three times to bring it all to the
dorm: blankets, winter gear, more matches, even something called
a "starter log" for the fireplace.

It was getting dark by the end of the fourth round trip. Robbie knew his way around New England weather, and thought himself up to date on the speed in which the daytime turned to nighttime in the winter, but on this day, he seemed to lose his feel for it. He was pedaling back in almost total darkness.

The rational choice would have been to stop over somewhere, but he was biking along the river and there *was* no place to stop over. He'd have to head away from the riverbank and into neighborhoods he wasn't familiar with, in the dark. That seemed like a worse idea than to just keep pedaling.

None of the wildlife knew quite what to do with the bike, and the wolves—he could hear them howling—were off hunting somewhere else, so it ended up being uneventful. When he made it back to hear that Touré hadn't returned, he was hardly surprised.

They kept busy the following day; they couldn't afford not to. And surely, they thought, Touré would turn up at any minute.

Bethany took Robbie's bike into Harvard Square to pick up more of the things "the menfolk" wouldn't have thought of. It turned out she *did* know how to ride a bike and just didn't want to. Or something. Robbie thought her reluctance to do so was directly influenced by her insistence on being contrary to Touré in all matters, but verifying that with her was probably going to end up being not worth the trouble.

Robbie, meanwhile, attempted to chop down a tree.

They had plenty of live trees to choose from. There were dead ones too, but they looked a lot like the one Robbie saw in the quad back on the first day: collapsed, and overtaken by some kind of invasive mossy ground covering. This same moss was fighting the grass in several places around the city. It was hard to tell who was winning, but the animals didn't eat the moss, which was a bad sign for the grass.

Robbie's attempts to scrape enough moss from one of the fallen trees to get at the wood underneath ended in frustration. If they wanted wood, it would have to be some combination of fallen branches and a live tree.

He decided on one of the trees near the river rather than near the dorm, reasoning that since he couldn't predict how a tree might fall, it would be better if when the tree did fall it didn't land on anything they liked.

The point was moot, because the tree never fell. He whacked at it for half of the afternoon, succeeding only in the creation of several blisters.

"We can take lumberjack off my list of possible professions," he said to Carol. She was on a bench a safe distance from the tree.

"But how will you feed your family of ten?" Carol asked.

"I'll have to go to the mines, like my papa and his papa before him."

She laughed.

He took two more whacks at the tree, then put the axe back down again. If a blister popped, he was done for, and all he'd managed to accomplish was a modest gash in the side of the trunk. It was nothing the tree couldn't abide.

"This is way harder than I expected," he said.

"It's a living thing," Carol said. "It's bound to fight back."

"Yeah. And it's winning."

"So. What *did* you want to do?"

"Today? I dunno, maybe grab a drink, see a movie."

"I meant, with your life. Now that we've excluded *lumberjack*."

He nearly said *Live to at least age thirty*, but thought pithy gallows humor was perhaps uncalled for under the current circumstances.

"You know, I've been thinking about it," he said. "I don't know what I wanted to do. I was heading toward CPA, but that would've been just to pay bills, I think. Maybe lawyer. My dad wanted me to look at law school after graduation. He didn't seem to think it was premature to drop those suggestions when I was still figuring out how to be a freshman, but that was how he rolled, so . . ."

"So not CPA."

"I didn't *want* to be an accountant. I *kind* of wanted to be a writer. I don't know if I'm any good at it, but if it turned out I was . . . that's the problem, though, right? I'm talking about all of it in past tense. I never wanted it to be my job to just *survive*. But here I am, hitting a tree with the sharp side of an axe and listening to the tree laugh at me. This is all I'm ever going to be now: someone who survives, or doesn't."

"Survival is important," she said. "And we need you to keep us alive."

"No pressure there."

"I'm not joking."

"I know. That just makes it worse. There are a lot of things I definitely *don't* want to be, and CPA is just one of them. I also don't want to be the one making important decisions with life-or-death consequences. I'd rather be in the back of the room, thanks."

"I know," she said. "But there's nobody else in the room."

"That's only true until we can find more people. Then I'll retire."

He swung the axe extra hard. It didn't help.

"Well . . ." Carol said. "You can still write. Nobody's stopping you. Get a pen and some paper and some candles so you don't ignite your work with a misplaced torch."

"I've thought about it. But for who? I want to succeed in a community that doesn't exist anymore."

"I suppose," Carol said. "But think of it this way: If you do decide to write, you'll be the world's greatest living author."

He laughed. "Sure," he said. "But the world's greatest lumberjack is calling it quits. I don't think the wood in this tree will burn anytime soon anyway. Firewood needs to dry out, right? We should have done this six months ago."

"You're probably right. Perhaps there's a better solution. Was there wood at the mall?"

2

Touré didn't come back the second night, either.

Bethany did, with a haul of products from some shop in Harvard Square. They were mostly hygiene-related: powders, perfumes, soaps, and two-ply toilet paper. She also brought a wide assortment of undergarments, clearly intended for her and Carol. And she had a gift for Robbie: a razor and shaving cream.

"Dude, you do not look like you're gonna pull off a beard," she said.

The next morning—after a cold-water shave that cut his face in two places—Robbie made another three trips to and from the massive hardware store at one of the Arsenal Street malls, this time for construction wood that looked like it might burn.

What he found was short enough to fit into the cart he was dragging, but too long to fit into a fireplace, so he also picked up a saw while he was there, thinking it was probably more appropriate for the task than the axe.

"I should search for him," he said that night, once it became clear Touré wouldn't be walking through the door.

"You can't," Carol said.

They were in the common room, sitting around the fireplace. There was no fire, as they hadn't worked up the courage yet, but the chairs around it were assembled in a way that was advantageous to conversation. They were each wrapped up in blankets, because as the winds picked up, it became clear exactly how drafty the building was.

"But he could be hurt," Robbie said. "If I can find him, and help him back here . . ."

"*You* not coming back sentences all three of us to die," Carol said. "That's the situation, Robbie, and I'm sorry to put it that way, but it's true. I'm worried about him, and I hope he's okay, but going into the same environment that appears to have waylaid him . . ."

"All three of us may die either way. Look, we might be the last four people on the *planet,* so I'm willing to value his life a little higher here."

What he didn't say was how much easier all of this was with Touré around. Not from a division-of-labor perspective, although that had merit. Touré made the end of the world bearable somehow, because he was the only one who seemed—oddly, Robbie would have to admit—*excited* by the idea. That was off-putting at first; now Robbie wasn't sure how to get through the day without it.

"It's too great a risk," Carol said.

"Once everything here is set, though . . ."

"He doesn't even *want* you to save him," Bethany said.

"What are you talking about?" Robbie asked.

"It's who he is, man. He wants to be the guy who saves everyone. He'd rather go down thinking he was a hero."

"I don't know where that's coming from," Robbie said, "but if it was me out there, he'd try and find me."

"Of course he would! Then he'd be the hero. That's what I'm saying!"

"We all need rescuing," Carol said. "We save one another."

"Yeah, Touré missed that memo," Bethany said.

"Right," Robbie said, standing. "Well, I think I'd rather get out there and ask him myself, thanks. Excuse me—I need some sleep."

3

Robbie didn't leave the dorm the next day, to look for Touré or for anything else. Nobody did, because that was when the snow came.

It was a tremendous storm, magnificent and beautiful as long as one was looking at it from the inside. It came with high winds and granular bits of snow that everyone familiar with this kind of weather recognized as the very worst. It was the sort of snow that piled up upon itself, buried entire landscapes, and either suffocated or froze living things, and it was carried in on the kind of storm that was supposed to come with a name.

The high winds buffeted the dormitory; it felt like the entire structure was tilting, and complaining about having to do so. The wind also exposed every last spot where the walls let through a draft, and in two places—dorm rooms, on the third and fourth floors—windows they didn't realize weren't intact allowed entire snowdrifts to form indoors.

Several times, they heard wolves howling somewhere distant, their voices carried by the wind. Other than that, it felt as if the world around them was dead.

They took to the higher floors to watch the snowstorm blow through. Robbie and Bethany tried to describe what they were seeing—a magnificent sight, from their perspective—to Carol, who mostly focused on the noises the building made.

Carol didn't like the storm at all, and said so, loudly, many times.

Such a chill settled in on the dorm that they finally tried the fireplace that evening. Robbie had to spend an hour sawing through wood first, and then came a comedy of errors, as it appeared the smoke wasn't going to go up the chimney. This was alarming; more evidence to support the thesis that they were simply terrible at preparing for long-term survival.

Surely an effort could have been made in advance of the storm, to determine if the fireplace worked. *During* the storm, escape to another building was perilous on a level only Touré might have considered trying. Yet they were evidently about to suffocate, so escape was the only option.

Then Bethany rechecked the flue, and then they were okay. Robbie, who grew up in a house with a fireplace but without any interest in using it, *thought* he'd opened the flue when he'd actually closed it. Bethany—still not sharing much about her past—was raised in a house with a working one, and also claimed without elaboration that she had extensive experience with fires.

They then came to terms with two other alarming facts. First, the fireplace was a barely adequate source of heat, and second, it consumed wood at a much greater rate than their available supply. There was enough to last the storm, *probably,* but unless there was a thaw before the next one (they assumed there *would* be a next one) they didn't have nearly enough wood to last the whole season.

Robbie, perhaps recalling the table leg he'd been using as a torch, pointed out that a lot of the furniture in the dorm was flammable, and that with the axe and saw on hand, they would probably make it through the year. After that, they could just move to the next dorm. In this way, they might never run out of things to set on fire.

It was a good point. A grim one, but still good.

The snows lasted two days. When it was over, the pile was so deep, they couldn't open any of the doors.

Carol

1

"Hey, we're out of food."

This was how Bethany greeted Carol and Robbie on the morning of the third day following the storm. The snow was still entirely blocking all means of egress, and snow shovels had not been one of the mandatory items on their list of needs. Not that it mattered. As Robbie said, it's really hard to shovel from the inside out; there would be no place to toss the snow.

"What do you mean?" Carol asked Bethany.

"Just what I said. There's enough Noot for this morning, and then we're done."

"Did you check the staff area?" Robbie asked. There were about ten places extra Noot bars could be lying around, because they weren't incredibly organized people.

"I checked everywhere."

"I thought we put those on the shopping list," Carol said.

"Yeah," Robbie said. "We did. It was on Touré's list. I didn't even think to check."

"We can make it a day or two," Carol said.

"No, I said, we're *out*," Bethany said. "Dude."

Carol assumed the last part was directed at Robbie.

"Yeah, okay. I'll gear up."

"What?" Carol said. "You can't. How will you get out?"

"I'll jump from the second floor. It's only a couple of feet. I should be back in a few hours."

"That's much too dangerous."

"It's sunny today, Carol," Bethany said. "We don't know what it'll be like tomorrow, right? What if there's another storm?"

They were right, but Carol was panicking anyway. If he didn't return . . .

"How will you get back?" she asked.

"I can practically walk up to the second-floor window as it is," Robbie said.

"I saw some rope in the basement," Bethany said. "I'll make a rope ladder for him, if he needs it. It'll be fine."

"And I have plenty of winter gear now," Robbie said. "It's really not that far."

"Yes, yes, all right, fine," Carol said. "But if Touré were here, he'd be telling you what a bad idea this is, especially now that you've said it will be easy."

"If Touré was here, he'd have picked up the food and we wouldn't be facing this problem," Robbie said.

It took Robbie an hour to collect the gear he needed, and then he was ready. Carol stood at the second-floor window and listened as he stepped through to hard snow just on the other side. They'd been truthful enough in that regard: The top of the drift really was high enough to make this feasible.

"Hurry back," Carol said.

"It won't be a hurry," he said, as he crunched away. "But I'll be back before sunset."

"That isn't the slightest bit comforting."

"I know. Sorry."

Bethany closed the window then and narrated Robbie's progress for Carol until he was out of sight.

2

Carol was mindful of the need to keep in shape. The safest way to do that was to go on walks, something that used to make a good deal more sense when she still had Burton. It was a little tougher now, especially outside. But indoors, in an abandoned dormitory, it was an effective way to remain occupied.

Walking also made her feel less useless somehow. It made no sense, as she wasn't doing any work that forwarded their cause, but it felt that way just the same. The only real benefit was that while she was doing it, nobody needed to look out for her, and maybe that was enough: an hour or two without her as a burden on someone else's time.

She'd already visited all of the floors at least once.

After the ground floor, there were another four, separated by stairwells on either end and a nonfunctional elevator in the middle. Each level had been checked for obstacles, so once she got the length of the corridors down, she was able to get up to a light jog.

But today was just for exploring and keeping busy so she didn't worry about Robbie.

On the windless days like this one—in stark contrast to the terrifying loudness of the storm—there was almost no sound. The snow muffled what might have come from the outside, save for the occasions in which a pile fell from the roof, or off a tree. Those periodic *whump* noises were to her ears the same as a truck dropping its rear gate, and so at first she misapprehended what she was hearing as proof of life, in a world that had no such proof to offer.

There was still plenty to notice. The fourth floor had a sour smell that kicked up whenever moisture got in through the broken window in room 421. It was also draftier than the other floors, although the fifth floor was pretty bad too. The third floor, for some reason, reminded her of the library she used to visit when she was ten. They'd had an audiobooks section that had almost nothing for ten-year-olds, so she'd just listened to what the adults were listening to. This led to a lot of awkward questions about what certain words meant, but, though scandalized, her mother never told her to stop listening.

The memory made her want to cry, so she stopped going to the third floor.

Sometimes she tried the dorm room doors. If one was unlocked —around one-third of them were—she'd wander in to discover what the last tenant had to offer. It was never much. Clothes sometimes, but no valuables. (Although, the definition of *value* had changed drastically of late.) If something seemed interesting but she couldn't identify it herself, she'd bring it to one of the others.

One such thing was a plastic disk that felt like a tiny satellite dish. It turned out to be a wireless cell phone charger. She'd never heard of such a device, and neither had Bethany or their resident tech expert, Touré. Robbie recognized it, and spent a few minutes going over the value of the product in a world with electricity. Then they set it aside.

She was on the fourth floor, checking out a new unlocked room, when she arrived at the conclusion that there was someone else in there with her.

Sneaking up on a blind person wasn't at all nice, and most people she knew didn't do it, or didn't do it on purpose. New arrivals typically committed to an incidental noise—throat-clearing was a favorite—to announce their existence. It was generally unnecessary, because for the most part, the person they were coming up behind already knew they were there. It was polite, though; a way to say, *I know you're blind* without having to say that out loud. But Bethany was just a kid, and Carol might be the first blind person she'd met.

"Bethany?" she said. "Is that you?"

The girl didn't answer, so maybe she wasn't there and Carol was just having a moment. It didn't feel that way, though. It was the same sense she got when the wolf entered the common room that first night: a vague quality in the air. *Someone is sharing this room with you*, the feeling said.

"Bethany, come on. This isn't funny."

Silence. Not even breathing. This had to be all in her head.

Except it wasn't.

The dorm rooms all had the same basic layout, with the choice of furniture placement an occasional variable. Carol had already felt along the desks and the bedposts of this room and was standing near the closet, which had a chest of drawers in the lower half and wasn't deep enough to hide a person. If someone was in the room with her, they had to be taking up hardly any space, and the space they were taking up was the other side, near the window. That meant it wasn't one of the wolves.

Not that it could have been anyway. A wolf couldn't have appeared inside a dorm room on the fourth floor without making a lot of noise. Not unless it climbed through the window. But the snowfall, while deep, wasn't *that* deep.

The room might also not be large enough for another human being, at least not without her having bumped into that person at least once.

It was probably her imagination.

She swung the cane around the middle of the room. There was nothing there.

Except *smells*.

The other dorm rooms smelled like mahogany, mildew, and dust. The wolves smelled like wet dog. The smell in this room was neither of those; it was closer to urine and sweat.

Someone *was* there.

"Hello?"

A shift in the air from a slight motion. A rustle of cloth on cloth.

That urine smell again.

"Look, I know you're there," she said. "This isn't amusing."

She felt along the wall for the corner of the closet. The room exit was on the other side of that corner. That was where she should be.

"Hello?" she said, again.

"Carol," a man said.

She nearly jumped through the ceiling.

"Robbie? Oh, Robbie, you terrified me. How did you get back so quickly?"

"Carol," he said again.

"No," she said, quietly.

This wasn't Robbie's voice, and it also wasn't Touré; that was the full extent of living men who knew Carol by name.

"Who are you?" she asked.

"You don't need to be afraid," the intruder said.

"What?"

She swiped her stick around the room, still not connecting with anyone. Directionally, it sounded as if he was right in front of her, but there was nobody there. Her four working senses were in total revolt.

"You don't need to be afraid. I'm here to warn you. It's coming back."

"Right. Yes, of course," she said.

The exit to the room was directly behind her now. She began backing up toward it, her stick pointed toward the middle of the room like a sword.

"It's coming back," she said. "I understand, thank you. I'd like to go now."

"Carol," he said . . . and then he touched the tip of her cane and pushed it to the right.

She screamed, pulled the cane away, spun around, and got her feet caught up with one another as they tried to engage in the act of running. She fell through the doorway, and landed on her knees in the hall.

"No, no," she cried, getting to her feet while expecting to be grabbed from behind any second. She turned and felt for the doorway, steadied herself, and grabbed for the doorknob. Then she slammed the door shut and held it.

Got you.

"*Bethany?*" she shouted. "*Come quickly, I need you!*"

Win

1

Winter hit Boston like a tsunami.

Win was a couple of miles from the gym when it happened, on a piece of land called Copp's Hill. Elton was munching on the grass while she took in the view and considered her options.

Touré was back at the gym, feverish, and babbling like a nutbar. She was pretty sure he wasn't going to make it, because she'd run out of ideas for how to help him and nothing she'd tried so far was working.

The morning after they started camping out at the gym, Win went out looking for whatever could take care of Touré's wound. It was a high-risk endeavor because the pigs were everywhere, and they were aggressive at all hours, but there were also five pharmacies within a mile of the gym. The best way to avoid a confrontation was to stay on Elton as much as possible and not linger out in the open, and so that was what she did.

From the shelves, Win grabbed antibiotic pills, creams, liquids to be injected, rubbing alcohol, and fresh bandages for the wound. Once she'd filled her bag, she returned to the gym.

None of the antibiotics had any effect. The area around the wound remained red, and Touré was in agony whenever Win moved the leg, touched the leg, breathed on the leg, or thought about the leg.

The fever started the second day. She had pills for that, too, but they weren't keeping it down. The mercury thermometer she'd scrounged—the digital ones wouldn't work—indicated his temperature was going in the wrong direction.

By this, the third day, Touré couldn't tell the difference between what was actually happening to him and one of several fictional adventures he'd narrated himself into. Sometimes, Win couldn't tell the difference either, frankly. Reality was pretty messed up without any embellishment.

"I have to bring the fever down," she said into the wind.

Copp's Hill was a high point in Boston's North End. Win remembered wanting to visit this city specifically for the Italian food of the neighborhood beneath her. It had proven a massive disappointment, but that was probably not the fault of the North End.

From the hill, she could also see part of Boston Harbor. At least some of what she was looking at was supposed to be dry land, but she couldn't tell which part.

She'd surveyed that area already before running into Touré. All the buildings erected at the edge of the harbor were at least partly underwater now, if they were standing at all.

One of those buildings was the New England Aquarium, which she *had* been to, on a class trip as a child. There was an enormous tank in the middle, viewed by walking around a ramp that curled, clockwise, all the way to the top. She wondered if the fish in that tank stopped to look at the fish swimming outside it and asked themselves what was going on.

She could see the dry parts of the city from the hill too. On land, pigs running around the streets was the new normal. There were other animals as well, but they were scattered; the pigs only respected the wolves and the substantially larger animals. Everyone else was potential food. The potential food appeared to be cognizant of this fact.

On this day, the streets seemed a lot emptier. She didn't understand why that was until the cold wind introduced itself. The animals knew something was coming.

Win left the edge of the hill and went back to find Elton. He looked up at her and snorted.

"I felt it too," she said. "I think it's snow."

She patted his neck.

"Hope you ate enough."

Win led him back down to the street. Copp's Hill was a burial ground, and she didn't feel like being around any more death today.

2

The snow didn't care to wait for them to get back to the gym.

It started before they'd made it all the way down the hill, and was—thanks to an incredibly strong wind—blinding in seconds. It cut right through Win's clothing, reminding her that she was dressed for a different season.

Elton allowed her onto his back for part of the return trip, but only the part he was comfortable with personally. He still wouldn't take the bit and considered her efforts to direct him in one way or another as suggestions rather than commands, so they were relying purely on his sense of direction.

Win closed her eyes, held on to Elton's neck for warmth, and let him find their way.

He didn't go far, stopping at the bottom of the City Hall steps. To the left should have been Faneuil Hall, according to the signs. That was another place she'd always wanted to visit. It was half underwater now too.

Elton had stopped not because of any barrier, but because he didn't seem to know where he was supposed to go next. Also, he was probably having about as much trouble seeing as she was.

"Okay, okay," she said, climbing down. "I'll lead. But I'm a tourist too, you know. You should pay better attention."

With her in front, they walked into the teeth of the wind, around and past the old State House—now missing the clock tower—up to Washington Street.

They were getting pummeled. Thankfully, there was no hail like there had been during the last storm, but the snow was whipping around so fast, it felt like being attacked by tiny needles. They were nearly snow blind and in extreme danger of becoming *actually* blind if they stayed out in this weather for much longer.

It was then—half blind, stumbling through the worst snowstorm of her life and wondering how it came up with so little warning—that Win saw the man in the window.

This was only a block from the entrance to the gym. There was an old building on a corner, with a small plaza in front of it, featuring bronze statues to commemorate . . . something. She'd never stopped to read the plaque, although she did mistake them for actual people once, in the twilight, which wasn't at all fun.

The first and second floors of the building were an open plan with look-through glass, the kind of design that made more sense for a department store or bookstore than for what this was, which was a bank. The second floor had desks so that (she guessed) the bank could showcase their happy customers signing loan documents.

The man was on the second floor. He wasn't signing anything; he was just looking down at her.

There were a lot of shadows going on. It looked a little like he had on a long overcoat or a cape and a little like he was wearing a mask or a helmet on his face, and Win thought maybe he had a hood.

Her first thought was that this was the angel of death here to pick up where he left off. But if that was true, the angel of death was awfully shy.

She steered Elton to the doors: There was a revolving door and a standard one for emergencies.

No way he was getting through either of them.

"Stay here," she said to Elton. "I'll be right back."

Win took the bow and quiver off the saddle, then smashed the emergency door glass with the knife — she'd gotten quite good at this — and stepped inside.

"Hello?" she shouted.

The way to the second floor was up a spiral staircase to her left, or via a nonworking escalator in the center of the room. She nocked an arrow and took the staircase.

"I saw you," she called out. "I know you're here. Come on out."

She got up to the second floor, reached the window, and discovered she was actively threatening a cardboard cutout of an extremely generic man in a suit who really, really very much wanted to tell her about how great the bank's interest rates were.

She laughed and then kicked the sign over so this never happened again.

"Thanks for wasting my time," she said.

Then, a flash of light on the other side of the window caught her eye.

Lightning again?

It wasn't lightning, unless it was extremely localized, extremely small ball lightning. A thousand sparkles of white light rushed through the wind currents in directions contrary to where the snow was blowing. She didn't know what was causing it, but it was beautiful.

As she watched, it aggregated into a shape that looked like it had two arms, two legs, and a head. She gasped.

"I've seen you before, haven't I?" she said. "You're my neon ghost."

As if in response, the lights charged ahead, passing through the glass and then through *her* before disappearing.

"Goodness," she said, once she felt like it was okay to start breathing again. "Buy a girl a drink first next time."

3

Elton hadn't run off, which was nice of him. They were back in the gym a few minutes later.

Touré was already talking.

"... big war, right? And these guys over here, like, there was this technology, okay, and it went, like, in the other direction from us, but to use it ..."

"Hi," Win said. "Who you talking to?"

He looked at her, confused. His face was flushed and his eyes bloodshot.

"Wasn't I talking to you?" he asked.

"I just got back," she said.

"Oh. I thought I was talking to you."

She went about the business of putting away what she'd come in with: Elton, mainly, but also more blankets, and a dead rabbit.

She had been cooking on the roof, but that might have to change, due both to the snow and to the dropping temperatures. A fire might be the only way to keep warm, and would make perfect sense if she could figure out what to do with the smoke. Short term, if she really had to, she could lie down next to Touré and put a blanket over them. He was generating enough heat to keep her warm through the night.

Probably not enough to cook the rabbit. But when she felt his forehead, she wasn't so sure—he felt like he was broiling to death.

Despite that, the wound actually looked a lot better. He screamed when she touched it, so it undoubtedly didn't *feel* better, but it looked like his body might be healing.

She just had to bring the fever down.

"Hey," she said.

"Present," Touré said. He spoke like there was cotton in his mouth.

"I think you should see the roof. Would you like to see the roof?"

"Love to."

"Great. But I can't carry you all the way, you have to help. It's going to suck."

"Then we'll stay here," he said.

"No, we have to go to the roof."

"Okay."

She helped him up. He screamed as soon as his leg moved and screamed some more when trying to put weight on it, but he didn't pass out, which was about the best she could have hoped for.

Reaching the roof meant going up another flight of stairs and then out through a maintenance door. She'd been up several times already—mostly for non-fire-related reasons—because the view was decent and she enjoyed looking at the stars. But those were good-weather trips. This time, the wind nearly took both of them off the ledge immediately.

"Hey," he said, "it's snowing. Merry Christmas, everyone."

"Here, right here, sit down."

"In the snow? Shouldn't I have on a hat or something?"

"No, just . . . lie down. Right here."

"Okay."

She helped him lie down in the snow, which was already six inches deep. Then she started packing the snow around him.

"Are you burying me?" he asked.

"I'm trying to get your fever down," she said. "I don't have an ice bath, but I do have lots of snow. How's it feel?"

He looked left and right, as if consulting the other Tourés on the roof with him.

"Not bad, actually," he said. "I think my leg is going numb. My fingers, too."

"We won't be up here long. I don't want to add pneumonia to your symptoms."

"Thanks, you're the best. We should . . . we have to tell the others."

"The others?" she asked, needing clarification. He had, in the past thirty-six hours, addressed entire roomfuls of people that weren't actually present. "You mean your friends in Cambridge?"

"It's coming back for us, that's what he told me."

"Who? Was it Elton? Were you talking to Elton again? Because he doesn't know what he's saying."

"Did you see the sparkly man?" he asked.

She was taken aback for a moment. He could be describing one of his many hallucinations, or he could be talking about her neon ghost.

Did he see it too?

"Yes," she said.

"You did?"

"Yes. Did the sparkly man tell you that it's coming back for us?" she asked. "Is that what you're trying to say?"

"No, no, he doesn't talk."

Whether or not any of this made sense, she thought it was a good idea to keep him talking, because if he dozed off and she couldn't wake him, she didn't know what to do next; she couldn't get Touré off the roof and down the stairs without his help.

All the same, it was hard to decide if he was speaking nonsense or if he'd seen what she had.

"Then who told you?" she asked.

"Doesn't matter. Have to warn them."

"Your friends."

"They're great. I can't wait for you to meet them. There's Robbie and Carol and Bethany . . . Well, we don't like Bethany, but she's okay I guess . . . and Noah. He's pretty cool."

"Sure. I can't wait."

She sat down in the snow, clutching his still-too-warm hand while she was personally starting to get a chill of her own.

From where she was sitting, she could see a department store across the street. As long as the pigs were hiding from the storm, she probably had time to run over there for warmer clothes, she thought. Before the weather got much worse.

She checked Touré's forehead again. There was no way to tell if this was working at all, but at least he *seemed* to feel better.

"I'll be honest, Touré, I don't know for sure what to do here," she said. "I don't think I can feed you all winter, and Elton . . . Do you know how much horses eat? Come winter, back at the ranch we had enough hay and grains stored to get the animals through when there wasn't any grass, but now we're in a city. He eats grass and vegetables, and all I have is protein. He'll have what I have, but it won't be near enough. I might have to set him free, make him find his own way."

"That's nice."

"Yeah. And then there's you. I don't have the medical training to get you through this, buddy. And I don't know if your friends would have an easier time, but I bet they would. I just have no idea how to bring you to them. It's too far."

"You gotta leave me," he said. "It's okay, I'm an NPC."

"A what?"

"A non-player character. Go ahead, I'll be here when you get back."

"I don't think so."

"No, but I gotta warn them. It's an engine, you know? It collects tickets."

"Sure," she said.

He squeezed her hand tightly.

"Take the train," he said.

"What?"

"If you wanna go to Cambridge, take the red line."

"That's an insane idea," she said, liking it already.

Carol

Carol had to shout for quite a while before Bethany finally heard her.

In that time, the man on the other side of the door didn't attempt to pull it open, which was almost worse; it could mean he exited during the three seconds Carol was on the floor prior to her getting the door closed. He could be standing in the hall, laughing at the blind woman.

By the time Bethany made it to the end of the hallway, that was exactly what Carol had convinced herself was going on.

"Is he behind me?" Carol shouted.

"Who?" Bethany asked. "What are you talking about? What's wrong?"

"There's nobody else in the hallway?"

"Just you and me. What's wrong with the door?"

"There is a *man* in this room. He called me by name. Are you armed with something?"

"Like what, my charm and good looks? Are you serious right now?"

"I am thoroughly serious. Go find a weapon."

"Okay, okay."

Bethany ran off.

Carol listened to her stomping down the staircase two steps at a time, jumping to each landing, all the way down. It was comforting, in its way, even if having Bethany fall and break her neck would make this situation that much worse.

It didn't sound as if Bethany was intercepted on her way down. Because that was the third, and least savory, option: If he wasn't still in the dorm room, or standing in the hall, he had to be somewhere else in the building. And if he was somewhere else in the building, he had the capacity to attack Bethany while she was making all that noise.

"She's coming back," Carol said, through the door. "With a weapon. And Robert's on his way. You'd better not mess with us or this will end badly."

It was a ridiculous bit of bravado. The only person less intimidating in this dormitory than the thirteen-year-old girl was the blind woman. Saying Robbie was the most formidable of them was saying almost nothing.

Bethany returned shortly.

"Okay," she said. "Open the door. Let's kick this guy's ass."

"What do you have?" Carol asked.

"Fireplace poker. Step aside."

Carol let go of the doorknob and moved to the left of the door. It did not fly open.

"One, two, three," Bethany said. Then she opened the door and jumped into the room, screaming obscenities.

Carol heard Bethany run around the room, yelling some more and swinging the poker.

It's option number three, then, she thought.

"There's nobody in here," Bethany called.

Carol entered the room.

"Are you sure?" Carol asked.

"I mean, yeah, as sure as I can be. Unless he's invisible. What's that smell? Did you . . ."

"Did I what?"

"It just, I mean it's okay, it smells like piss in here, so I was asking. You know, never mind."

"That isn't me," Carol said. "It's *his* smell."

"Well, he's not in here, so I don't know what to tell you."

"All right. Let's wait for Robbie in the common room. Until he's back, we go nowhere alone in this building, do you understand?"

"Geez, sure, Mom."

"Then you *don't* understand. I'll make it clearer. There was a man in here who knew my name. If he's not here any longer, he's in another part of the building. Since the snow has blocked all the entrances, he was here for the storm, and may have been here with us this entire time."

"Okay, well, now I'm not getting any sleep tonight."

"I may never sleep again. We'll have to find rooms we can lock from the inside."

"Or move somewhere else."

"Yes, or move somewhere else."

Robbie

1

This is what's going to get us killed, Robbie thought, as he waded through chest-deep snow. *Not the big things; the stupid little things we forgot because we took them for granted.*

Of particular annoyance to Robbie was that this was only a round trip of about a half mile, in total. He could have done it any other time in under an hour. With snow, it was going to take the entire day.

That was assuming he made it there at all. He was walking through snow, on top of snow. The stuff at the bottom was sufficiently compressed to support his weight, which was fine, except he had no idea how deep the drifts really were.

Occasionally he'd hit a soft patch, and then he would know. These came up without warning and dropped him another two or three feet straight down, well past where the top of the snow was over his head. The first time it happened, he panicked, which just resulted in him sinking deeper. He got out by calming down and performing a sort of sideways-and-up swim move.

It happened three more times, but once he understood the best way to extricate himself, it got easier. With each step was the fear that the *next* time, he'd slip so far down so fast that his legs would end up pinned until a thaw released him or a predator found him, whichever came first.

But still — it was only a quarter of a mile each way.

2

One of the other issues he failed to take into consideration was that the snow blocking the door to the dormitory would of course also block the door to the supermarket. He realized this after nearly walking *past* the supermarket.

"Geniuses," he said, to nobody. "That's what we are."

The top of the snow met the lip of the roof. If he'd thought to bring one of the shovels he'd neglected to pick up from the hardware store, he might have been able to dig out the side door enough to open it, but he'd need about five more hours than he probably had. That was *with* a shovel. With just his hands? Forget it.

He pulled himself up onto the flat roof.

There should have been at least as much accumulation up on the roof as anywhere else, but for some reason there wasn't; it was only a couple of feet deep. Robbie figured wind had to have been a factor in keeping it from really piling up there. He was grateful, anyway, because the lower snow cover meant he could see the roof access door.

Between kicking around snow and scooping it up with his hands, he had the space in front of the door cleared out in just a few minutes. Then he tried opening it.

Unsurprisingly, it was locked.

"Honestly, I don't know what I expected," he said. "Of course it's locked."

He pulled on the doorknob a couple more times, just in case the door changed its mind. Then he looked around for something to hit it with, which was also not helpful, because the entire roof was under a layer of snow. There could be a loose axe lying around and he wouldn't see it.

"That's what I need. An axe."

Getting one meant going all the way back to the dorm, coming back again, chopping open a door that looked like it was made of metal anyway, getting the Noot, and going back. All before dark. Based on the sun — he deeply missed being able to know what time it was still, but had become accustomed to estimating how much day he had left using the sun's position — he didn't have enough time to do all of that.

But they had to eat. If he waited a day, he might not have the energy necessary to accomplish this trip a second time, so he probably had no choice but to do this *today*. If not, the other realistic option was to hope the snow melted very soon . . . and that no other storm came along to replenish it.

Robbie was thinking about all of this when he heard a click from the door. Puzzled, he turned and stared at it for a few seconds.

"Did you just unlock yourself?" he asked.

Robbie tried the door again. This time, the knob turned and he was able to pull it open.

Okay, so either my pulling on it jarred something loose in the lock, or someone unlocked it from the inside, he thought.

"Hello?" he shouted, into the void on the other side of the doorway.

It could be Touré.

Touré could have made it back as far as the store and gotten stuck here. Or he was injured and couldn't make it any further. They hadn't returned to the market since Touré disappeared — clearly, since they'd run out of food in the interim. So it could be him.

But Touré would still be standing here.

"Touré?" Robbie shouted. "It's me, Robbie."

Nothing.

"All right, I'm coming down."

There was a doorstop—a barrel of cooking oil—on the inside of the entrance. Robbie moved it to the roof to hold the door open. Then he used the sunlight to help guide his way down what was an unpleasant-looking metal ladder.

The ladder deposited him into one of the storerooms in the back of the market. He could barely see, but recognized the space because he'd been in it before, looking for any evidence of non-Noot products. Today, the place smelled more like body odor than he remembered, which meant either someone else had been in there or he just hadn't noticed it before.

"Hello?" he said.

Still nothing.

In the only light he had, he bent down and pulled a torch from his (thankfully) waterproof bag and got it lit. The room flared into view and for a second . . .

No, that can't be right, he thought.

For just a moment, he thought he saw a figure in the corner of the storeroom, right near the exit to the sales floor. He was taken back to when he thought he saw someone staring at him from the parking garage off Mass Ave. But no, this was just his mind playing tricks.

"Just me," he said. His voice echoed back, as if affirming this conclusion.

He exited to the main part of the store and started going aisle by aisle, just to confirm that he was indeed alone in the place.

"I guess you're just my imagination," he said. Like the door earlier, his imagination didn't talk back.

He made it to the front, shoved five Noot bricks into his bag, and went back out the way he'd come in.

3

Robbie returned with the five Noot bars late in the afternoon, having taken even longer to return to the dorm than it took him to reach the store. The snow was becoming softer as the day progressed, which increased the number of soft patches, each one more exhausting than the last.

A couple of times, he considered just staying there in the snow. He had food, and he had water, and the snow covering provided some insulation, if not a kind of warmth. He didn't do it, both because that was a preposterous idea and because Carol and Bethany were relying on him.

He didn't like being the guy everyone turned to for help, but until there was someone else around for *him* to turn to, this was how it had to be.

When he finally did make it back to the front of the dorm, he discovered a new problem: The snow was melting a lot faster than was okay under the current circumstances. On the one hand, fast-melting snow was excellent news—the kind they'd been waiting for since the storm ended. On the other hand, when he stood under the window he'd left through in the morning, he was two feet further from the bottom of the sill than expected. And he still wasn't close enough to the ground to use the front door.

He chucked snowballs at the window for a while, shouting sparingly—not interested in attracting the attention of any wolf in snowshoes . . . or a hawk maybe—until Bethany showed up.

"Oh, hey, I have a rope," she said, disappearing inside. She returned a minute later with thick twine that barely met the definition of *rope*. It was sturdy enough to lift the food to the window —which was how they used it first—but barely capable of supporting Robbie.

"Where'd you find this?" he asked.

"It was holding together some furniture in the basement," she said. "It'll work. I put some knots in it for you."

There were a number of things Robbie hated having to do when he was in grade school, and that he was also objectively terrible at; in those cases, he either didn't make any effort to accomplish them and thus failed, or he *did* make an effort to do them and *still* failed. He used to argue with the teachers, counselors, gym instructors, his parents, or whoever, that surely learning how to do *this thing* he was unable to do wouldn't be important later in life.

Years later, his life depended on an intermediate rope-climbing exercise.

It didn't end up being all that bad. There was a wall to help him along the way, so rather than go knot to knot in a free climb, he scaled it as he might a mountainside. The one setback came when it turned out the furniture Bethany tied the other end to wasn't heavy enough to support his weight. He fell, but only five feet, and into soft snow.

Back inside, exhausted, he felt like he'd actually done some heroic hunter-gatherer stuff.

Behold, I have slain five Noot beasts, he thought.

He got out of the heavy wet clothes and into some dry ones, then plopped himself down in front of the fire with a blanket, looking forward to an evening without any additional physical labors.

Then the women told him they wanted to move.

"You want to *what?*" he asked.

"As soon as possible," Carol said.

"Why?" he asked. "And also, no, don't be ridiculous; it's impossible to get anywhere out there. But more importantly: *why?*"

Then he got the story of the man in the room on the sixth floor.

He turned to Bethany first.

"Did you search the building?" he asked.

"What? No, dude, are you insane?"

"We agreed to not be alone," Carol said. "If he confronts one of us he will confront both of us."

"Yeah, that makes sense. God, I wish Touré were here. Okay, I'll go floor to floor while you two stay put. We never did a full search of the place anyway, right?"

"Hey, maybe it's a ghost," Bethany said, uttering the most not-helpful thing he'd heard in his entire life.

"*Please* don't say that," he said. "That would make this so much worse."

4

A debate ensued regarding the exact definition of a full and comprehensive search.

It was eventually decided—on a vote Robbie lost—that the very best way to do this was to open every locked door. But while they did have someone accomplished at getting through locked doors, Bethany needed to stay with Carol, and taking all three of them along on this search would just elongate the whole endeavor.

So, Robbie took the axe instead. He needed to have a weapon anyway, and most of the doors were made of wood, so it all worked nicely.

Using an axe to get through a wooden door hadn't been a part of Robbie's grade school curriculum either, but if it had been, he would have failed at it, too.

The first door he encountered—the third door on the second floor—took ten swings and a lot of punching. But by the tenth or eleventh door he'd gotten quite good at it.

He finished the search of the dorm rooms just before sunset. That left only a sublevel storage room, which they checked together with the help of a torch and Bethany's lock-picking skills. It was a boiler room, and, like everywhere else, it had no one unexpected inside.

"Okay, the place is clear," Robbie said, once they were back in the common room. He'd collapsed on a couch. He could hear his hands throbbing and could barely move his arms. "Can we stay now?"

"Oh, no, we can't," Carol said. "He could have avoided you; you were making so much noise."

"Carol . . ."

"I'm willing to wait until the front door is clear, but after that, I would like to go, please. I no longer feel safe here."

He sighed and sat up.

"I have to ask—" he began.

"No, Robert, you don't."

"I do. Someone has to. Is it *possible* you imagined this?"

Carol delivered the most withering stare a blind person was capable of. Robbie was too tired to care. He looked to Bethany.

"Tell me you aren't thinking it too," he said.

"Yeah, sure," Bethany said, "but it doesn't matter."

"Of course it does. Either there was someone here or there wasn't. There's no gray area."

"No, dude, what matters is, she believes it. There's only three of us, right? That's her reality or whatever, and we're stuck in it with her."

He sighed, sat back, and held on to the next thing he wanted to say. If there was ever an occasion to bring up *the wolf,* this was it. Except he was sure it wouldn't go well.

The morning after their first night in the building, Carol insisted a wolf had gotten inside, but that she petted him and he went away. He'd never challenged this, but it sounded a lot like someone who missed her dog very much had a dream about him. Now she was interacting with people who weren't there and making suggestions that could put their lives in danger, and he didn't know what to do.

"What if adhering to her reality gets us killed?" he asked Bethany. "Isn't this how we lost Touré? You said yourself he was trying to play the hero, when the truth is, he needed us to have his back. Now he's gone and probably . . . I mean, it's *bad* out there. If he was hurt . . ."

"I will not be compared to Touré, thank you," Carol said. "I miss him too, but don't do that. *Someone was here,* Robbie. He frightened me when he didn't need to, and that makes this worse. I'm leaving as soon as I can, alone or otherwise. Excuse me."

Carol, and then Bethany, got up. They left together.

Robbie sat alone, listening to the wind through the tiny crevices in the walls.

"Well . . . *crap,*" he said.

NINE

Win

1

TOURÉ'S FEVER BROKE AFTER ALMOST A WEEK, RIGHT around when Win ran out of snow to cool him down with. That was because of a thaw that started the day after the storm, when a blazing sun appeared and pretended that whole winter thing was a scheduling error.

The sunlight turned the city into a steam bath, despite which they didn't see grass or pavement for five days, among rivers of water running for the sewers. Since it appeared half of those sewers were backed up, this resulted in a lot of standing water, but it was drinkable *fresh* water, so nobody much minded.

Certainly, none of the pigs did. They were the first to show up once the sun came back out. If anything, it seemed like there were more of them than before.

Instant population boom, Win thought. *And I have to get us past them.*

Elton walked up next to her, looked through the window, and snorted.

"Yeah, I know," she said. "They look hungry, don't they?"

Elton huffed.

"Yes, you're hungry too. But I don't think this town's safe for either of us. Let's get you out of Boston. Then you can decide if you're better off foraging than hanging with me."

Elton looked at her.

"Cambridge?" She nodded toward Touré. "That's what he thinks too."

Touré groaned from the other side of the room. He was wrapped up in nearly all the blankets they had, like a baby in a receiving blanket. This was to try to combat the violent chills that had been wracking his body for the past day. Win didn't understand how someone could have a 104-degree fever and complain about being cold, but she wasn't a doctor.

The fever was down to 100 now. He wasn't entirely lucid yet, unless he was *always* like this.

"Figured it out," he said, ostensibly to her. There was no guarantee, because while she and Elton were the only ones there, Touré also held conversations with people who weren't strictly real.

"What did you figure out?" she asked.

"We weren't home," he said. "That's how come."

"We weren't home?"

"Right."

"You aren't making any sense," she said.

She knelt down next to him and tried his forehead. Yes, much better.

"Probably not," he said. "None of it makes any sense. You're pretty."

"Thanks. Don't make me regret not leaving you in that snowdrift."

"Oh, wow, that was real? Thought I imagined that."

"That was real. Listen. I was thinking of taking you up on your suggestion."

"I've made a lot of suggestions."

"The one about the subway."

He furrowed his brow.

"I don't remember this," he said.

"I think we have a window. The snow's melted, it's warm, and we need to get out of the city before the real winter cold hits."

"Subways," he said. "I remember. You want to take the train out of town. But we can just ride the horsey out."

"The streets are overrun with pigs."

"Cops run this town, man."

"Touré."

"I'm here," he said. "Tell me what you're thinking."

2

He didn't like the plan. Elton also didn't like the plan, so Win had to sit down with both parties, laying out the facts as she understood them, until they both reluctantly agreed.

First, though, they had to clean Touré up. For starters, he needed new pants: The wounded leg portion of his old pair was torn open from when Win had bandaged him, which by itself made them essentially useless. Worse—and what necessitated a completely new set of clothes—was that he'd soiled himself.

Against his protests—she was not going to go to Newbury Street to pick up *something cool*—he dressed in sweats obtained in the gym's terribly convenient branded products shop. He also self-performed a sponge bath in the ice-cold water of the men's locker room, in between outfits.

Win had a bath too, and a change of clothes, and would now be riding into battle in yoga pants and shorts. It wasn't remotely practical for winter, but the clothing was comfortable, the weather was warm enough for it, and there'd be opportunities to change in Cambridge if they made it there.

Touré hopped out of the locker room an hour later looking like a living representative of the species for the first time since he and Win had met.

"I could use a shave," he said. "My whole face itches."

"Later. How do you feel?"

"I'm here. When's my first lesson?"

"There's only one," she said. "Don't squirm too much when I tie you down."

"Aw, not again."

"You'll be upright this time."

Win walked Elton outside first, then took Touré down the stairs and helped him into the saddle.

Elton protested.

"We talked about this," she said to the horse.

He griped, but didn't run off or try to buck Touré loose, which were two other entirely possible outcomes with historical precedent.

"I think he actually likes you," she said as she tied Touré's legs to the saddle.

"I'm likable," he said. "Ask anyone. Hey, watch the wound."

"I know. How's that feel?"

"It sucks. Only seven on the suck scale, though. It was a ten before."

"Good enough," she said. "What I meant was, the first time I got on his back, he ran for something like two hours straight to try to shake me off. You he's fine with."

"Then I'm very glad he likes me. You're not gonna tie my arms down again, are you?"

"No. Hold the rope, there and there."

"Got it. Two hours straight ahead gets us out of Boston."

"You'll never make it that far."

She slipped the quiver onto her back, and with the bow in her right hand, she took Elton's lead with her left.

"Which way?" she asked.

"Are you asking me, or Elton?" Touré asked.

"You."

"We want the red line, so, that way."

He pointed. Not far away, a subway station entrance erupted from the ground, with a Downtown Crossing sign that was half red and half orange.

"Easy enough," she said. "It goes the right way?"

"It goes four ways, but one of them is the right way."

There were a ton of pigs in front of them. It remained the case that they didn't know what to make of Elton, so at least initially, they were more interested in getting out of the way than in squaring up to attack.

"It's like the boars of Pamplona, man," Touré said.

"I was thinking more Hitchcock," she said.

"*The Birds*! You're right. The ending. You're right. Yeah."

"Keep your voice down."

The station was practically next to the gym entrance, in terms of actual, measurable distance. Measured by boar headcount, it was a lot farther.

But they made it. At least as far as the top of the stairs.

So it was all going great, except that Elton took one look at the subway station entrance, whinnied, and refused to go down.

"*Come on*," she said. "I know, it looks bad, but we don't have any other options. We *had* this conversation."

"Maybe he didn't know it was an underground train," Touré said. "They could just have an el where he comes from. Are you from Chicago, Elton?"

"You aren't helping," she said.

Behind them, a phalanx of boars had formed, led by perhaps the largest one of them she'd ever seen. It looked big enough to take on a wolf, maybe big enough it would think it had a chance with a horse.

"Touré," she said as she let go of the lead and nocked an arrow. "I'm going to need you to encourage Elton to go down."

"Why?" he asked, trying to turn in the saddle.

"No, don't turn around. Elton might turn with you. Just get him down."

"How do I do that?"

"Hit him in the sides with your heels."

The lead boar's attention shifted to her. It was simply massive, snorting like a bull about to charge, as if they actually *were* at Pamplona and this was going to be a stampede.

"Yeah, that's right," she said to the boar. "Look at me. Show me those big eyes."

"It's not working," Touré said. "He just complains louder."

"Elton, buddy," Win said, "you have to trust me here."

She could hear them inching closer. The goddamn pigs were flanking them.

Win took a step closer to Elton. "Touré, can you reach the quiver?"

"Yeah, I think so."

"Take an arrow out."

"You want me to throw it at one of the pigs?"

"Just do it."

He did. She stepped away again, looking for a safe space be-tween the horse's hindquarters and the pigs.

"Okay, now what?" Touré asked.

"Now stab Elton in the butt and hold on for dear life."

"Seriously?"

"Very seriously. And keep your head down."

What happened next might have been funny if it didn't involve everyone nearly dying at about the same time.

As soon as Touré jabbed Elton in the rear with the tip of the ar-row, the horse whinnied and reared up, nearly hitting his own head against the low entrance to the station. Touré failed to hold on with adequate sincerity; his arms flew back, along with his head and up-per torso, and he lost the arrow, which clattered to the ground a few feet from Elton.

Touré would have landed right next to it if he wasn't tied down. As it was, he screamed in pain, because one of the things keeping him attached to the horse was his wounded leg.

The next thing Elton did was charge down the stairs, his rider still bouncing along helplessly on his back, trying to sit up and grab ahold of the bridle.

The lead boar seemed to recognize his prey was escaping into the city's sublevel and *charged*. Win released the arrow she had nocked, and watched as it found a home in the beast's right eye. The effect was dramatic and immediate; a two-hundred-pound unstrung marionette with a rhino's momentum. That momentum carried it to within a few feet of Win.

There was no time to appreciate what was a righteous kill, though, because while having their leader dropped caused all the pigs behind him to hesitate, another boar from her left didn't care. It charged.

Out of the corner of her eye, Win caught the movement at the last second and stepped back, kicking it in the head, narrowly avoiding being gored. Then she spun around, and ran down the steps.

Elton and Touré had made it to the bottom in one piece, but neither of them was the slightest bit happy about the situation. When Win made it down, she found Elton pacing angrily in front of the turnstiles he couldn't fit through, with Touré bouncing along on his back. It was all dark on the other side of the turnstiles.

"Help, help, help," Touré was saying, quietly.

She didn't have *time* to help, at least not right away. As soon as she reached the last step, she drew another arrow, turned, and waited.

None of the boars had followed them.

"They don't like it down here," she said.

"Neither do we," Touré said.

3

The way to get Elton past the turnstile was to take him through the handicap gate, but in order to do that, he had to agree to talk to Win again, which he seemed reluctant to do.

Elton did allow her close enough to help Touré, who was still flopping about on the horse's back. Touré had lost his grip on the rope at the top of the stairs, and—as long as Elton was still moving around—had given up even trying to sit up in the saddle.

"Thanks," Touré said, once he was upright. "I was thinking about just passing out, but this is much better."

Once Touré was settled, Win took out a couple of torches and got them lit.

You have to be careful with fire around horses, for obvious reasons, but Elton had mostly gotten used to it by now. Win handed a torch to Touré and then walked around on the other side of the turnstile to show the horse that he had not been led into some kind of equine hell.

The rats scurrying around at her feet probably didn't help sell the story. They appeared to be the only animal interested in residing in the subway tunnels — she wondered if this was why the pigs didn't come down — and there were *a lot* of them.

They were also very, very large. It certainly made the underground *look* hellish.

The rats didn't appear interested in eating any of them, but the question of what they *did* eat was definitely on Win's mind.

"This is . . . disconcerting," she said, kicking rats as she walked. She held open the gate for Elton, who looked like he felt the same about the scurrying rodents underfoot.

"Yeah, I'm glad I'm up here, thanks," Touré said. "We could probably put a saddle on one of the rats for you, if we had an extra one."

Win used the torch flame to clear the way as they walked, which made her feel slightly better about the overabundance of rats. Elton appreciated it too.

Soon they reached the first set of tracks, which unfortunately were not the tracks they needed.

"We're looking for the red line," Touré said. "Over there, down that next flight."

"*More* stairs?"

"Yeah. You want me to stab him again?"

"No, you lost my arrow the last time."

She got ahead of Elton, grabbed the lead rope from his neck and started pulling. He complained, *a lot*, and dragged her back a few feet, but eventually agreed to go.

It was a good thing he didn't charge down this flight like he had the last one, because the stairs ended at a landing to tracks that were underwater.

"How deep do you think that is?" Win asked.

"Three feet?"

"I think it's closer to five."

"Sure, okay. Hmm ..." Touré studied the water. "We're totally sure the power's out, yeah?"

"The whole city's out," Win said. "How much surer do you need to be?"

"It's just, there's a third rail under that water—you get me?"

"I do."

Win kicked a rat into the water. It plopped in, surfaced, and started swimming in a way that clearly indicated it wasn't being electrocuted.

"Satisfied?" she asked.

"Yeah, that works."

Elton lowered his head and sniffed the water, huffed, and tried to turn around.

"No, no," she said. "You were warned."

"You know he doesn't understand you when you tell him things, right?" Touré asked.

"Sure he does. He's just being stubborn."

"I can't believe I'm the crazy one in this relationship."

"You were having conversations with people who weren't there," she said. "I'm talking to a horse. It's completely different."

"Right."

"Elton, look at me," she said. "I'll go first, okay?"

Win handed her torch to Touré—who held both of them in his right hand, opting to keep holding on to Elton with his left—and secured her bow and quiver on the side of the saddle. Then she stepped in, going under entirely.

"Whoa!" she said, on surfacing. "Yeah, five feet's closer. It's cold."

"You sure are making it sound appealing," Touré said.

"Come on, Elton. This is the way out, let's go. Water's great!"

She reached up, grabbed the lead, and pulled.

Reluctantly, the horse jumped in. Win went under again, and would have been crushed to death by Elton had he not angled his jump to land ahead of her. And the only reason she wasn't swept in the wrong direction by his wake was that she held on to the rope.

"Win, where are you?" Touré shouted.

She breached behind him and spat out a mouthful of seawater.

"Here," she said. "Wow, this was a really bad idea." Win looked north, then south. "Are we facing the right direction?"

"Toward Alewife. Yes."

"Hand me a torch?"

He leaned over and passed one to her.

"So," he said, "according to my wound, this is definitely salt water."

"That's how it tastes. Does it sting?"

"Yeah, I might faint, just so you know."

"That's why you're tied down, cowboy. Try to keep the torch dry."

4

They continued ahead in the same basic formation as before, with Win on Elton's right. Instead of a weapon in her right hand, she held the torch, which Elton was being very cool about. She wished there was a way to reward him properly once they got out of the city.

"Hey, so you and your buddies, with your bikes . . ." she said. "You and Noah, or whoever."

"Noah?" Touré asked. "Robbie, you mean. Where'd you get Noah?"

"Whatever. Did you guys find any gardens?"

"No, but we didn't go very far. To be honest, we weren't thinking real clear. We were just trying to figure out where everyone went, and we had the Noot bars, so we figured there was time. Carol was the only one keeping us straight. I think we'd all be dead without . . . Well, they *might* be dead now, actually."

"I'm sure they're not," she said. "What's a Noot bar?"

"You don't want to know. Oh, hey, we made it to Park Street."

He held his light up against a sign that said exactly that.

"Good, what does that . . . *whoa*."

"What's wrong?" he asked.

"Something just brushed past my leg."

"*Something?*"

"Yeah, there's fish or . . . I mean, I *hope* it's a fish?"

"Are the walls getting closer? I know this movie."

"Let's just hope Elton—"

Win didn't finish the sentence, because whatever was in the water did indeed rub up against the horse's legs. Elton, perhaps on his very last nerve, completely lost his shit.

The horse bolted. Win, standing to his right with her left hand wrapped in his lead, nearly lost that hand and the shoulder it was attached to. She *did* lose the torch, but that wasn't even close to her most pressing concern.

Drowning was the big one. They were in water that was now less than five feet high, which was just enough to keep her from getting dragged on the tracks behind Elton—although the level had been going down steadily, so if he didn't calm down soon and she managed to not drown, getting dragged was definitely her next most pressing concern.

Win got her right hand up to the bridle, swapped it with her left, then got her free hand up and out of the water.

Touré discovered her grasping hand, locked in a grip, and pulled. Then she was up on the saddle behind him.

She blinked seawater from her eyes and found she couldn't see.

"I'm blind," she said.

"No, you're not," he said. "I lost my torch too. Sorry."

"All right."

She got her arms around Touré and grabbed the makeshift reins.

"We need to slow him down," she said.

"I agree, but I can't find the brake pedal."

"Elton! It's okay!" she shouted. "It's okay, you're okay! Tell him he's okay."

"You're okay, horse," Touré shouted. "You're awesome."

A light appeared ahead. Win's first reaction to it was panic—that it was a train heading their way.

"Are we at the end already?" she asked.

"Charles Street station's aboveground."

"I thought you said this was an underground train."

"Yeah, but not the whole time," he said. "Be happy the tracks go over the river instead of under it."

"What about the pigs?"

"I think the runaway horse we're attached to is a bigger problem right now, don't you?"

"He'll calm down."

They reached the end of the tunnel. It was literally an uphill climb getting there, which took them out of the water entirely.

One would think Elton might stop running then, because without water there was no threat that another mystery aquatic creature could brush past his leg. And he did, but not until after he passed the Charles Street station landing and got halfway across the bridge that led to Cambridge. He only stopped then because there was a large collapsed tower in his way.

A reasonable argument could be made that he never did calm down; he just ran out of a track upon which to express his displeasure.

"Okay," Win said, dismounting, "*now* where are we?"

"Great place to watch the fireworks," Touré said. "And no pigs."

"What happened here?"

"One of the towers came down," Touré said. "I noticed this when I came in."

"On this bridge?"

"No, no, on the Mass Ave. bridge, over there." He pointed across the water to their left, at a bridge that looked like a much easier crossing.

"There used to be four. The other ones must have fallen into the water."

Win climbed onto the brick pile and got a good look in every direction. Clouds had formed in the sky since she'd last looked at it, and the wind down the river—which they were now standing over—cut through her wet clothes like they weren't even there. Yoga pants, she decided, had definitely been the wrong way to go.

"We have to get off the tracks," she said.

"I agree."

The bridge was laid out with the train tracks down the middle, with roadways for car traffic on either side. There was a hard barrier running along both sides of the tracks, to keep cars and pedestrians from accidentally intersecting with the train.

It was also an exceptional horse deterrent. She thought she could probably climb it, but Touré couldn't.

"So where do we go? I'm open to suggestions," she said.

"Do horses have an eight-foot vertical leap?" Touré asked.

"They do not."

"I didn't think so, but, you know. Figured it wouldn't hurt to ask. We'll have to double back."

"Into the tunnel?"

"No, no, not that far. Just to the station landing. He can get up there, right?"

"I hope so. Then what?"

"We go out the station, to the street, and then back onto the bridge the way a car would: up the on-ramp and down the car travel lane."

"There might be pigs on the street," she said.

"Or we can move all this rubble with our hands."

"All right," Win said. She took a look at the roadway Touré was talking about. There were a half-dozen cars on it. They weren't parked; just stopped. She thought back to the scene on the turnpike, and the jawbone in her bag.

More graves, she thought.

"We'll hope for no pigs," she said.

5

It had been a good plan, but unfortunately Elton couldn't be coaxed into jumping up to the landing.

Win thought it was probably within his abilities, but this was a stunt even a trained horse like Max might have balked at.

It took some work, but she was able to find a steel plate hanging up against the wall. Its original function was to bridge the gap between the train and the platform, for wheelchairs, and was resting next to a hydraulic lift that was there for the same reason. The lift wasn't of any use, but the ramp could be repurposed successfully for horse relocation.

Elton balked again at a doorway that was neither wide nor tall enough for both him and Touré, so Touré had to climb down and hop to the other side. Win tied him back into the stirrups once they were out of the station.

The road under the overpass was a foot deep with water, and thankfully had no pigs. Elton took one look at the water, shot an *Are you kidding me?* look at Win, but then stepped into it without a word from either of them. He seemed attitudinally prepared to write off humanity entirely. But given that Win and Touré might be the last two examples of the human race, it wasn't as profound a statement as it would have been otherwise.

They found the Longfellow Bridge on-ramp and headed back across again—on the outbound side, which the collapsed tower wasn't blocking. Elton stopped whining.

The cloud cover, meanwhile, had become substantial.

"Another storm's coming," Win said. She was shivering from the wind and looked forward to finding some cover. "Sure hope Cambridge is the land of milk and honey like you've been saying."

"The wheat and corn just plant themselves," he said. "You know I was delirious, right?"

"I do."

"Did I mention the wolves, at least?"

"You did, yes. You said they were as big as Elton. I assumed you were exaggerating."

"Only a little. Whoa, hey, did you see that?"

"See what?"

He was squinting at the horizon.

"Straight ahead," he said. "I saw a flash, I swear."

"Like lightning?"

"*Like* lightning, but *not* lightning. Come up here."

She took his hand and climbed onto Elton. Touré directed her gaze to a not particularly interesting spot in the air above Cambridge.

"Near Kendall," he said.

"I don't know where that is."

"It's straight ahead."

"I don't see anything."

Then there was a flash.

"Huh," she said. "Definitely not lightning."

"Definitely not," he said. "Could be, someone in Cambridge has electrical power. Wanna go find out?"

Ananda

1

A lot of information that had made no sense before suddenly made a whole lot of sense after Ananda discovered she'd lost a hundred years.

There were still plenty of questions left over, though, along with a number of new ones, such as: *How did I get here?*

Presupposing that this was currently unanswerable, Ananda spent more time looking at what her discovery *did* answer: the vegetation overgrowth, the general deterioration of the buildings and roads, the wildlife population explosion, the lack of power, and even the stubborn refusal of batteries to function.

Of course, a lot of that depended upon precisely *when* all the people died.

She hadn't found any corpses, but such a find would have been of limited use, as she had no forensic experience; looking at remains and estimating how long a person had been dead wasn't really something she could do with any confidence. Not to say examining a corpse would yield no information, exactly, because a corpse would provide clear proof that at least some of humanity had *died* at a point in the past as opposed to just *vanished*. Further, she might learn a little about what killed them based on what that hypothetical corpse was in the midst of doing when they died. Were they running, sitting, lying down, driving a car, defending themselves, etc.? Were there wounds, either on the body or inferred by the clothing?

Without remains on which to base an investigation, it was theoretically true that the proposed extinction of the human race (or near extinction, as she continued to be human and alive, to the best of her self-understanding) was unproven. More to the point, if a hundred years had passed, perhaps in that hundred years, humankind simply left the planet.

Frankly, a century wasn't long enough for that to be very likely, not for the kind of technological advancements that would have been necessary to relocate a significant portion of the species off-world. Also, there would have surely been terrestrial evidence of that momentous leap forward. Her only discovery that remotely met such criteria was the Noot bars.

That didn't seem like enough.

"While you were away," she said to herself, "we invented interstellar travel and this gelatinous rectangle. Sorry about the taste."

Ananda was staring at a whiteboard in one of the conference rooms in the electronics building. She had been spending most of her time there because it was the only part of the campus she'd been able to power.

That became especially important during the snowstorm.

None of the buildings had heat, and a fire was largely out of the question, both because of a dearth of material available to burn and an active concern that if she tried, she'd burn down the campus. Yet heat was obviously a concern, with the impending winter cold. Plus, Ananda was still wearing her Monday clothes, after about three weeks. (Or, a hundred years and three weeks.) And they were clothes meant to be adequate for springtime, not winter.

She considered visiting her apartment for a change of clothing until it occurred to her that after a hundred years, it probably wasn't her apartment any longer. That got her to wondering if she'd been reported as missing and if there had been a funeral for her. Did all her belongings go to Luke and Jakob? Thinking of her husband and son—and indeed the entire train of thought that led there—left her unbearably sad.

It might have been a sane decision to go scrounging for clothes in one of the nearby stores, or one of the thousands of apartments in the area, but Kendall Square had essentially nothing in the way of clothing shops, and the risk/reward of making that much noise to break into an apartment that *might* have clothes was too great for her to seriously consider.

Still, clothes worn for that long were bound to develop a stench, and even if she couldn't smell it herself, the wolves surely could. So she washed them every couple of days, with dishwasher detergent, and wrapped herself up in a blanket until they were dry.

So, without winter clothes or any way of safely using fire for warmth, during the storm, she stayed where there was power. The electricity kept the space heaters on.

The storm lasted two days, and for the entire time it dumped snow on the campus, Ananda confined herself to a three-room space with adjoining doors that was closed off from the hallway.

A lot of her time was spent on the radio, listening for other signs of life. Paul was still silent—with the snow, she just assumed the worst. The coywolves continued to lodge protests about the radio, but they had proven incapable of getting through the door, so she opted to ignore them.

Her perseverance was not rewarded. Despite several instances when she thought she might have heard something humanlike over the air, it never panned out.

If there was anyone else alive out there, they weren't using a radio.

The rest of Ananda's time was spent staring at the whiteboard, trying to work out (1) what she definitely knew, (2) what she didn't know but could figure out, and (3) what she didn't know and probably could *not* figure out.

The observation about the batteries was a key one.

Batteries had a shelf life after which they were no longer of any use. The shelf life of an unused battery undoubtedly varied from battery to battery, and, for instance, if it was alkaline or lithium or something else, but a longer-lasting-and-yet-dead battery might provide her with an "at least" threshold.

It was already clear that whatever had happened to all of the people, it hadn't happened recently. It also hadn't happened on the Tuesday that Ananda thought she was waking up to, because there was clear evidence of non-recent anthropogenic change in the area: The downed building and army blockade, the sulfur dioxide injected into the atmosphere, and the Noot bars were all good examples of this. In short, whatever happened was neither recent nor too far in the past.

Thus, if she knew that the shelf life of the car battery Paul complained about was thirty years, then she could say with some measure of confidence that what happened to everyone happened *at least* thirty years ago.

It was a start.

2

One of the items in the *don't know, can probably figure out* category was *What happened between the Monday when all was normal in Ananda's life and the day everyone died and/or vanished?*

There would be records. Granted, most of those records would have been archived for posterity on computers, but generally, notes were kept on scratch paper. Or at least they had been when Ananda performed sundry acts of science; possibly, her colleagues advanced entirely to paper-free handheld devices in the intervening years. She doubted it, but it was possible.

Those records, if they existed, were sitting in offices throughout the MIT campus. That was the good news. The bad news was, there was no telling which offices contained anything useful or how to recognize something as *being* useful. Ananda's own notes, when she took them, were basically informative only to her . . . and pretty much unreadable to anyone else. She suspected it was the same for everyone.

But it was worth trying. If she collected all the notes in one place and took the time to go through them, she might be able to figure out what some of them meant.

This was how she discovered that the world still had people as of 2039; that was the year they broke the two-degree barrier.

She got this out of an early excavation of the Department of Earth, Atmospheric, and Planetary Sciences.

Since the department was quite large—all of the MIT departments were—she concentrated first on the climate science labs. It seemed a reasonable place to begin, given the red sunsets.

She didn't expect to find answers to the big question; surely no matter how bad things had gotten with the environment, climate change couldn't be responsible for this particular mass extinction of the human race. But maybe if she knew where things had left off prior to the extinction event, she'd have a better handle on what to expect from the weather going forward. There had already been a severe hailstorm and a massive blizzard, and if she had the time of year right, it wasn't even winter yet.

The climate lab had a gigantic, entirely outdated printer that re-corded data from a weather satellite week by week. The paper had spilled over from the bin and onto the floor long ago. That the climate science department (of all departments!) employed this out-dated, wasteful dead-tree technology to keep (now-deceased) members of the human race up to date on how quickly they're kill-ing the planet was a delicious bit of irony.

The previously printed sheets—the ones not amassed on the floor—were stacked neatly at a desk on the other side of the room and marked up with a pen. The last date on the last sheet on the ta-ble was from 2039.

The numbers circled on that last sheet—by some long-dead climate specialist—along with the notes in the margin, indi-cated these numbers meant that the two-degree barrier had been crossed.

Ananda wasn't an expert in climatology, but she knew enough to be scared. For the sake of present-day energy needs, the human race was—or had been—heading into a future of extreme priva-tion. That the same human race did end up ceasing to exist, but for an entirely different (unknown) reason, was another great irony.

Likewise, that extinction probably meant the conditions now weren't as bad as they could have been.

Probably.

She was living in the future, but only a tiny part of it. She had no way to assess the global changes, but as bad as the storms were, the local weather wasn't living up to worst-case scenario expectations so far. Conditions might be a good deal worse elsewhere.

One thing she'd come to appreciate over the past few weeks, alone in a future that had forgotten about the human race, was that without an energy source, the planet was entirely too hostile. At the same time, the aggressive acquisition of energy was what may have made it so hostile in the first place.

This was the third great irony.

3

The weird object at the construction site was currently in the *don't know and probably can't figure out* category, along with Ananda's hundred-year leap forward. It wasn't a fair category for either of them; that column really existed for the items she couldn't even get her mind around when working on *how* to figure them out. Once she did, she supposed she'd have to rename the category.

She wasn't sure she should even go near the object. There was ample evidence a lot of people had decided that that was a bad idea before they died and/or left the planet (or whatever). It could be radioactive; there was equipment at the scene to measure radiation, so she could use that to check . . . except it required electricity and she didn't have a power cord that long.

To even begin to understand the device, she needed a better idea of what it *did,* if indeed it did anything at all. The kid she saw the first night who had been hitting it with a stick seemed to have some information in that regard, but he never came back and she hadn't gone looking for him.

Ananda settled on observing the object from afar, a practice she took up before the blizzard, suspended briefly during it, and resumed as soon as the storm was over. This involved making it to the roof of the computer science building, which was next to the one she'd claimed as her own. It was taller and had a better angle on the site, and she had a telescope.

The hope was that by checking on the anomalous object at different times of day and night, she might see it do something that would provide an insight as to its function.

On a couple of occasions—both late at night, when such a performance was more visible—the odd light show that first drew her attention to the scene occurred again. On neither occasion did it last for long; both events lasted perhaps a half an hour each.

It didn't tell her anything new. The second time, she thought she saw a figure standing nearby, but that was probably a trick of the shadows. No one was hitting it with a stick again, certainly.

Eventually, Ananda had to admit that the only way to gain greater knowledge about the device was to get close enough to examine it. She'd already seen a human get that close and not die instantly, which was her minimum safety requirement. She'd also seen plenty of wildlife walking around near the device, and while deer and whatnot didn't have any kind of built-in radiation detectors, it clearly passed their okay/not okay threshold.

There was even a way to reach the scene with hardly any risk: the tunnels.

In addition to the aboveground corridors linking most of the

MIT buildings, there was a more comprehensive set of underground tunnels that connected very nearly the entire campus. Conveniently, getting to them meant passing through a door and going down a flight of stairs—and the wolves couldn't open doors.

She'd been using the tunnels only sparingly, because there was no light down there and her mammalian brain was trained to fear darkness. The last time she went down, for instance, she became convinced there was someone there with her.

Confirming that this was a misinterpretation of available stimuli would have taken a lot more work than what she did, which was to exit the tunnel immediately. But it surely was the case that she'd been alone and only imagined the whole thing.

She knew she could take the tunnels from the building she was in all the way to the Ford Building, which was across the street from the anomaly, and when she tried it, it worked fine. It landed her close to her destination, unmolested by any wolf, and she knew it would work at all hours.

She didn't go any closer to the object the first couple of times, staying at the fence and working up the courage to go nearer.

But when she finally did go in, it happened on the same day she learned that she was not alone in the world.

4

The object was about thirty inches tall; it came up to about the height of Ananda's hip.

It had no handle, no opening. It was white, with rounded sides that had no seams. The top cap was rounded as well, like a bowl turned upside down.

From a distance, she had thought it was metallic, but that

seemed less certain the closer to it she got. Metal-*like*, perhaps, but there was a softness to it that implied it was composed of some other material. *What* other material was an open question.

She moved closer.

The rounded cap on top extended slightly past the edge of the cylinder beneath. When she got down on her knees and looked up at the underside of the lip, she saw what looked like a vent.

"Are you there to take something in . . . or to let something *out?*" she asked.

In need of a probe other than her finger to examine the opening further, she scrounged about until she found a loose twig. With the end of it, she was able to confirm that there was indeed an opening and it went all the way around the cylinder. Interesting, certainly, but not very informative.

She put the twig down, sat on the ground, and spent several minutes studying the surface of the object.

It wasn't soft, she realized. It was *fuzzy*. Not hairy: indistinct. It seemed as if the object hadn't entirely decided if it was really there.

The side also wasn't perfectly smooth. There were pockmarks on the half facing away from the street. They seemed to be scattered randomly and looked more like damage than a utilitarian feature.

She got to her feet and took another look at the top cap. The kid had been hitting it with a piece of rebar. She remembered at least five or six blows. Yet the cap had almost no damage on it; just a couple of dents. The light show from that first evening was also absent.

She wondered what would happen if she hit it herself.

From an experimental standpoint, the idea had merit. She could learn how soft the surface was, and whether striking it caused the lights to appear. The former might provide further insight into what the object was made of, and the latter might lead to a better understanding of its function. That assumed the lights were a component of its function, which seemed a safe assumption. From a safety-in-the-workplace perspective, it made about as much sense as taste-testing radium.

What the hell, she thought. *The world already ended. How much worse can things get?*

She disproved one hypothesis before she even began: After she found the rebar the kid had been using, but before she'd struck the object, the light show manifested above her head.

"Oh, hello," she said.

It looked like a swarm of … Well, it was difficult to say. Angry fireflies without form, or sparks from a welder. They circled above the object and dove at it. Colliding with the object caused neither thing any obvious harm, and when they dove at *her* they also seemed to cause no harm. In fact, there was a complete absence of sensation altogether; it seemed as if they passed through her a couple of times, yet it didn't tickle, pinch, or even hurt. In fact, had she been blindfolded, she would not have been able to pinpoint the moment when this interaction was even happening.

She decided that this was actually an excellent argument that what she was witnessing was purely optical and otherwise not real. It could be, in other words, that her eyes were seeing something that wasn't there.

The second test was a lot more interesting. Hoisting the rebar over her shoulder—it was quite a lot heavier than it looked—she walked up to the object, raised the metal rod over her head, and slammed it down on top of the dome cap.

The force from the impact vibrated along the rebar, into her hands and right down her arm, causing pain at every joint along the way. She let out a cry of surprise and dropped the rod on the ground, where it couldn't hurt her anymore.

She shook her hands for a few seconds until the numbness subsided, as the light swarm spun around her head like cartoon stars signifying a concussion.

A reexamination of the cap revealed something fascinating. The two possible outcomes—or so she thought—were (1) she would have created a third dent, or (2) she wouldn't have hit it hard enough to damage it.

Yet there was now only *one* dent. She hadn't damaged the object; somehow, she'd *repaired* it.

"Well, *that* doesn't make any sense," she said.

The lights appeared to agree with her.

She retrieved the rebar and tried it again, wincing with the impact, but also better prepared for it. When she was done, there were no dents at all.

Ananda lifted the metal bar to try it again, thinking the weird but somehow logical thought that now that it was repaired maybe she could put new dents in it, when someone behind her spoke.

"Greetings!" a man shouted.

She dropped the rebar and spun around.

There was a guy on a horse being led by a woman holding a bow. All three of them—the horse included—looked like they had been having a Very Long Day.

The woman in particular: She looked cold, worn out, and dirty, and was wearing some entertainingly out-of-place yoga pants. Her hair was up in a ponytail, and her eyes were sharp. She looked quite capable of violence.

The man on the horse did not. He looked sallow and tired. His face betrayed some pain. He was, she realized, not riding the horse. Not exactly. He was *attached* to it.

She'd never seen two more beautiful people in her entire life.

"Oh my God!" Ananda said. "Oh my God, oh my God."

"Hi," the woman said. "Are you okay?"

"No, I'm not."

Ananda ran to the fence.

"Are you really here?" she asked.

"We're real," the woman said.

"What's with the light show?" the man asked.

"I don't know," Ananda said. "Are . . . are you Paul?"

"I'm Touré," he said. "That's Win, and this is Elton."

"Hello, Touré, and Win, and Elton," she said. "Don't move, okay?"

Ananda scrambled along the fence until she came to the opening she'd used to get inside, ran back again, and by some miracle they were still there. She hugged Win, not at all caring if Win wanted a hug or not.

"Whoa," Touré said, not as a comment on the hug, but on the lights. They suddenly swarmed around him.

"I've seen this before," he said.

"In Boston?" Win asked.

"Before that. Up the street in the back of a hardware store. Robbie was with me. It came in the shape of a person then."

"A person?" Ananda asked, breaking off the hug. "Are you sure?"

"Yeah, pretty sure. It was kind of memorable."

"That's peculiar."

The lights dissipated. Touré looked upset.

"Aw, come back," he said.

"I take it you're the only one here," Win said to Ananda.

"Yes," Ananda said. "I'm sorry. About the hug."

"It's okay, I understand."

"Does that thing make the lights?" Touré asked.

"I don't know," Ananda said. "I was just trying to work that out."

"Oh. I was hoping it was a power source."

"If it is, I don't know how to use it like that. But I have power inside."

"You do?" Win said.

"Solar. I have heat, too. And some food."

Win reached into a sack attached to the horse and pulled out something that looked and smelled like pork.

"Food, we have," she said.

"How about antibiotics?" Touré asked. "And some medical training?"

"And some answers," Win said.

Ananda looked at Touré first.

"You're injured," she said.

"The fever nearly killed him," Win said. "I found medicine, but none of it worked."

"Yes, of course; it wouldn't," Ananda said.

This caught Win off-guard, clearly.

"'Of course'?" Win asked. "Why, 'of course'?"

"I do have *some* answers," Ananda said. "Not of the big questions, but I know why antibiotics don't work. It's the same reason batteries don't work. I'll take you inside, but first, I have to ask: What year do you think this is?"

There was a pause as her new friends stared back at her for a little too long.

"What a terrifying question," Win said.

TEN

Robbie

1

THE SNOW WAS GONE COMPLETELY TWO DAYS AFTER THE blizzard, which wasn't nearly enough time for Carol to abandon the idea of moving.

For Robbie, spending two days in the dorms with Carol and Bethany when they were angry at him for asking sensible questions was pretty tough. But if it came to pass that they were actually stuck there for the winter—if, for example, another storm came along before the first was finished with them—he was pretty sure they'd relent eventually. When there are only three people left in the world and you happen to be angry with one of them, you can't really afford to stay mad for long.

Plus, he really didn't think he'd committed some kind of grave sin. He perhaps misread the degree to which Carol was rattled by her (possibly imaginary) encounter with an intruder, but that was all.

Robbie shouldn't have minded moving all that much. They had collected entirely too much to move in one trip, but they were already storing their goods in multiple locations, with their only food source sitting in a vacant supermarket down the street. As long as they were staying in the Cambridge area, he could quite feasibly relocate Carol and Bethany, and then make trips back and forth until the whole supply was moved. As long as the weather held.

He *did* mind, though, because moving meant admitting Touré was probably gone forever. And he resented, just a little, that he was the only one who felt that way.

So he wasn't in a good place when Bethany came at him with a map, alone, the morning after the thaw was complete.

"Where's Carol?" he asked. "I thought you two had an attached-at-the-hip system going."

"We did, but we're driving each other crazy," Bethany said. "She's in the bedroom, door's locked."

The women had taken to sleeping in the same dorm room on the second floor, mainly because it had a lock on the inside. He had no idea how they dealt with having to use the bathroom during the night—the dorm didn't have individual bathrooms, and the central bathrooms on the second floor had no running water—but didn't want to risk asking the question and sparking a new argument. He'd been sleeping on the couch in the office off the common room, the same place they'd crashed on the first night they came to the dorm. He was on that couch when Bethany showed up.

"I'm here to talk about the move," she said.

"Oh, that," he said. "We're still doing that?"

"C'mon, you know how she is."

"And *you* know it's more likely that this intruder was just in her imagination."

"Sure," Bethany said. "And I think she did imagine it. I thought that when it happened, too, but I knew better than to call her on it."

"So we're still moving is what you're saying. I'll have to go out and scout a new location. It may take a while. We have no idea when the weather will turn again."

"Nah, we're gonna do this all at once." She put the map down on the desk. "This is dumb," she said. "Do you have any idea how cool some of the homes around here are? And we're sleeping in this old dorm like it's the only option."

"It's where we're safe," he said.

"It's where two Harvard kids feel safe, but c'mon. I'll show you."

He got up and took a look at the map. Her finger was on a neighborhood he and Touré had never visited.

"This section here's got it all, okay? Individual houses with fireplaces and yards. Big enough to sleep all of us, small enough to search quickly in case Carol gets another dose of the heebies. Over here is another grocery store, so maybe there's more Noot bars in case no one figures out how to hunt by next year. I mean, I *hope* we do. I could use a steak, you know?"

"We haven't seen a single cow," he said.

"Deer steak, then."

"Venison."

"Yeah, that."

"There are other neighborhoods closer to that store," he pointed out.

"Sure, but that's not all. Over here is Harvard Yard, and this?" She jammed her finger down on one location. "This is the public library."

"I don't understand."

"*Books,* man. Come on, between you, me, and her, we don't know how to do *anything,* right? Let's go to the library and *figure it out.* If the public library's gone or, well, not useful, like I said, Harvard Yard's just over here. There are libraries there too, right? And there's a museum right here, and two more there. We keep waiting around for some survivors who know how to *do* things to show up and save us. Let's just admit nobody's coming and see what we can do for ourselves before one of us breaks a leg and we don't know how to handle it."

He looked at the map again.

"You make a good argument," he said.

"Thanks. I feel like I'm taping a PSA for the school system, but, I mean . . . I'm bored out of my skull here. I think we all are. No point living if it's this boring, right? Reading is a solution."

"You obviously haven't been looking at the same textbooks I have," he said. "I see your point. But . . ."

"Dude, *what?*"

"What about Touré?"

She squinted at him. He could tell she decided to not say two or three things.

"What about him?" she asked.

"He'll come here looking for us."

"Write 'Croatan' on the wall or something."

He didn't know what that meant but decided not to ask.

"I'll leave him a note," he said. "Once we have a new address."

He just had to be alive to find it.

2

They already knew it, but there was something seriously wrong with the weather.

First, there was the epic snowstorm that dropped more in two days than any of them could remember having experienced. (Robbie and Bethany, in particular; Carol never had to worry about snow in Florida.) And then six days later? A heat wave.

Before going anywhere, Robbie and Carol—who was speaking

to him again now that he had agreed to move—debated the best way to get about town. He favored using a tandem bicycle from the shop, but since it was just him, he'd have to walk there, find one—he didn't know if they even had a tandem there—and ride it back solo. The walk was a mile; doing this would burn up a decent part of the morning. But with a tandem, he could put Carol on the back seat and speed up the second part of this process.

Robbie was outvoted once Bethany made the perfectly reasonable argument that the neighborhood she picked for them was also only about a mile away, albeit in a different direction. It would be easier to spend the morning looking for a place to live and set Carol up there, and then Bethany and Robbie could go back and forth.

This would mean going to the bike shop to find Bethany a bike of her own *anyway*, but that didn't seem to bother anybody other than Robbie.

They still left a lot later than they probably should have, because they couldn't decide what absolutely, positively had to come with them on the first trip, assuming they found a new place to live on the first go. (For example: Did they need to bring winter gear when it was like eighty degrees out?) Then, after getting all that sorted out, they were a hundred feet from the dorm before Robbie realized they'd forgotten—yet again—to worry about food. So, they turned around, made room for a few Noot bars, and restarted.

Bethany was leading Carol, which freed up Robbie to walk ahead with the axe he'd grown to enjoy the company of. He only knew how to use it against inanimate objects so far, but it probably looked scary enough to keep away the average midsize predator, should they come across one.

"It feels like spring," Carol said.

"Yeah, hey, maybe that was it for winter," Bethany said.

A warm breeze cut across the lawn. Robbie checked out the sky, which was cloudless. The air looked brown.

"Probably not," he said.

"I was kidding," Bethany said, reacting to his tone. "Relax."

I'll relax when we're safe again, he thought.

The path from the dorm to the area around Harvard Yard and the public library was all uphill. They took side street after side street, with Bethany telling Robbie which left and right and straight to take as they went. Rather than stay on the sidewalks, he took them right down the middle of the torn-up street, a practice he'd begun with the bike and now hardly thought at all about.

Touré was the one who'd convinced him there was no reason not to just saunter down the middle of the road, since no cars would be coming. It was sort of funny, given that on the first day, Robbie was almost struck by a vehicle the first time he tried it. It was definitely funny that Touré was the one who almost hit him.

Touré was also the only other person who would find that funny.

"This used to be kind of awesome," he said.

"What was?" Carol asked.

The apocalypse, he thought.

"Nothing," he said.

It was slow going. They passed nail salons, restaurants, an eyeglasses place, a black box theater, a bagel shop, and a secondhand clothing store. Robbie was lingering in front of each spot, ostensibly to wait for the women to catch up, but really to have a quiet breakdown.

This was a vibrant city. Burger shops, bars, coffee shops, bookstores, secondhand stores, pizza places, movie theaters, all the stuff he used to have to drive a long way to get to, and he would have had all of it in walking distance from his new home at the college. He had been looking forward to living here for his entire life. Now, before he'd gotten a chance to live in it, it was a ghost town, because the world ended.

Robbie had to stop to collect himself. He sat down at a table in front of a gastropub with a menu on the wall outside that described a burger he would give anything to try.

"You okay?" Bethany asked.

"I'm fine," he said. "I just need a second."

Five wild turkeys walked past, tails fanned out and strutting. On the other side of the street, in a small patch of green, two deer were grazing. The sun had gone away already; a large bank of clouds turned up out of nowhere, just large enough to get in the way. He was pretty sure it was a rain cloud. Also, everyone he ever knew was dead.

It was a bad time for an existential crisis, but it turned out you couldn't plan for one.

He was crying before he realized it. He wiped his eyes as Bethany sat Carol down in a nearby chair and pretended she didn't notice him.

"How do you cope with this?" he asked, quietly.

They looked confused.

"Who are you speaking to?" Carol asked.

"Everyone's dead," he said, ignoring the question.

He got up and threw the axe into the front window of the gastropub, eliciting a yelp of surprise from Carol, to whom this must have sounded like an attack.

"Everyone!" Robbie said. "I mean, this is *it*—this is our lives now. I don't *want* it. I want the life I was promised."

"We all want that," Carol said, levelly. "Breaking things won't make that happen."

"Well . . . it makes me feel better."

"Then break your things and we'll continue."

"Right."

"Robert, like it or not, we have to keep trying to survive, because that's all we *can* do."

"Just that? Nothing more? You know what we were doing before? Me and Touré? We weren't just trying to find someone else who knew how to do this better than we do. It was to prove there was *more*. Because if there *aren't* more people out there ... why bother? Who are we staying alive for? Our families? I had a mom and a dad, and my little sister ... She was in prep school, and she's dead now. They all are. I had a girlfriend too, back home. We were broken up because I went off to college, but she was real and she was nice, and I liked her. Her name was Tina, and she's dead too. So are her parents, and all the kids we were in school with, and all of their parents. I can't ... I just ... I just want to know: How are you two dealing with all this? Because I can't anymore."

"Robbie," Carol said, "it's all right."

She walked over and gave him the hug he evidently needed a great deal. He was crying like a child on her shoulder, was embarrassed to be doing it, and yet couldn't stop.

"I *don't* cope," Carol said. "Not very well. But I don't have to; you do it for both of us. We need you to keep doing that."

"I don't think I can," he said.

"There isn't anyone else," Carol said. "I'm sorry, but that's how it is."

"I think we're the ones who're dead," Bethany said, suddenly, loudly, as if saying this was something not entirely within her control.

"Not now," Carol said.

"I mean it. I saw my own obituary."

Robbie pulled away from Carol to focus on Bethany. He had to rub his eyes to do it.

"You mean that literally?" he asked.

"I woke up in my own house," she said. "Not a dorm, like you guys, and not on a couch, like Touré. There was a shrine, to me, because I'm a missing person. You guys probably are too. My family thought I was dead and had a funeral. I don't know if that makes this worse or better, but they got to say goodbye, at least."

"You said you thought we were in purgatory," Carol said. "I assumed you were speaking non-literally."

"I kinda was."

"Why didn't you tell us this before?" Robbie asked.

"Because I keep expecting to wake up from it, man. Don't you?"

"Yeah," he said. "I guess I do."

"Maybe we'll luck out one morning," Bethany said. "Until then, she's right. You're who we've got. Cry yourself to sleep at night like the rest of us do, try not to attack so many restaurants during the day, and let's get moving. It looks like rain."

Robbie laughed.

"Terrible pep talk, thanks."

"You're welcome," Bethany said. "Meltdown all done?"

"For now. Hey, maybe we *are* missing persons," he said.

"I don't know what that could even mean," Carol said.

"I don't either, but the library's sounding like a better and better idea. Lemme get my axe."

3

The rain came just as they reached the neighborhood Bethany had proposed relocating to.

It was a heavy downpour, but it was also warm, and the houses they were looking at all had porches, so it didn't end up being too terrible since they were able to take refuge on them. Robbie found his spirits strangely lifted by the whole process, actually. It was as if they were Saturday-afternoon house-hunting in a neighborhood where everything was available.

It was just the kind of silver lining in the apocalypse Touré would have appreciated.

What they settled on was a musty place that Robbie decided had been owned by a professor—he wasn't really sure why he thought that, but it felt correct—with creaky wood floors covered by worn area rugs. It seemed warm and lived-in, even though it was actually cold and drafty. Though every place was going to be drafty until they figured out how to acquire and apply some weather stripping to the windows.

They found canned food in the pantry. Not a lot, but they'd been eating nothing but Noot for weeks, so the discovery was hailed as if it was the greatest treasure imaginable. There was also wood for the fireplace on the enclosed back porch, plenty of blankets, three beds, and a full liquor cabinet.

"This was definitely a good idea," Robbie said, plopping down in a dusty easy chair.

"Right?" Bethany said.

Carol was on the other side of the living room, at a desk facing away from the front windows. Robbie imagined the professor who'd owned this place sitting at that desk and grading papers, using the afternoon sun through the porch for illumination.

"There's something on the floor over here," Carol said.

"Let me take a look," Robbie said.

Her cane was hitting the side of a pair of men's shoes. They were resting under the desk at the end of a pair of pants that were draped over the side of the chair. In the chair was a shirt, a jacket, and a pair of eyeglasses.

Seeing all of it assembled in this way hit Robbie hard, because he realized in an instant precisely what he was looking at.

Someone died in this chair, he thought, *and this is all that's left of him.*

"What is it?" Carol asked. She had her hand on the side of the chair and was about to sit.

"Just a pair of slippers," Robbie said. "Hang on, there's stuff in the chair. Let me clean it off."

"Guys," Bethany said. She was holding up two umbrellas. "I know it's raining, but who wants to go check out the library?"

"We only just arrived," Carol said, clutching Robbie's hand. "I'm sure this was enough for one day. Tomorrow we can bring more over from the dorm, and then maybe we'll make time for the library. How about that?"

"It's literally right over there," Bethany said. "We're about as close to it as we were to the river before. *C'mon,* sunset's not for a couple of hours, and we have umbrellas."

"We went through a lot just to go this far," Carol said.

"Please. I'm begging you. I am *so bored,*" Bethany said.

Carol was clearly expecting Robbie to say no, which was a good guess considering his reluctance to go *anywhere.* He appreciated her speaking up for him.

"What the hell," he said. "Let's go."

"Then I'll go as well," Carol said. "I'd rather not stay here alone until I've gotten used to the noises this house makes."

4

Robbie sort of wanted to visit Harvard Yard first, if only to finally complete the trip he'd begun when he woke up on the first day of the apocalypse.

But Harvard's libraries were scattered, and slightly less useful to a layman trying to understand how to make electricity or set a broken leg. For example, there was an entire law library they weren't likely to ever have any use for. That was probably equally true for the theological library.

Also, the public library was closer. As Bethany said, it was only a couple hundred yards away, at the bottom of the street.

The library was an odd-looking place. On the left side, it was a slate-gray brick building that looked like an old castle. On the right, it was a far more modern edifice made of glass. The newer half could have been mistaken for a greenhouse, which was what Robbie at first thought he was looking at. Both buildings were dirty, and dealing with climbing moss, but that was more obvious on the glass structure. The castle side looked like it was *supposed* to have stuff growing on it.

There was a large, overgrown lawn in front of both parts of the library, with crisscrossing paths damaged by vegetation the same way the city's sidewalks had been. Thanks to the rain, only a few animals were loitering around outside.

"We went past this place," Robbie said. "Me and Touré. I thought it was part of the high school."

The city's high school was indeed in the background, behind the older side of the library. It consisted of one long building, a smaller building that looked like a theater, and a courtyard beyond that, fronting another street.

The whole area stood between two major thoroughfares: Broadway and Cambridge Street. They met at a spot closer to the Square, with a firehouse sitting at the point of the V. Opposite the firehouse was a tunnel that had Cambridge Common on the other side.

Robbie had been through this section on his bike at least three or four times.

"Yeah, I was going there next year," Bethany said, in reference to the high school. "Looks like it's homeschooling from here on out. C'mon."

They headed across the lawn, past a curious family of geese, to the glass door of the new library.

Up close, the glass looked several years overdue for a cleaning. Robbie could just make out vague shapes on the other side. Those shapes looked like bookshelves, so he didn't let himself get freaked out, though the whole thing did seem inexplicably creepy.

"Cover me," Bethany said, handing off her umbrella to Robbie. She knelt down in front of the door and got to work on the lock.

"What are you using to do that?" Robbie asked.

"Paper clip works, most of the time," she said. "I usually make do with what's around if that doesn't work. I used a barrette once, or one time the tooth on a belt buckle."

"I figured you had some sort of professional kit."

"Right. Saved up my allowance and everything. Dad wouldn't even let me have a *cell phone*—don't think he was springing for a locksmith's kit." She stood. "Yeah. I can't open this," she said.

"Why not?" Carol asked.

"Didn't really think I'd be able to; it looked like the wrong kind of lock. Thought it was worth a try."

"What's the right kind of lock?" Carol asked.

"Not this kind. It's too new."

"Now what?" Robbie asked. "I could break the door down."

He held up the axe to emphasize his point.

"No, man. Now we look for another door. Nobody ever swaps out all the locks. There's always a basement door, or a laundry room, or an employee exit."

She took back her umbrella and started toward the older wing.

Robbie reached out, grabbed the handle, and tried pulling the glass door. It didn't budge.

"I tried that first," Bethany said, without turning.

"I thought we'd feel pretty stupid if it was unlocked the whole time."

"I agree. That's why I tried that first."

The miniature castle wing had several doors to choose from. The main entrance was both locked and chained, with a sign indicating the porch they were standing on was unsafe, and to please use the entrance to the new wing instead.

Next, they found a normal-looking door around the side, at the bottom of five stone steps covered in mold. Standing at the door meant wading into inch-deep standing water.

"Yuck," Bethany said. She leaned over to get a good look at the lock. "Yeah, I can do this one."

She stepped into the muck, while Robbie stood above her and to the side, extending the umbrella as well as he could. Carol waited nearby, under her own umbrella.

They were all getting wet, despite the umbrellas, because the wind had begun to pick up significantly over the past several minutes. Twice Carol nearly lost her umbrella to a particularly stiff wind.

"I'm beginning to think we should try this on a better day," she said.

"No, I've almost got it," Bethany said.

Then, quite abruptly, the wind stopped.

"Whoa," Robbie said. "Somebody turned off the weather machine."

"Shhh," Carol said.

There was a roar in the distance.

Robbie gazed up at a cloud bank that was doing things he'd

never before seen a cloud bank do. It was low and swirling, and if he were a religious person, he'd say it looked like the hand of a deity was trying to reach down from the sky.

Then the rain tripled in intensity.

"Do you hear that?" Carol asked.

"Hear what?" Robbie asked. "The rain?"

"Not the rain," Carol said. "Over the rain. Bethany, you need to hurry."

"Almost there," she said.

"Wait," Robbie said. "Is that . . . is that a *train?*"

That was what it sounded like: the *chucka-chucka* sound of an old locomotive. But there were no tracks anywhere near them.

Also, everyone was dead.

"It's not a train," Carol said. Then a powerful gust of wind knocked her over and took her umbrella away.

Robbie ran over to help, leaving Bethany unprotected.

"Hey!" Bethany said.

"Sorry!"

"I'm okay!" Carol shouted, over the wind and rain.

He closed the second umbrella before it was swept away as well, and got Carol to her feet.

"We're in!" Bethany said, yanking open the door. "Quick!"

Robbie got Carol to the steps and handed her down to Bethany, who guided her the rest of the way in.

"My cane!" Carol said. "Robbie."

"I'll get it."

It was on the ground a few feet from where she'd been knocked over. He crawled over to it, to stay out of the wind as long as possible. Then he saw what was making all that noise.

There was a funnel cloud touching down on the street behind the high school.

"Robbie, come on!" Bethany shouted.

He scrambled to the steps and down through the doorway. Bethany closed the door behind him, plunging them into complete darkness.

"This is fine," Robbie said. His voice echoed back to him, indicating they were in a large space. "I don't know what's down here, but it's gotta be safer than what's out there."

The building groaned, unless it was the wind that was groaning, which was somehow more terrifying.

"Damn, what *is* that?" Bethany asked. "Are there dinosaurs now?"

"It's a tornado," Carol said, from the other side of the room. "We'd better stay here until it passes."

Bethany

Carol's admonition aside, there was no way Bethany was simply going to be staying in a basement when an honest-to-god tornado was passing by her future high school.

"*No way*," she said. "Get me out of here. Where's the staircase?"

"Tornadoes are really very dangerous," Carol said. "Are there any windows? We should stay away from them."

There were half windows at the top of the walls, but a ton of muck was built up on the other side, rendering them unusable.

"We're okay," Robbie said. "We should really stay here."

"Sure, *you* say that," Bethany said. "*You* got to *see* it."

Bethany opened up her bag. It was a great find, that bag. Easily the best thing Touré scavenged. It was meant for cyclists, so it was weighted funny if you weren't on a bike, but it was also waterproof, so the matches were still dry and so was the torch.

She dug out the lighter fluid to prep the torch, and lit a match.

"Ahh!" Robbie said. "Warn me before you do that."

"Sorry."

She touched the match flame to the end of the torch. They'd been using table legs. Bethany had the end of it wrapped in a sheet that caught easily, with spare sheets in the bag so she could reuse the torch.

She'd gotten good at it, having learned early to let the sheet burn a little before holding the torch upright, or bits of it would fall on her hand. This meant letting hot ash fall on the floor, but that had never been an issue, not even in the dorm hallways, which were carpeted.

Considering the library floor splashed when she walked, she was probably okay, she figured.

As long as it was water and not gasoline.

"Be very careful with that flame," Carol said. She was on the other side of the room, next to a stack of old newspapers.

"Yeah, wow," Robbie said. "Everything down here's flammable."

"Including us, yeah," Bethany said.

There was a wooden staircase to Carol's left.

"I'm getting out of here, guys," Bethany said. "I wanna see the tornado. You can tell me it's dumb and childish later."

The door at the top of the stairs was locked, but not with the kind of lock that would give her trouble. She got through it in under a minute and didn't even have to put down the torch.

"Hey, you guys coming?" she asked.

She continued without waiting for a reply.

Her childhood was on the other side. The door let out into the old wing's children's section, a basement-level area that used to be equal parts books and play area. Bethany remembered being taken down here when she was five, just as she was learning that the symbols under the pictures meant something.

All the books were gone now, but a lot of the displays—a giant green caterpillar, a gigantic horned monster, a few superheroes—remained. That only meant the building was closed down not long after her last memory of the place. The new kids' area in the modern wing probably had more current artwork.

Robbie and Carol made it up the stairs.

"Where are we?" he asked.

"The tomb of my misspent youth," Bethany said. "I used to love coming down here."

She handed Robbie the torch and took up a position at the window facing Cambridge Street.

"Aw, man, where is it?" she asked. She couldn't see the tornado anywhere.

As if in response to her question, a powerful wind shook the glass in its frame.

"Where are the books?" Robbie asked.

"I think this whole wing might be condemned," Bethany said. "Long time ago. Last time I came, I wasn't allowed down here. I think only the stacks are used now."

"The stacks?" Carol asked.

"Archived stuff. Cool place. I'll show you if you want."

"I think we should find some books," Robbie said. "Recent ones. I take it that would be in the new wing?"

"Yeah, come on. I think I missed the fun outside."

She took back her torch and led them up a staircase that was embedded in one of the things that looked—from the outside—like a castle turret. The windows were thin and tall, and out of reach. Decorative and not too useful for archers.

At the top of the steps was the old lobby. She remembered this place twice over. Before the new wing existed, it was what you'd pass through to get to the basement. As she got older, and the books moved, she still went through it, only then it was to get to the stacks.

A breeze hit them as soon as they reached the lobby; one of the windows had been broken.

"I guess we could have gotten in through there," Bethany said, as wind and a little rain tickled her arm. The condemned porch was on the other side.

"I think the storm must have done that just now," Robbie said. "It wasn't like that before."

"Kind of it to leave the other windows alone," Carol said.

The entrance to the former center of the main library—where all the boring adult books were located—was to the right of the down staircase. Those doors were closed now. On the wall opposite the lobby desk was a set of steel doors leading to the stacks. Next to *that* was the entrance to the new wing.

"That's where all the up-front books are," Bethany said, pointing to the new wing. "If you guys don't mind, I was gonna head to the stacks first."

Robbie opened the steel door and peeked inside. Cold air came out. All either of them could see was a metal grate floor and the beginning of a railing.

"Seriously?" he said. "What for?"

"I'm in the middle of a couple of series," she said. "It's hard to explain."

"I guess," he said. "Just, I don't know, be careful. That window could have let something in."

"Back atcha," Bethany said. "I'm going on the other side of a steel door. You guys don't have one of those in the glass house over there."

Robbie

The first thing to greet them on the ramp connecting the old to the new was a sign that read WE'VE GONE SOLAR above a bank of light switches. Excited, Robbie tried the switches.

It didn't do anything.

"Of course not," he said.

"What is it?" Carol asked. She was on his left, with two fingers on his outstretched elbow.

"Nothing. I'm going to keep trying light switches until I find one that works."

"Yes, well. I think we've established that the power grid has been offline since the start of the whateverpocalypse."

Robbie laughed. It was Touré's word. It still cracked him up. "According to this sign," he said, "the library isn't on the grid; it's solar."

"Hmm. That *is* interesting. I wonder what would cause a solar panel to fail?"

"I don't know. But we can go ahead and rule out *lack of sunshine*."

The glass walls weren't doing a great job of letting in the afore-mentioned light, although there wasn't really any to let through, for a couple of reasons: (1) There was the torrential rainstorm outside; and (2) there was a real possibility that it was already late enough in the day for the sun to start setting. If it *was* getting dark, they might have to spend the night in the library, although the house wasn't far.

Robbie noted that the extreme rain wasn't doing a lot to wash the windows. That was because it wasn't just dirt—the windows were tinted. And probably treated, to keep the sunlight from discoloring the books. Either way, he couldn't see through them, and as a result the whole library was pitch dark.

"Hang on," he said. "I can't see."

"You'll get used to that."

"I believe you," he said, laughing. He was well past feeling awkward about his sightedness around Carol.

He stopped in the walkway and, using the fading light from the old section, started assembling his own torch.

"How'd you know about the tornado?" he asked.

"Didn't you feel it?" Carol said. "The pressure, in your ears."

"I did, I guess. Wasn't something I thought about at the time."

"One learns to respect sudden barometric changes in Florida," she said. "Or at least I did."

The torch caught.

"Okay, we're good," he said. "Where to first? I take it you're looking for a section of books in Braille."

"Unless you think books on tape is a viable alternative, yes."

"Okay, I'll bring you there, and then give the place a once-over. I was going to see about finding a current newspaper."

"Are you concerned that Bethany is right?"

"What she said didn't make sense, so I don't know how she could be, but I'm not going to dismiss it completely."

The Books in Braille section was halfway down the center corridor of what was a two-level library, with little bullpen areas segregating fiction and non-, and subgenre by subgenre.

The idea of picking up something to read recreationally—which was surely what Bethany was doing, and probably Carol—seemed utterly alien to him. He was far too hung up on what was wrong with the actual world to concern himself with the tribulations of fictional people.

He made sure Carol was all set, then started wandering around, trying very hard to keep the flame from his torch away from the books.

"We definitely should have done this on a sunny day," he said. He had to raise his voice to be heard from halfway across the library, which felt strange, given it *was* a library.

"It makes no difference to me," she said.

"Yeah, true. Finding anything good?"

"One of my favorite romance authors has a new book. So yes."

"Romance? I didn't peg you for that."

"And what do you read? Manly tales of misogyny?"

"Don't knock manly tales of misogyny until you've read one."

He found a section on medicine, but a quick look made it clear that if he wanted to turn himself into a doctor, this wasn't the place to begin. He *didn't* want to turn himself into a doctor, but the others were right in pointing out that someone was going to have to learn how to do some of this, and they didn't have a lot of candidates.

There really weren't a lot of books *anywhere*, medical or otherwise. It was kind of bothersome. Cambridge was a big city, with lots of educated people who must have been invested in their local library on some level. Yet the pickings in this place were pretty thin. Even when he went upstairs, he found a lot more sitting space than books.

Maybe they archived the rest, he thought, *and Bethany had the right idea going to the stacks.*

He returned to the first floor and walked up to the front desk, near the entrance with the lock Bethany hadn't been able to pick.

There was a sign on the counter that explained a lot. It said that due to a government paper reduction act, "ninety percent of all new media will be available in electronic form only." Then it listed the library's online resources. A second sign suggested visitors talk to a librarian about free public resources for those in need of Internet access.

That was disappointing, because not only did he not have Internet access, but there was no librarian available to take that up with.

There was one detail about the sign that made him go cold. The date of the United States government's Paper Reduction Act was May 7, 2035.

"Hey, Carol? What year is this?"

"That depends," she said. "Do you imagine we've made it through December yet?"

"Let's say no."

"Then it's still 2016. Why do you ask?"

"Because it's 2019," he said.

"Well, that's ridiculous. Whatever you're looking at, someone wrote the date wrong."

"That's not the problem. What I mean is that I went to sleep on a Tuesday night in 2019, and until a few seconds ago, I thought you did too."

"That isn't funny, Robert," she said.

"I'm not joking. And I think we both might be wrong."

"Well, I'm not playing this game, whatever it is. Are you in the science fiction section?"

It had always been in the back of his mind how weird it was that everyone had a different understanding of what month they were in. He figured it was going to be one of those things that stayed in the pile of unknowns, along with *What happened to everyone?*

It didn't even occur to him to check the year.

"Carol, do me a favor," he said. "That new romance book you were talking about? Flip to the copyright page."

His eyes drifted to other messages on the front desk. All of them were saying the same thing: *This is not the year you thought it was. You're in the future.*

"This doesn't make sense," Carol said.

"What's it say?"

"Twenty thirty-one."

"I'm looking at a desk calendar that's telling me that that book is thirteen years old."

Bethany

Age ten was around when the nanny started looking for places to drop Bethany off for extended periods, for free, without getting into trouble for neglecting her charge.

One of her favorite stunts was to stick Bethany in the library while she went and got her hair done at one of the Harvard Square salons. This was a special event reserved for days in which Bethany's little brother was occupied—at a friend's house or the like—for the day.

Bethany didn't have any friends she was that close to, as she was pathologically antisocial, although that wasn't how ten-year-old Bethany thought of it. She just figured some people made friends and others didn't and that was how it was.

Her antisocial instinct started to become obvious around twelve, at approximately the same time Bethany learned to *pretend* to be social with the people in her neighborhood, just so she could hear them complaining about the cat burglar, and to maybe get introduced to their new watchdogs. Pretending meant learning how to mimic people who *were* sociable; in that mimicry, she realized how far away she was from the minimum necessary standard.

It was for the same reason—at least at first—that she gravitated away from the new library wing and toward the stacks.

For one, it was cooler in the stacks. The new library wing was all windows. Those windows were treated to keep out the "you vee" radiation (whatever that was), but even with air-conditioning it felt sticky on the hotter days.

There were no windows in the stacks. Just four floors of metal catwalks and a bunch of books that nobody wanted. (Or so it seemed. Bethany was told otherwise by a librarian who explained once that most of the books in the stacks were one of a kind and couldn't be checked out. Bethany preferred her Island of Misfit Toys interpretation.)

Now thirteen, and on the other side of the end of the world, Bethany stood alone in the stacks, wondering if the ten-year-old her felt a kinship to these books.

The child nobody wanted.

This wasn't at all fair to her parents, who'd built her that nice shrine. But the nanny—the substitute parent they'd hired—had certainly made *her* feelings clear.

Secondly, the books in the stacks were more interesting.

This wasn't true of *all* of them, of course. There was an entire floor of encyclopedias, which were definitely not interesting, and another half floor of law library indexes.

But then there was *Pogo*.

There was a section in the stacks where anthology collections of old comic strips were left to die. These were strips that hadn't run in a newspaper since the 1930s. Their creators were long dead, and probably so were nearly all the people who remembered reading them as one-per-day episodes.

The first time Bethany found this section, she didn't understand what she was looking at. She didn't even know there *were* comic strips in the newspaper, because she almost never got to see the newspaper at home. (And when she did, it was a paper that didn't have comics.)

She didn't know what they were, in other words. She went to the stacks initially because there weren't any kids in that part of the library, and she'd found a section nobody—adults *or* children— was interested in, full of books with pictures and word balloons, and (in some) developing story lines. That was the appeal. She read something called *Prince Valiant*, something else called *Terry and the Pirates*, and . . . well, all of them. Whatever she could find. She didn't even leave the stacks. She just sat down on the metal grate and read them where she was.

Pogo was her favorite. She couldn't explain why. There were talking animals who lived in a swamp, and that was it. She had no clue what they were talking about most of the time, which mattered not at all. She read every word anyway.

It was her secret kids' section.

There was no need to go back and find *Pogo* again, and yet she was doing exactly that. She'd already been through all the available volumes, and there were never going to be new ones added to the shelf. That was true even before the end of the world. It was still going to be reassuring to see it there, waiting for the ten-year-old version of Bethany to show up.

She didn't count on the stacks being quite so dark and cold on this trip. It was always cold, but if she was there in the winter, she would be in winter clothing, and if it was summer, she would be enjoying a break from the heat. Now, she was soaked through from an unseasonably warm downpour and a damn tornado. The stacks got downright chilly, really fast.

"You cannot afford to be sick," she said to herself.

Her voice echoed a ton. She remembered footfalls echoing, but nobody ever spoke when in the stacks, so she had no idea how bad it was.

The darkness was somehow worse. There were enormous fluorescent lights in the ceiling of each level, but of course they didn't work anymore. All she had was her torch.

She went down the spiral staircase to her right, one level, which was where she remembered the secret kids' section being located. It was three-quarters of the way down, on the left, in a position she used to think was entirely random but probably wasn't. Roughly halfway down, she decided this was a dumb idea.

That came with the creeping sense she wasn't alone.

No, it was more than that. It wasn't just a *sense;* it was legit. Someone else was in the stacks.

And they were crying.

The sound was muffled, like whoever was doing it was trying not to by putting a hand over their mouth.

"Hello?" she said. "I can hear you."

She heard more crying, then, somewhat more restrained. Higher pitched now, like a whine.

This is some kind of haunted house business, she thought.

Admittedly, a ghost would be someone new to talk to, and that wasn't something to be discarded outright.

It's not a ghost, she told herself. *Grow up.*

"If you're hurt, we can help you," she said. "We're really cool like that."

She heard running on the catwalk above. *Clang-clang-clang.* It was impossible to move silently in this place, because you were always standing on a metal grate. But this person wasn't even trying.

The sound was leading away from her . . . and away from the door.

There was another spiral staircase at the halfway point of the catwalk. Bethany ran to it. A chain was over the entry, with a sign that read DO NOT ENTER. She hopped the chain—maybe the stairs were unsafe, but it was an unsafe world—and scampered up. Now she was on the same level as the exit . . . and possibly also the same level as the ghost.

Not a ghost, she reminded herself. *Not. A. Ghost.*

She stood at the edge of the staircase and listened. She heard heavy breathing. One more level up, but it was close.

"Come on," she said. "What are you afraid of?"

"Not my fault."

It was a male voice. A young man. Maybe just a kid.

She remembered Robbie and Touré chasing someone around town a week or two back. She had assumed that whoever they'd seen—or thought they had—would have been long dead from exposure, given all the exciting weather that had happened since. But maybe not.

"Sure, man," she said. "Not your fault. It's not anybody's fault. I don't even know what we're talking about."

"I tried to stop it."

"Stop what?"

"It knows about the machine."

His voice was almost directly above her now. The grates were see-through, and sound traveled right through as well, which was why it echoed so much.

"What machine?" she asked.

He hissed. Whoever this kid was, he was long past gone.

"It's going to happen again," he said. "The shadows said so."

"Right."

Bethany was beginning to feel really uncomfortable about sharing a room with this guy.

"Tell you what," she said. "I'm gonna go and tell my friends what you said. It sounds really important."

Clang-clang-clang. He was running again . . . straight for the exit.

"Noooo, no, no," she said, breaking into a run.

Center aisle, left turn, straight on till morning, she thought. Her misspent childhood in the stacks was coming in handy, because she knew exactly how to get around this place.

She was almost to the door when he jumped down from the last step of the staircase to land directly in front of her.

He didn't look . . . *human.* He was a gasping skeleton in baggy, torn clothes, with blood around his mouth.

They both screamed. She was probably louder. She also fell backwards about five feet, nearly went under the railing that was there to prevent people from falling down a level, and dropped her torch.

She heard the door engage and watched as her torch skittered along the catwalk.

"A vampire," she said. "I just saw a vampire."

It was heading for Carol and Robbie. She retrieved her torch and ran to the door.

She had to save them.

Robbie

1

Robbie heard a lot happen at once, and none of it made any sense.

First, he heard Carol get pushed over. This was a loud *oof* and a thump, and then she gasped in surprise and called Robbie's name.

"What happened?" he asked.

Next came Bethany's voice, and the secondary lighting from her torch. She was coming down the tunnel that connected the old library to the new.

"Vampire, vampire!" she screamed. "There's a vampire in here!"

"Carol?" he said. "Are you all right?"

"Someone knocked me over," she said. She was using that too-calm voice that meant she was actually in the middle of a serious panic.

"Bethany, check on her," he said.

Robbie ran from the front desk to the main corridor, stopped, and listened. He heard the women to his left, and . . .

"Hey, you," he said. Someone was in the A–M Fantasy Fiction section on his immediate right. "I can hear you. It's all right—we're friends."

"We are not friends with the undead, Robbie!" Bethany shouted.

"You aren't helping," he said.

He turned the corner with his torch in one hand and the axe in the other. This probably didn't come off as all that friendly.

What he was confronted with was a starving teenager. He looked manic, and from the blood on his clothes and face, his diet probably had something to do with it.

"What have you been eating? Squirrels?" Robbie asked.

"It's coming back," he said. "The shadows told me."

His breathing was coming out in ragged gasps. Robbie thought he could see the kid's heart beating, he was so thin.

"Come on now," Robbie said. "There's no need to freak out. You recognize me, don't you? You and I, we saw each other before, outside of the hardware store. My friend Touré, he tried to catch up with you. We're okay people. We have . . . We can feed you better than what you've been getting by on. And we have shelter. Here."

Robbie put the axe down and extended his left hand.

"Take my hand. It'll be okay."

The kid looked confused.

"What's your name?" Robbie asked.

He was trembling, and blinking slowly, as if he had to tell his eyes to do that because they'd stopped doing it on their own. And he was having trouble thinking of his name.

"Ray," the kid said, quietly. "Raymond."

"Raymond, I'm Robbie. You already met Bethany and Carol. Well, you kind of ran down Carol, but that's okay. I'm sure she'll forgive you."

Raymond rubbed his forehead, like there was a treasure hiding under the skin of his brow.

"It hurts so much," he said.

"Look, you must have followed us here, right?" Robbie said. "You broke the window to get inside. You came here so we can help you. Let us help you."

Raymond was crying. He seemed to want to agree that this was indeed how they'd ended up in this situation, but something wouldn't let him relax.

"When is this?" Raymond asked. "Do you know? Do you know when this is?"

"I don't. I thought it was 2019. When do you think it is?"

"No, no, *no*."

"Raymond . . ."

"Just another future man, future man, no, no, no."

Robbie took a couple of steps forward, meaning to comfort the kid, who was reverting back to psychotic break mode. It was a bad idea. He didn't think there was any kind of strength left in Raymond, because it looked as if a light breeze was all it would take to knock him over.

He was wrong.

Ray barreled into Robbie, shoving him backwards and sending the torch into the air. It landed in Mystery and Suspense, the flame touching books that were twenty or thirty years old.

And very, very dry.

The fire spread immediately, jumping from Mysteries to True Crime in an instant.

"Carol!" Robbie shouted. "Bethany! Where are you?"

If they answered, he didn't hear it, because of how loud Raymond was.

Somehow, Ray was on fire . . . and screaming.

The reaction of his body was to start running, but his legs didn't seem to know where to take him first, so he just bounced around from row to row, spreading the fire as he went.

Robbie got a good look into Ray's eyes as the young man shrieked past him in agony, unwilling to surrender to what were definitely going to be the last moments of his life. It was a mix of horror and pain Robbie would be taking with him to his demise . . . which would be happening in another couple of minutes if he didn't get out of the building.

He took two steps in the direction of Carol, then remembered his axe and doubled back.

A–M Fantasy Fiction was already on fire and in the process of falling over. He barely recovered the axe before it was buried under an avalanche of books.

Then he ran.

The middle corridor was the widest book-free part of the library, so he was safe as long as he stayed in it . . . at least for the moment. There were flames coming up on both sides, and the smoke was getting bad, fast.

He collided with Bethany and Carol, and the three of them fell over in a heap.

"Are you okay?" he asked, of whoever felt like answering.

"We're okay," Carol said.

"Did you torch it?" Bethany asked. "The vampire."

"We have to go back that way," Robbie said, pointing to the old wing of the library.

"Fire's cut it off," Bethany said.

"Right."

He grabbed the elbow of Carol—who had ahold of Bethany—and pulled them past the front desk, to the glass door exit Bethany couldn't pick. That was back before a tornado, a vampire, and a raging inferno, so it seemed as if it happened ages ago.

He hit the door, hard, thinking the crash bar would unlock it. It didn't.

"I have some real fire safety concerns about this town," he said. "Stand back."

"There's a fire behind us," Bethany said. "Not much room to stand back."

"Get back and duck below the smoke," he said, raising the axe. "I don't want to hit you with the backswing."

He flipped the axe around so the dull side was facing the door, and then swung it as hard as he knew how.

The glass, to the credit of whoever designed this building, didn't shatter. He put a mean dent into it, though, with threads crackling away from the epicenter of the strike.

He swung again.

Then a third time.

On the fourth swing, the door burst. Robbie jumped back and covered his face, and then got blown over. A rush of air swept past him and into the library, where it supercharged the flames.

And suddenly it seemed like all of the books *exploded*.

"Where are you?" he shouted from the floor near the exit, amidst broken bits of door glass.

He could barely see. Smoke was billowing out from the raging fire, blinding and choking him. They were only a few steps from fresh air, but he wasn't positive which way that was.

Then he felt a hand grab him by the elbow.

"Come with us," Carol said.

They pulled him to his feet, and the three of them staggered out together, collapsing onto the cool, wet grass once they made it far enough away from the fire that they couldn't feel the heat on their backs any longer.

"Oh my god," Robbie said, rolling onto his back.

It had stopped raining, of course. Rain would have been useful in putting out the fire, so naturally they couldn't have any *now*.

He ran his hand across the wet grass and used the moisture to clean out his eyes.

"Are we all here?" he asked.

"Yes," Bethany said, coughing.

"We're here," Carol said. "But I don't think we're alone."

Robbie sat up and looked around.

"You're right," he said. "We're not alone."

Their eyes glowed in the firelight. Three pairs, or four, or six; it didn't matter. It was more than they could handle.

They were surrounded by wolves.

2

Robbie had once been closer to the wolves than he was now, that one time near the dorm on the first day, but it had been so dark that he hadn't been able to see what he was running from.

He had no problem seeing them now.

The library fire was lighting up the whole area, attracting creatures great and small … especially the seven wolves who were about to eat the last three people on Earth.

They'd looked bigger from a distance. Not that they weren't plenty big enough, but he remembered seeing something that, from afar, had appeared horse-size. And up close, through a metal gate, with no light and a lot of imagination, he was certain the creature on the other side of that gate was simply *massive*.

These were slightly larger than a Saint Bernard.

He didn't even know if they *were* wolves. They were large canines, and they were wild animals who hunted in packs. In his admittedly limited understanding of the species variants, that made them wolves. Probably there was a book in the library that would clarify matters, except the library was burning to the ground.

"What do we do?" Bethany asked. "Should we try to run?"

"To where?" Robbie asked. "The nearest place is on fire."

The animals were taking turns circling them, not yet certain if the humans were capable of launching a counterattack. To that end, they might have been if Robbie hadn't left the axe in the entryway.

Carol, on her knees between Bethany and Robbie, was tilting her head and listening to the pack. "I know what to do," she said.

Then she stood and took two steps toward the nearest wolf.

Robbie reached up to grab her, but she whacked him with her cane.

"Don't," she whispered. "It will be fine."

Carol was in the habit of making a particularly bad joke about how it would be best if they just put her on an ice floe and sent her down the river. It wasn't funny, but it was easier to laugh off than to confront what was clearly a concern for her. Aside from pointing out that the Charles River didn't have any ice floes, Robbie never knew exactly what to say. He'd just assumed she was joking.

Now that she appeared to be sacrificing herself, he was starting to think it hadn't been a joke at all.

He looked at Bethany, who just shrugged and shook her head.

Carol took another step closer, and now all the wolves were focused on her. Then she crouched down, held out her hand, and spoke.

"Puppy," she said. "Hello, puppy."

Not one of the seven wolves and two humans witnessing this appeared to have any idea what was going on.

"Puppy," she said again, waving her hand. "Hello, puppy."

One of the wolves started into a growl that tapered off into a whine.

"Puppy," she said.

The vocal wolf broke rank, walked around Robbie from the left, and positioned himself inches from Carol's outstretched hand.

She smiled.

"It's okay, puppy," she said.

The wolf edged closer, sniffed her hand, and then put his head under it. She started scratching him behind the ear.

"What a good boy!" she said.

He whined and licked her face.

The other six wolves didn't look all that impressed by this.

"Yes, hello," Carol said. In the same singsongy voice, and while still apparently addressing the wolf, Carol said, "Robert, are they stepping away? Can you escape?"

Another wolf made a tiny motion forward in a way that Carol's wolf took poorly to. He turned his head and growled.

Stay away was the clear message.

It didn't look like it was in charge, though. For the moment, the rest of the pack remained uncertain, but they weren't going anywhere, either.

"I don't think we can," Robbie said, under his breath.

"Maybe we should all adopt one," Bethany said.

The biggest wolf—the leader, perhaps—barked twice. Carol's wolf barked back, and then whined again and licked her. Two other wolves barked.

It seemed as if they were caught in a negotiation, which was fine, but the wolf representing the humans was outnumbered and appeared to be interested in defending only one client.

I object, thought Robbie.

He started looking around for a safe place he could sprint to. Maybe he and Bethany could make it to safety and, as crazy as it sounded, Carol could escape by becoming a member of the pack. But the closest safe haven was a pizza parlor with a chain on the door, across a lot of open grass. They would never make it that far even if there was a way past the chain.

"Hey, who's that?" Bethany asked. She tapped Robbie on the shoulder and pointed.

There was someone walking up Broadway from the direction of Harvard Yard. Robbie assumed at first it was Touré, back at last, at the very worst time.

It *wasn't* Touré. This was a big white guy with a scarred face and tattered clothing. He walked with a limp and didn't appear to have full use of his left arm.

There were two long guns on his back and a large duffel bag over his right shoulder. He looked a little like a soldier returning from war, only he'd forgotten to stop and see a paramedic before hopping the boat home.

The man reached the edge of the lawn and assessed the scene.

Then he calmly lowered the duffel, drew a handgun from his belt, and fired it once, in the air.

This got everyone's attention. Carol screamed in surprise and dropped to the ground, covering her head. All the wolves, including her favorite, turned and walked toward the man, growling.

"Was that a gunshot?" Carol shouted.

"Sure was," Robbie said.

"C'mere, dogs. C'mere," the man said. "Know what a gun is, do you?"

"I don't think the wolves do know," Robbie said. "They're not afraid of anything."

He looked over at Robbie.

"I know that, son. It's a common problem these days. And these aren't wolves; they're coyotes."

The pack drew closer.

"They don't fear people," he said. "And they don't care if it's day or night. They're smart. They need to be taught things, but they can learn. What do you say, doggies? You ever see a shotgun before?"

"Robbie," Carol whispered. "Don't let him."

The man drew one of the long guns from his back, held it with his right hand, and stabilized it over his left forearm.

Robbie couldn't have stopped him if he'd wanted to, and right then he didn't know if he did want to or not. He reached out and grabbed Carol's hand and squeezed.

"Guys, we can escape now," Bethany said. "We have an opening."

"Are you paying attention?" the man asked.

The coyote-wolf creatures were about ten feet away when he fired. He had it aimed at the grass between them. Shot kicked up the dirt and grass, for a display of cause and effect.

One of them yelped and started limping around, caught in the foot by a stray pellet. The other six backed way up.

"There's another barrel," he said. "The next lesson's gonna hurt more. Now *git*."

The big one, the one Robbie had pegged as the leader, took two steps forward and growled at the man. The man literally growled back. Then, after a short staring contest, the coyote-wolf broke off and the pack dispersed.

The man stood his ground until he was certain that the wolves had no plans to double back. Then he fell to one knee.

Robbie handed Carol off to Bethany and ran over to their rescuer.

"Hey, hey, are you all right?" Robbie asked.

"I'm looking for Ananda," the man said. Then he collapsed into Robbie's arms.

Robbie nearly fell over himself; the guy was pretty big.

"Help!" he shouted. "Need some help here."

Bethany came running over.

"Is he okay?" she asked.

"I don't know."

The two of them managed to get him off of Robbie and onto his back.

"I think he's just unconscious," Robbie said. "Yeah, he's breathing."

"Wow, what happened to him?"

Something large had bitten his shoulder sometime in the recent past. The blood seemed pretty fresh. Another, older scar, on the left side of his face, looked like a gift from a large cat.

Robbie pulled open the man's jacket, expecting to find dog tags or a flak jacket, or maybe a police badge or a Superman costume. What he found instead was a black shirt with a clerical collar.

"Huh," he said.

Carol found her way over. She looked deeply shaken.

"Is he all right?" she asked.

"I don't know—he's pretty messed up," Bethany said.

Carol nodded wordlessly and took a few steps closer to the fire.

Robbie was no expert in psychology, but he thought that what she just went through must have felt a little like losing Burton all over again, even though the dog that just ran away was still alive and in fact wasn't a dog at all.

"We have to get him off the street," Robbie said. "Before everyone in town shows up to watch the fire. Any ideas?"

"An ambulance," Bethany said.

"Any ideas we can *use?*"

"No, I'm just saying this guy needs an ambulance."

Bethany

Getting the preacher man out of the streets became one of those puzzles Bethany remembered from grade school, with the canoe, the duck, the wolf, and the wheel of cheese.

Between them, they couldn't lift and move the preacher more than a couple of feet without his help, and he was out cold. Robbie wanted to go out, in the dark, and find something they could use to carry the man back to the house, but he also wanted Carol and Bethany to go back home, where it was safe.

They also couldn't leave the guy alone and defenseless for however long it took to make it back to the house and to find something that could help get the man out of the street.

Then Carol said Robbie was in no position to demand she go back, because she wasn't defenseless, and they started *that* argument again, until finally Bethany volunteered to go find something herself.

"You can't," Robbie said. "We don't go anywhere alone, remember? Not outside, especially."

"There aren't any better choices," she said. "One of us has to be left alone. It's you, me, or the wheel of cheese."

"Excuse me?" Carol said.

"Never mind."

Bethany picked up the handgun lying next to the preacher. It was heavier than expected.

"I'll take this," she said.

"Whoa, whoa, be careful with that," Robbie said.

"I'll be fine. It's point and shoot, right? I've played video games before."

"Have you ever fired a gun?"

"Nope," she said. "But it makes a loud noise. Nobody likes loud noises."

"Just don't shoot yourself," Carol said.

"No, I'll point it the other way."

"This is a bad idea," Robbie said.

"You don't have any good ones, unless you want to sit out here all night with him. Hey, maybe we can. We already have a fire going. Look, all you need is a . . . a wagon, right? A wagon or a wheelbarrow. Do you have any idea how many gardens this town has? I'll be back in a couple of minutes."

Robbie looked torn, but he had to appreciate the logic of her argument.

"All right, but please hurry," he said.

"I plan to."

She shoved the gun in her bag and took off before Robbie changed his mind. Not that he was in any position to tell her what she could and couldn't do, but life was a ton more annoying when Robbie and Carol were mad at her.

Bethany headed straight into the neighborhood they'd just been house-hunting in. The front half of it—before the hill—was still bathed in light from the library fire, which made searching pretty simple. It also meant she knew quickly that nobody on the street she'd picked had a wheelbarrow in their yard.

There were plenty of gardens, although none of them had anything edible: just flowers or long-dead vegetable crops. The only evidence that someone intentionally grew plants in most of these yards was the landscaping, and even then, a lot of the intentional stuff—the railroad ties and tiered gardens and whatnot—was seriously falling apart. In one such yard, she spent a couple of minutes picking a lock on a shed, thinking the contents would be helpful, but the gardening tools stored there included nothing on wheels.

Having exhausted the easy options, she got back to the sidewalk and headed over to the other side of the hill . . . and immediately ran out of light.

Bethany hadn't spent any real time outdoors once the sun went down, so she was stunned by exactly how dark it was. The cloud cover completely blocked out the moon and stars, and without them she had nothing except the matches in her bag to light the way. She *had* a torch, but lost it somewhere in the middle of the library fire.

She was beginning to understand why the others thought it was a bad idea to go anywhere after dark, alone or otherwise.

Robbie may have been right about this one, she thought.

She lit a match. It killed what little night vision she had, but it was *very* little, so whatever. The match didn't help at all, though, except maybe to notify the local animals of her exact location.

She spent a few seconds looking for a loose branch to light on fire, but everything she found was wet. Then the match was at her fingers, so she put it out.

"It's either head back and find another street before the fire dies," she said, "or wait a few minutes for the moon to come back out."

She sat down next to a tree to give the moon a minute to think about it. If it didn't make an appearance soon, she'd double back.

While waiting, her hand went into the bag and found the grip of the gun. She wrapped her fingers around the handle, just in case any of the wildlife tried something funny.

She almost dozed off then, thanks to some combination of the adrenaline crash after all that excitement and the fact that she literally could not tell if her eyes were open or closed. She'd been wondering if the fire had spared the stacks or not, and then her focus drifted and she was *in* the stacks, reading *Pogo* to a guy in a cape with fangs, which was definitely not actually happening.

Then she thought she heard someone call her name.

"What? I'm awake," she said, with a start.

She looked around, but there still wasn't anything to see. She could make out the house in front of her, and the tree she was leaning on, and the street and sidewalk. Not much else. There could be a boa constrictor on the lawn and she'd miss it.

Then she saw a flash from somewhere up the driveway. A light, or the reflection of a light, or maybe just her eyeballs malfunctioning. Or she was still dreaming.

She got up anyway, made sure the gun was still in her hand, and headed for the flash.

What she found . . . was a wheelbarrow.

It was on the side of the house, just sitting there, right-side up, waiting to be discovered. It had a plastic wheel that was intact and in no need of being inflated.

It seemed like a highly improbable discovery.

"You were caught in a downpour, Mr. Barrow," she said. "How come you're not full of water?"

She tipped it onto its side to confirm that there wasn't a gallon of rainwater in it, set it back upright, and considered whether this was also a dream, or if the universe was just choosing this moment to show a little charity.

Gift horse or not, this was really, really weird.

There was a shift in the wind, which carried a familiar smell.

Piss, she thought. *Same as the dorm room.*

He's here.

Carol's apparition was in the yard with her, somewhere, somehow. And at a moment when Bethany was just as blind as Carol.

But maybe not as defenseless.

"Hello?" she said. "I know you're there."

He *was* there. He didn't respond, but he was there, and he was right behind her. She was positive.

He was reaching for her, out of the darkness.

He was real.

She screamed, spun around.

And fired the gun.

Robbie

1

The library fire didn't show any signs of letting up, even when the roof collapsed.

Robbie kept expecting to hear sirens, but there weren't going to be any. Not even from the fire station two blocks away. What really would have helped was another torrential downpour. It seemed this was the day when everything happened out of order.

"Where's the boy who knocked me over?" Carol asked. "I thought I heard him screaming. Did he get out?"

"No, he definitely didn't," Robbie said. "But he was . . . he was in rough shape."

"Bethany called him a vampire."

"Yeah, he looked like one. Half dead from starvation. And there's this guy. He looks like he fought every animal in the state to make it here."

"Is it that bad?"

"It's pretty bad. I'm wondering if this is the kind of survivor we should expect from now on. Dying because of a lack of something: food, water, someone to watch his back."

Carol smiled. "Humans are pack animals," she said. "That's why we're still here. And why we get along so well with other pack animals."

"Yeah, I'm sorry he scared off your new wolf friend. Or new *coyote* friend, I guess. Assuming we can believe a guy who's probably delirious from blood loss."

"It's okay," she said. "I'll find him again."

"Don't take this the wrong way, but I hope not."

She nodded and fell silent as they listened to the fire crackle and distant howling. The hunt was still on.

"Robbie, before we set the library on fire . . . what you were saying about what year it was—that wasn't a joke, was it? Or a typo in the copyright? It was . . . it was *real*, wasn't it?"

"Yeah, I think so."

Carol sighed. "I'm starting to run out of things I can count on to be true," she said.

"I think it actually explains some stuff," he said. "Other than us, I mean."

A gunshot interrupted their conversation.

"Crap," he said. "I was afraid of this."

"Was that Bethany?"

"She's the only one we sent into that neighborhood with a loaded weapon, so probably."

He grabbed the shotgun and started fiddling with it. The owner of the gun had fired off one round and said there was another barrel. Robbie hoped that meant it didn't need reloading.

"Do you have any idea what you're doing?" Carol asked.

"Not a clue. I've used a shotgun in a couple of video games, that's about it. He's got a bag full of ammo here, so I think if I need to reload it, I'm supposed to shove some kind of canister into the back of the barrel."

"I mean, what are you planning to do with that?"

"Go after her, I guess. What else can I do?"

"You can stay here and hope she comes back."

"She could be in trouble."

"You're going to run into an unfamiliar landscape with a shotgun you don't know how to use, to rescue a thirteen-year-old who is running around that same neighborhood with a loaded handgun and who may not be in any need of rescuing?"

"Well, yeah, I was, before you put it that way."

"I'm okay!" Bethany shouted from a good distance away.

Robbie couldn't see her, but he could hear her coming down the street, along with the sound of something loud and wheeled.

"We heard the gun," Carol said. "You're really okay?"

Bethany came into view, pushing an actual wheelbarrow.

"I got spooked," she said. "Lost the gun and hurt my wrist. Man, firing a gun *sucks*. Don't ever try it. But hey, look what I found."

2

Getting an unconscious adult human into a wheelbarrow ended up being the hardest task any of them did that day.

Or maybe it just seemed like it given it was the *last* hard task at the end of a very long day. It was accomplished, eventually, after multiple one-two-three-go's, and a possible concussion for Father Guns-A-Lot (Bethany's nickname for him). Then there was the problem of seeing in the dark well enough to find the house again, which was resolved when Robbie excavated the edge of the library fire until he found something both still on fire and portable. It looked like it used to be part of an armchair.

After all that, with Bethany using the makeshift torch to guide them home and Robbie struggling to keep the wheelbarrow from tipping over, they had no actual plan to move the unconscious man up the stairs and into the house.

"Maybe we should have picked a place with a handicap ramp," Bethany suggested.

"It's not too late to look for one," Robbie said.

"It's a little too late *tonight*," Carol said.

"All right. We got this far—why don't we just carry him up to the porch, like before."

Before was attempt number seven of their efforts to get him into the wheelbarrow. It involved Robbie holding one of his arms and one of his legs at the knee, with Bethany holding the other arm and Carol holding the other leg.

It worked—until it didn't. Carol missed a step, since nobody was paying attention to the blind woman, and anyway, they could barely see themselves. They stumbled, and dropped him on the porch, rather than placing him there gently.

He grunted. "Oof," the preacher said. "How about if I take it from here?"

ELEVEN

Paul

PASTOR PAUL WOKE UP IN AN OVERSTUFFED BED UNDER SEVeral blankets with the smell of a fire in his nostrils and a sense of ease he hadn't felt in a long, long time.

It was so jarring that for a few seconds he wondered if he'd been forgiven—for what transgression he still did not know—and accepted into the bosom of the Lord.

Then he tried to move his left arm.

"Are you all right?"

The speaker was a young Asian woman in a rocking chair a few feet away, staring out the window with eyes that couldn't see.

"What?" he asked.

"You cried out just now. Are you all right?"

"Did I? I apologize."

"Don't apologize for being in pain."

She got up and found her way to the side of the bed with the help of her cane, and put her hand on his forehead.

"We don't think you have a fever," she said, "but we can't find a working thermometer. How do you feel?"

"Like I've been chewed up, spit out, and run over by a stampede."

"Mm. I'm told that's how you look as well."

"You're blind."

"Yes, I am. I have been since birth."

"I didn't mean any offense," he said.

"I'm not offended. I know I'm blind."

She held out her hand, which he took.

"I'm Carol," she said. "The others are Robbie and Bethany. They aren't here right now."

"I'm Paul," he said.

"And you're a priest?"

"I'm a nondenominational preacher, ma'am. Or I was. I guess I can claim to be whatever, the way the world is now. Are you a doctor?"

"No, unfortunately we don't have a doctor. We found some bandages for your wounds and made do. What happened to you?"

"Depends on which part of me we're talking about, I guess."

"The shoulder, then."

"A bear bit me."

"A . . . bear?"

"Yep. Big one. They're all big now—have you noticed that? Those coyotes you stared down last night . . . Wait, *was* it last night? Or have I been out for a while?"

"It was last night, but I don't blame you for asking. We're all missing time around here."

He didn't know what that meant exactly, but let it pass.

"Eastern coyotes are a hybrid breed, but they've always been mostly coyote and coyotes don't grow that large," he said. "That's what I mean. Everything's larger than it should be."

"So, a larger-than-average bear bit you," she said.

"Yup. He should have had me. I put the double-barrel under his chin and pulled and that was that. I wore his pelt for warmth for a few days. Did you get that snowstorm up here too, or did the Lord send that just for me?"

"We got it, although . . . if you don't mind my saying, if I did believe in a god at one time, I wouldn't now."

He laughed. It made his whole body hurt, so he stopped right away.

"I don't mind at all, Carol," he said. "To be honest, it's been so long since I spoke face-to-face with another person, you could curse my mother all afternoon and it would be the sweetest sound I heard in my life."

She smiled.

"Are you sure you're a man of the cloth, pastor?" she asked.

"Got a chapel in New Hampshire to prove it."

"I think you're too charming to be a religious man."

"Sometimes that's all we have going for us," he said.

She felt around behind her until she located the chair, which she sat back down in.

"All right," she said. "A bear. What about the face?"

"Mountain lion. Came at me from the trees. My own fault for not sticking to the highway, but I needed shelter. I shot him too, with the pistol. Knife would've been faster, but I couldn't get to it."

"And when you say 'sticking to the highway' . . . how far did you walk to make it here? Not all the way from New Hampshire?"

"No, I didn't walk all of it. I had my truck running for a bit. Did you get a hailstorm?"

"We did. We appreciated it from indoors."

"That's the way to do it, yes ma'am. That was me being punished for pride, I think."

She laughed.

"I think you *should* be punished for your pride," she said. "Especially the part where you believe regional meteorological events are meant for you specifically."

"Yeah, I can hear how it sounds. Same time, there aren't a lot of other folks around for the Lord to direct His wrath at."

He wanted to tell her about the angel that manifested before him and sent hailstones to destroy his truck. It seemed like this was a bad time to have that conversation, though, so he kept it to himself.

"Anyway," he said, "that storm wrecked all I had except for the guns and the Bible in my pocket. I've been walking here since."

"Why's that?" she asked. "What made you decide to come here?"

"Here is where the Lord wants me. He had too many opportunities to claim my life on the way, and He didn't take any of 'em. On that, at least, you've gotta agree. If not, I'll tell you where the boar stabbed me, and the snake bit me, and we can just keep on going."

"Well, as I said, we don't have a doctor, but I do agree it's surprising that you're still alive after all of that. I suspect few would be."

"You folks seem to be doing okay."

"We've been very lucky. And even so, one of us has been missing since before the snowstorm."

"I'm sorry to hear that," he said. "Hey, you were the one petting the coyote, weren't you?"

"Yes, that was me."

"That was a little foolish, if you don't mind my saying."

She smiled. "That would be the majority opinion, yes. It seemed a reasonable choice, from my perspective."

"I'm sure it sounded like a dog and felt like one, but those animals aren't tame. They could have killed you."

"Again, you're not the only one to have said so. But if anyone was going to . . . I mean, if one of us were to go . . . No, never mind. I don't think you would understand."

"Go on and say what you were going to say," Paul said. "I'll keep it to myself. You want to check my neck? It's a real collar."

She nodded and carried on an internal debate for a while before answering.

"It would be easier for everyone if they *had* killed me," she said. "Don't you think? Robbie and Bethany would have gotten away and that would have been for the best."

"Best for who?"

She nodded. "For everyone else," she said. "Before the world turned into this, there were systems in place to make it possible for someone like me to live independently. There were bells and alarms, and I had a trained dog. I wasn't a burden. The others won't say it, but I know: I'm a burden. Touré . . . he might have said it, eventually. He was rude, but honest."

"Is that the one who's missing?"

"Yes."

"Well, I think you're wrong, Carol. And I think if you told the others that, they'd say the same thing."

"Of course they would. That doesn't mean it's what they *think*. You haven't been here. The choices they've had to make . . ."

"You're right, I haven't been here. But looking at this from the outside, you're the best evidence I've seen so far that there's hope for all of us. I don't know Rob, or . . . What'd you say the girl's name was?"

"Bethany."

"Bethany. I don't know them yet. Other than a few seconds last night, we haven't been introduced. But I'm betting it didn't once occur to them that what you're talking about is even a possibility. Animals eat their wounded, and we *don't*; you understand what I'm saying? The Lord can damn us to an eternity of this, but as long as we're taking care of someone like you, I think we'll be okay."

She nodded, slowly. "Thank you, Paul. I think you might be a man of the cloth after all."

"Was that too corny?"

"It was a little corny."

"I'm out of practice," he said.

She stood. "I'm going to find you something to eat. We have Noot bars and water. Will that do?"

"What in the heck is a Noot bar?"

"It's what those of us who didn't think to bring guns and knives to the apocalypse feed ourselves with."

"Well, I'll try it, then. I'm not in any shape to hunt, and I ran out of meat two days ago."

She stopped at the door.

"You haven't told me *why* yet," she said. "You came so far, and said God wanted you to go on foot for some reason. Why didn't you stop? Find a home in which to outlast the weather and stay there?"

"I had a good reason," he said. "Her name's Ananda, and until last night I thought she was the only other person left."

Carol looked torn between asking if Ananda was, strictly speaking, real, and encouraging him to elaborate.

"And where is she?" Carol asked.

"Depends on how far we are from MIT."

Bethany

Bethany tromped downstairs, and was out of the house by sunrise.

Robbie was also awake by then and already packing up to head back to the dorm for what would likely be the first of many visits. They would need more Noot bars, especially with a fourth person now in the house, and . . . well, who knew what else the day might bring? Cambridge had *tornadoes* now.

He asked where she was headed. She lied and said she wanted to see if any of the library was salvageable. She *did* want to see if the stacks were still there, but that wasn't what was really on her mind.

"Well, be careful" was all he said in response. She was expecting a lecture about how they had to stick together, but maybe he'd gotten tired of saying it over and over.

She did start at the library. It was burned to the ground, and still smoking. The old brick castle wing looked like it had weathered the inferno surprisingly well, though.

What she was there to do was reconstruct the path she had taken the night before. The spot where the preacher fell was marked by blood from the man's shoulder, so she started retracing her steps by standing there and turning in the approximate direction of her departure.

I ran down THAT street, she decided. It was on the other side of Broadway, which was the road fronting the library.

She headed up the street. About halfway, she found the shed with the lock she'd picked the night before, confirming that she had this right.

Up and over the hill, she looked for a house on the left side of the street, with a driveway on the right and a tree out front.

There.

She sat at the base of the tree and felt the same knot in her back she'd felt last night. This was definitely it.

Up the driveway, the gravel made a familiar crunch under her shoes. She could see the skid marks left behind by the wheelbarrow, too. That gave her pretty much the exact position where she'd been standing.

She stood there again, counted down from three, and then spun around.

"Bang," she said.

There was a bullet hole in the garage door now. It wasn't a stretch to assume it hadn't been there before.

But where'd the gun go? she thought.

She'd been woefully unprepared for the degree of kickback when firing a gun for the first time. Her wrist—which she thought at first was broken—still hurt, and probably would for a while. She also fell backwards, into the wheelbarrow, causing the skids in the driveway. And, of course, she lost her grip on the gun.

The next thing she did after that was get up, right the wheelbarrow, and get the hell out of there as fast as she could.

So where did the gun land?

Looking for it the night before would have been a waste of time had she even hesitated to consider the notion. But clearly it landed somewhere that was not out in the open.

Unless someone else had come by overnight and picked it up.

She walked around the front lawn, which was skirted by overgrown shrubs, until her eye caught something silvery beneath a bush. She got down on her stomach for a better look.

"*There* you are," she said.

The gun had flown a remarkable fifteen feet from where she'd fallen over. This was surely a record of some kind.

She reached under the shrub and grabbed the revolver, then walked back over to the middle of the driveway and pantomimed her prior actions once again, this time with the gun in her hand.

Stop, spin, fire, fall down, she thought, while neither firing nor falling down.

Next, she walked the bullet's trajectory to the garage door. Theoretically someone had been standing somewhere along the path when she fired, assuming she hadn't imagined it all.

She had to admit, she probably *had*. Just like Carol had in the dorm. In fact, that was by far the most likely explanation for *all* of this: (1) Bethany got the idea of Carol's bogeyman rattling around in her brain; (2) alone in the dark, she let her fear get the better of her; and (3) she shot the gun at a figment of her imagination.

There *was* something that felt wrong about the driveway, though, now that she was looking at it in the light. The surface was still damp from the rain the night before, but it was a soft pebble driveway rather than tarmac, and from a certain angle, it looked like one spot had been rubbed in the wrong direction, like a thick pile carpet brushed against the grain.

A patch of the driveway was a different color from the rest of it, and it was right in line with the flight of the bullet. If the discoloration had been *red*, Bethany would have been all over the idea that this was blood, and therefore proof that she wasn't losing her mind, that she really hadn't been alone, and that she'd even clipped the guy.

But it was *yellow*.

Robbie

It took Robbie most of the morning to get one load of blankets together and into the cart.

Not because blankets were a particularly difficult challenge, in terms of packing, but because first he had to make sure everything they wanted to bring was collected in the same place. It would give him a good idea of the volume he was dealing with, to assess how many trips he would need in order to move all of it to the new location.

They hadn't been in the dorm for more than a few weeks, but somehow they'd managed to spread stuff out all over the place, between four bedrooms, three bathrooms, two rooms in the basement, and the common room. It made him wish they'd thought to pack before leaving. Although if they had, they probably never would have come across the heavily armed priest.

Having the pastor around was an incredible relief. Or it was going to be once the man was ready to get out of bed again. Assuming he survived the wounds they found him with.

The guy had walked through hell in order to make it to them, doing what none of them had the skills or the tools to do. He could hunt, and he had guns. And thank God for both, because there wasn't enough Noot to keep them all alive until spring. Not unless they found more, or figured out how to plant and grow their own Noot trees.

"Or we could just grow *actual* food," he said to himself. "Crazy, I know."

The bike was loaded and waiting at the front of the dorm for the first of many trips. Robbie was at the back of the dorm, meanwhile, on the other side of the gate, looking at the river.

It was a beautiful day. Despite the now-leafless trees, it was easy to see how they'd been confused about precisely which season they were in the middle of. The weather was manic; it couldn't decide what it wanted to do from minute to minute.

He would have liked to be able to spend more time close to the river if only to have this view now and then. At the same time, it wasn't that far from the house, and Bethany had been right; the new place was definitely safer, and easier to defend and heat.

"All right," he said. "Enough sightseeing. Let's do this."

He was about to head back inside when he heard … Well, it sounded like a *horse*. It probably *wasn't* a horse; it was probably something terrible, not unlike when he thought he heard a locomotive and it turned out to be a tornado.

But in this case a horse was exactly what it was. Far more important, someone was riding the horse.

"*Touré?*" Robbie shouted.

"Robbieeee!"

Touré and the horse came to a stop in front of the gate, and Touré climbed down as fast as he could. Which wasn't fast at all, as he appeared to have a bum leg.

"I can't believe it!" Robbie said. He was crying and this time didn't care who saw.

"Dude!"

Touré hopped over, Robbie met him partway, and they hugged for a while.

"I thought you were dead," Robbie said. "I can't —"

"I know, I'm sorry. I got attacked. Oh, man, I have so much to tell you."

"Me too!" Robbie said. "And you have a horse? How do you have a horse?"

"Don't call him that. His name is Elton."

"Don't call him a horse?"

"Yeah, he doesn't know."

"When did you even learn how to ride a horse?"

"*That's* what you wanna ask me?" Touré asked.

"It's the first thing I thought of. I have more."

"Okay, well, I'm not really riding him, I'm kind of hanging on. I can't believe he even got me this far; I thought he was gonna jump into the river instead. And he's not mine."

Elton snorted.

"Sorry, man," he said, petting the horse's neck. "Elton doesn't belong to anyone, but I'm not the one who put that saddle on him. Her name is Win, and she saved my life a lot."

Touré looked past Robbie, to the dorm.

"Hey," he said, "um, you're not . . . Are the others . . . ?"

"Oh, no, no," Robbie said. "They're fine. We moved. And we ran into that kid from before. Yeah, he's dead now, and we set the library on fire, after a tornado. But we met this priest, who seems pretty cool, and all that was just *yesterday*."

"You met a *priest*? I met an astrophysicist. Look, we have to get you guys over to MIT. Win's there now. We have electricity, and heat. Ananda says she thinks we're in for a crazy bad winter."

"Ananda?"

"The astrophysicist."

"Oh, cool," Robbie said. "I think my guy is looking for her."

"The priest or the dead kid in the library?"

"The priest."

"Wait, wait, wait . . . Is his name Paul?"

"I left before I asked."

Touré laughed, and then Robbie hugged him once more. He really never did expect to see Touré again, and it had been killing him for so many reasons. Today in particular, because he had been gestating an idea and Touré was the only person in the world who would take it seriously.

"Look," Robbie said, "we have to go over all of it, but I think I've worked out what happened to us."

"Is it a crazy theory that makes no sense and is probably impossible?"

"It is."

"I've got ten of those," Touré said. "Hit me."

"It's about how we survived."

"Uh-huh. Go on."

"I think . . . This is going to sound crazy," Robbie said. "You'll think I've lost it."

"That's the *best* kind of idea. Are you kidding?"

"Here's what I think. I think we survived because we weren't *here* when it happened. The mass extinction, I mean. We didn't die because we weren't here."

"Here, where? Like, in Cambridge?"

"Bigger than that," Robbie said.

"Not on the *planet?*" Touré said.

"Bingo."

Touré laughed. "I love it," he said. "So how did we end up off-planet for the apocalypse?"

"That's the crazy part," Robbie said. "I think we were abducted by aliens."

Touré hugged him hard.

"I am so glad I found you again, man," he said. "You're not going to believe this, but I was thinking the same exact thing."

PART THREE
DUNGEON MASTER

TWELVE

Paul

1

"DO YOU HAVE THE SHOT?" WIN ASKED.

The deer was standing in the middle of Lexington Common in front of a monument to honor those who died in a battle long ago, erected by a community of people who effectively no longer existed.

The animal looked largely indifferent to the historicity of the environment.

There was a small patch of grass near the monument, at the border between the cement walkway and the rest of the battle green. It was formed by the runoff from the snow that—while melting— was still very much a major presence in the area.

"I do," Paul said.

He was lying on his belly on a porch across the street from the green, watching the deer along the barrel of his Remington. The porch he was on was probably also historic—there was a plaque on the side of the house, partly obscured by an overgrown tree— but Paul was largely disinterested in the details. He'd been camping out in Lexington for a week now, and only realized where he was five days into the stay. It explained why the wood floors in some of the houses were warped, and the doorways so low, and the door-knobs and whatnot so antiquated.

"Good, that's out of my range," she said.

Win was kneeling next to him, behind a support beam, with that compound bow of hers nocked and ready to loose.

"It's fifty yards. That's not out of your range," he said. "You're better with that than I am with this."

The doe raised its head and looked around, perhaps sensing it was the subject of a conversation taking place nearby, or perhaps just naturally edgy.

Paul exhaled slowly and squeezed off a shot. The deer's head rocked to the left, and then the animal collapsed into the snow. The shot echoed through the neighborhood, sending various other critters fleeing in a collective scurry.

"I can't hit a deer in the eye like that from this range," Win said. "Nice shot, by the way."

"Thanks," he said. "You would if you had to."

He set the Remington aside. It was the only rifle he made it out of the wilderness with, of the three. He managed to hang onto the double-barreled Winchester, but the Mossberg made it about half-way; he lost it around the time the bear bit him. He lost the Ruger in the hailstorm, and the Glock in a fight with a cougar. The Smith & Wesson and the Heritage both made it all the way, but the former was currently in Bethany's possession.

He rolled to his left and held out his hand, while Win got to her feet so she could help him to his.

There were things about Paul's recovery from the many wounds he'd endured on his walk from the New Hampshire border to the city that everyone took to be true, absent the formal opinion of the medical professional they did not have and could not consult.

Those included (1) that he would never regain full range of motion in his right shoulder, (2) that he had cartilage damage in his left knee, (3) that the scarring on his face had healed about as well as it was ever going to, and (4) that it was an actual miracle he hadn't died from an infection. This last seemed especially pertinent given Touré nearly *did* die from only *one* such wound.

Paul thought the Lord refused to let him die for reasons known only to Him, and he was in no position to question His wisdom. But by Paul's reckoning, miracles were supposed to be positive things, and this seemed to have been performed out of some kind of divine spite. He did not feel graced.

"I'll get him," Win said, once Paul was up. "You look like you need to work some kinks out there."

He squeezed his right hand to try to get some blood back in his fingers, and flexed his knees. The left one tended to just give out altogether without warning. If it really was cartilage damage, it was bound to improve. Until then, he wouldn't be using any of the bikes the others used to get around.

Luckily, they had a horse.

Win dropped the quiver and bow and headed across the street to fetch the deer carcass. A few months back, Paul probably would have argued that a woman like that was too slight to lift the deer. But she'd proven him wrong more than a few times already.

It wasn't actually a few months. It was a few months and *a hundred-odd years,* but he wasn't going to be getting his mind around *that* anytime soon, no matter how often Ananda offered to explain it. The problem was, her explanations were all centered on the proof of the fact but were short on the *how* part. Until someone provided him with that part of the story, he was holding on to some skepticism.

Win made it to the body of the deer—but suddenly froze because a wolf had emerged from the blind side of the Revolutionary War monument.

Paul bent to retrieve his rifle. Win raised her hand, which was a signal that said: *Hold on, I have this.*

She pulled out that knife of hers and crouched down over the deer.

"Go on," Paul heard her say, faintly. "This one's mine. You don't want a fight."

Win was a head shorter than Paul, and probably half his weight. She was supposed to be wearing pantsuits and working for a public relations firm in Providence, not facing down wolves in the snow. There were times when Paul saw that woman in the pantsuit, when Win relaxed. There were other times, like this one, when he saw the world-class archer who lived off the land, alone, for weeks, and would straight-up murder anyone that got in her way.

They seemed like entirely different people. Paul didn't know which one he preferred.

The wolf growled. She was locking eyes with him, which was not something Paul would have recommended unless you were aiming to challenge. It worked for her, though.

"You'll lose, doggie," she said. "*Shoo.*"

A long standoff ensued, and then the wolf whined and loped away. It was thin, hungry, and alone for the moment. If it had been with its pack, that might have gone differently.

Winter hits us all hard, Paul thought.

With the weather surveys Ananda found as a guide, they were anticipating the worst kind of winter, from a constant onslaught of nor'easters carrying outrageous amounts of snow to days and weeks of subzero temperatures. But with that as context, it had been a pretty mild season so far. There had been one really bad storm, and a week where the mercury thermometers registered as below zero (absent a windchill calculation) but it wasn't epically, end-of-the-world terrible.

That was good, since so far as they knew, the only building in the world with heat was at MIT, and some of the temperatures Ananda was talking about were legitimately life-threatening. That it didn't happen—and now winter appeared to be winding down—was a small kindness.

Out on the green, Win slung the deer over her shoulders and headed back.

"Are you set up in here?" she asked, nodding to the front door.

"Yep. Already have a fire going. You want some coffee?"

2

The idea of establishing remote outposts to hunt game and prep it for wider consumption came out of the need to find sustenance for Elton.

What they wanted was an area where people might have kept horses, so they could take advantage of whatever stored hay and grains might still exist. That meant leaving the local area, because outside of the Boston mounted police, nobody in the city kept a horse. (They didn't know where in Boston those municipal horses might have been kept, anyway. And after what happened to Win and Touré, nobody was interested in exploring the downtown, except to go boar-hunting.)

Lexington, Concord, Lincoln, Bedford, and Carlisle were all close enough to travel to in an hour—by bike or by horse—and had plenty of farmland to choose from. Some of it looked promising as potential sources of actual vegetables, too, come spring.

There weren't any barns in downtown Lexington, but there were plenty less than a mile off the main road. Paul was only set up downtown because it was near the central drag—Massachusetts Ave.—and it was about time for Paul and Elton to head back and rejoin the living.

Win dropped the deer on the marble kitchen countertop the prior owners had undoubtedly been quite fond of, and the two of them got to work cutting up the carcass. This was done wordlessly and with the efficiency of lots of practice, helped along by the carving implements they'd collected from a butcher's shop in Cambridge.

A couple of hours later, the meat was all carved up. Half would go back raw, packed in snow. The other half, they were cooking in the fireplace.

This was another nice thing about the houses out beyond the city: They all had fireplaces.

"How's everybody doing?" Paul asked as he passed a rocks glass to Win. They were sharing an expensive bottle of bourbon from the homestead's extensive liquor cabinet. Alcohol was just about the only good thing about discovering themselves inexplicably vaulted ahead a century: All the stuff that got better with age had done so.

"Ah, you know—the same," she said. "Ananda's still assembling answers to the great mysteries. Robbie and Touré bring her new material all the time, now that Touré can move around on that leg. I think they're working on some secret project—it's hard to tell with them."

"Secret project?"

"Or something. Touré won't talk about it, which for him is . . . I mean, you know how he is. He's excited about it, I can tell you that. I'm not going to press him on it. I think those two just need this to be an adventure in order to keep moving. Touré does, anyway."

Paul nodded. He didn't quite get Touré. The kid came off as weirdly juvenile at times that didn't call for that kind of attitude, which Paul just found off-putting. But Paul had enormous respect for Win, and she talked about Touré as if describing a different person entirely.

He had a higher opinion of Robbie, who was the closest this odd little collection of survivors had to a leader. What was interesting was that everybody seemed to know this except for Robbie.

"So they're off keeping each other sane," Win said, "and that's fine. Carol's doing her own thing a lot of the time too. She found a library with books in Braille. I don't know what she's teaching herself. Bethany, we don't see her for days sometimes."

"She can take care of herself, that one," Paul said.

"Well, you let her keep a gun. I'm sure she *thinks* she can."

Bethany had asked to keep it, and Paul had agreed on the condition that he give her some training first. Not everyone liked this decision; Bethany had already fired the gun once when she'd gotten spooked by something that wasn't there. Nobody wanted to be nearby the next time that happened, especially if it was one of them instead of a shadow.

Let the moody teen be the one to carry around the deadly weapon just seemed like bad company policy. Paul could see that. But nobody really felt comfortable telling Paul he couldn't do it—their governing structure consisted of the occasional vote during the occasional meeting, and gun distribution was never brought up—so Bethany got to keep the handgun.

He wasn't worried. He'd trained many kids her age and younger on proper gun use. Some of them were too eager and not interested in paying attention to the part about safety. Those kids got sent home with advice to the parents to give their child another year or two to mature. Bethany wasn't one of those.

"She'll be fine," Paul said. "I'd be more worried if Touré was the one who wandered off on his own for a spell."

Win laughed. "Yeah, so would I. How's Elton?"

"Well, speaking of wandering off on his own, that horse doesn't care for fences or barns. He seems to forage for himself okay, and he comes back at a whistle if he's in earshot. Everybody leaves him be out here. He's closed up in a barn down that way, just for the night. Didn't feel like spending another couple of days out here waiting for him to show up again. Although now you're here; he'd probably turn up for you."

"I think he's sweet on me," she said. "You ready to come back?"

"I enjoy the solitude as much as the next guy, but I think I've had my fill for a while, yeah."

It was a month before Paul could walk around well enough for them to seriously consider the plan that was now in play: sending him back off into the wilderness for the winter to hunt game and keep an eye on Elton. During that time, Win was the only human Paul interacted with. It wasn't all *that* different from when he lived on the mountain, except back then his isolation was easy enough to break whenever he felt like it. And there was always Sunday. This felt more like exile.

He also no longer knew when Sunday was. Once he realized he'd lost track of that, he just designated one particular day as Sunday, celebrated it as such (albeit alone, as nobody else seemed interested) every seven days, and was mostly okay with that. It troubled him a little that he might be honoring the Lord's Day on a Tuesday, but since the Lord was being pissy with him anyway, he figured it didn't matter all that much in the grand scheme.

"Oh, hey," Win said, pointing to the window to the backyard. "Looks like the shimmer is back."

She was referring to the collection of lights that had formed on the deck. Win got up for a better look. Paul checked over his shoulder just in case it was different this time. It wasn't.

"Yeah, I've seen 'em around here," he said. "First time they've stopped by this house, but, you know. Another thirty seconds, they'll be gone."

"This one looks like it wants to be human-shaped," she said.

"Yeah, they do that."

She watched until it dissipated. "Still think it's an angel?" she asked.

He laughed. "Don't make it sound like we got a bunch of other guesses as good as that," he said.

"That's fair. First time I saw it, I thought it was a ghost."

"A glowing one?"

"Sure, why not? Anyway." She put her empty glass down on an end table and checked the venison. "This looks ready," she said. "We should get some rest. Long couple of days ahead."

Robbie

1

"We have to cut left at this junction," Touré said, waving his torch to emphasize his preferred vector. "We went right last week and ended up going nowhere."

"That wasn't nowhere," Robbie said. "Everything here goes somewhere."

"You know what I mean."

"The right led to an upstairs full of wolves. That's your definition of nowhere."

"Okay, it led us into one of the dens, and I don't have enough hit points to make it through there," Touré said. "Neither do you."

"It's not a dungeon. It's a school."

"You keep saying that. You'll think differently after we come across a dragon."

They were on a quest—Touré's word, but in this case, a reasonable choice—to locate as much handwritten material as possible across the entire MIT campus. Or rather, the entire part of the campus they could access, which was very nearly all of it. A great wizard—Ananda—charged them with this quest. This idea came not long after their initial meeting, in that first week in which all seven of them were together.

In that same meeting, the group pooled together all that they'd discovered, whether it made any sense at all, to see if any of it fit together.

Some of it *sort of* did, and some of it sort of did not.

For example, Robbie thought it was 2019, and both Carol and Win thought it was 2016. It was Bethany's opinion that it was 2013, Touré said 2014, Paul believed it was 2018, and for Ananda it was 2020.

This made everything complicated, because while Ananda could assert—correctly—that it was *about* a hundred years from when she thought it was, that already meant it was *about* 107 years from when Bethany thought it was, and so on. Since Ananda's calculations couldn't get her any closer than the roughly one-century difference, basically nobody knew what year it was, but they *did* know it wasn't exactly the year they thought it was.

The gap in the timeline went a long way toward explaining where everyone had gone. Cambridge had been evacuated—they didn't know why, but they had plenty of evidence that it had been —so the lack of bodies was explicable, locally. What made less sense were the piles of dusted human remains they'd encountered outside of the city.

Win had showed them all the partial jawbone she was carrying around. It was, so far, the only human bone any of them had encountered. Everything else was piles of dust.

Everyone agreed that a dead human body, if exposed to the elements, could disintegrate completely, given long enough. But nobody knew how long that might be, and everyone agreed that there should still be a lot more bones lying around. Paul brought home this point by describing a scene in a barn in which he found the remains of a cow. The bones were still there, even if nothing else was. So what happened differently with the dead humans than with that dead cow?

They later worked out the best available estimate, that there were people on the planet up until around 2044. They got to this number not by one of Ananda's calculations, but because it was the date on a chemical engineering class syllabus Robbie and Touré discovered. They had been turning up artifacts with progressively later dates for a month, transforming the exercise into a perverse kind of inverted archeology study: the newer the better.

This particular discovery meant the Apocalypse Seven (as they'd taken to calling themselves) didn't wake up right after the extinction of the human race: It was more like fifty or sixty years later. It also meant whatever explained that extinction would also have to explain what happened to the bones.

Another topic on which they only partly agreed was the shimmer. Everyone had reported having seen it at least once except for Bethany (and, technically, Carol, although she didn't count); Touré, Robbie, and Win claimed to have seen it take human form, and Paul thought it was an angel. Ananda had only seen what she described as a swarm and dismissed everyone's humanoid sighting as an optical illusion. They didn't challenge her, but after the meeting, Robbie wished he'd asked her to elaborate on why she held that opinion. The idea that it was humanoid seemed no more out-landish than anything else, certainly.

Other parts of that meeting didn't add up quite so neatly. The dying words of Raymond the erstwhile vampire, the yellow splotch in Bethany's driveway, Carol's man who wasn't there, and Robbie's door that unlocked itself didn't all add up into a common under-standing of, well . . . *anything*.

Robbie knew for a fact that not everyone shared all they knew, or suspected, in that meeting. Paul believed the Rapture had hap-pened, but didn't say that out loud. Bethany thought this was some secular version of purgatory, but kept that to herself. And critically, Robbie and Touré thought aliens were involved, but didn't say so to anyone but each other. And there were probably more ideas that he didn't know about.

They all had their reasons.

2

Ananda was convinced there were answers out there still; they just had to find them. For Robbie and Touré, getting answers always meant taking the bikes farther and farther from the city, but that was because they thought they were answering *Where are all the peo-ple hiding?* and not *How did all the people die?*

"At least twenty-five years' worth of data is out there," she'd said, at that same first meeting. "Find it and maybe we'll figure out why we're the only ones left."

Win rightfully pointed out that even back in ye olden days of 2016 most things were recorded in computerized form, and that this was likely even truer in Ananda's distant future of 2020, and that therefore it was more likely still in 2044.

"And we can't get the computers running," Win said.

"For *now*," Ananda said. "But there will be notes. There are always notes. Diaries, field notes, pages and pages of numbers that don't mean anything to anyone except whoever wrote them down. We can do something with those; we just have to find them."

"Where?" Robbie asked.

"If I knew, it wouldn't be a long search," Ananda said.

They were all still getting used to one another at that stage. Paul was weird and gruff, clearly in a lot of pain, and prone to long speeches that prominently featured God. Ananda came off as clinical and dismissive, and was probably on some kind of spectrum. Win drifted between *happy to meet you* and *I'm remembering the time I killed a guy*. It was impossible to tell how much any of that had to do with what they all had gone through alone before the seven of them joined up, and how much was just a part of who they'd always been.

It made Robbie wonder how he, Touré, Carol, and Bethany would have ended up if they hadn't been relying on one another from day one. Like Raymond, probably.

"What I mean is, where do you expect us to search?" Robbie asked.

"On the campus," she said. "I've searched these rooms, and parts of some other buildings, but I've been limited by time, by too many places to check, and by my study of the object."

"On the campus with wolves roaming the halls?" Touré asked.

"The wolves don't go into the tunnels," Ananda said. "You can use those to get around."

"What tunnels?" Robbie asked.

"There's a network of tunnels connecting most of the buildings."

"Hold *on*," Touré said, "are you telling me MIT has a secret dungeon level?"

"I guess you could call it that," she said. "It's not really a secret."

"I didn't know about it," Touré said. "Robbie, did you know about it?"

"Nope," Robbie said.

"Anyone else?" Touré asked.

"Stop being a nerd," Bethany said.

"Then it's a secret," Touré said, ignoring Bethany.

Ananda looked at Win, as if Win were responsible for Touré. She shrugged.

"I'll find you a map," Ananda said.

3

Robbie pulled out his copy of the map and held it up under the torchlight.

"So you want to go left," he said.

"Because going right leads to wolves."

The issue was probably that Touré still couldn't run. He got along on his leg really well these days—they could only explore nearby buildings in short trips at first—but when it came to running, he mostly hopped a lot.

"That's only because of where we went upstairs," Robbie said. "We could keep going, and *then* turn left."

"Where would *that* get us?" Touré asked.

"Um . . . Buildings One, Three, and Five."

"What's special about them, aside from being prime numbers?"

"Nothing, except we haven't been in them yet," Robbie said. "And one isn't a prime number."

"You can only divide it by itself and by one. That makes it a prime number."

"You're wrong, and is the plan okay?"

"Going right? Yeah, okay, I guess. But we're going to have words about prime numbers later."

"I'm sure we are."

The tunnels really did feel dungeon-like, especially when illuminated by torchlight. They were also incredibly cold. This could have been due to the time of year, but Robbie thought probably not. The ground surrounding them was cold, and there was no sunlight getting in, so he imagined this was how it would always be. A positive: They could probably store meat in the tunnels during the summer.

The ceiling had fluorescent lights built into it. Ananda seemed to think they would eventually be able to restore power to the entire building, using only the hypothetical extra solar panels that were hypothetically stored somewhere on the premises in a room they had yet to discover. Robbie wondered if when that happened, he would find the tunnels more pleasant.

He and Touré passed under the stairwell leading to Building 10. That was where they'd left off last time, and as Touré said, it had been a mistake. The main wolf den (or technically *coyote* den, but nobody called it that) was up there, in and around the Great Dome. This time, they kept going to the stairwell on the other side, which, according to the map, led to Building 3.

"You sure about this?" Touré asked, now whispering, out of respect for the collective ton of murderous canines just above.

"I'm not sure at all," Robbie said. "I'm just checking off buildings we haven't seen yet."

This was actually a modest overstatement of their accomplishments. They'd visited about half of the buildings at least once, but every one of them consisted of several floors, each with several offices, only some of which were locked. They'd been marking the doors to the rooms already searched in order to keep them straight. At some point, they were going to have to circle around, hit the floors they'd never made it to, and get into the unmarked rooms. But that wasn't as fun as getting acquainted with a new place every few days.

"Right," Touré said. "I guess that's fair. Okay, let's go have a look."

Touré climbed the first two steps, then hesitated.

Robbie caught a whiff of something both familiar and not. It was something they'd been smelling a lot lately.

Touré turned and looked at Robbie. *I smell it too,* he was saying.

Their shadow visitor had returned.

4

One of the things Robbie had never shared with anyone, aside from Touré, was what happened that day near the parking garage when he had become convinced the darkness was staring back at him.

Aside from quoting Nietzsche, Touré had taken it well, but not seriously, even when Robbie tried to connect that moment to another thing he hadn't shared with anyone else: that he thought they'd been abducted by aliens.

Then they started going through the tunnels regularly and Touré began to believe. Because every now and again, he'd have the same sense, that someone or some*thing* was behind them, or ahead of them, or just to the side of them. Sometimes Robbie was the only one to feel it, sometimes Touré was the only one, but *every* time, it was accompanied by the same bad body odor smell.

They'd been using the tunnels for almost two months, and had thirteen distinct encounters, in thirteen different parts of the dungeon.

They called it the intruder.

After the last time they encountered the intruder, they decided to put together a plan.

It consisted of this: Step one—charge.

There was no step two.

5

"All right," Touré said. "I'm going."

This was for the intruder's benefit. Meanwhile, on his hand —from a position only Robbie could see—he counted down, *Three . . . two . . . one . . .*

On one, they both spun around and ran down the stairs, Robbie running right and Touré hopping left.

Robbie had his torch in his left hand. When he turned, his right arm swept through the space behind him and contacted something solid. Soft, clothed in fabric, but solid.

Surprised to have even accomplished this much (as this was a plan he entirely expected to fail) he next used the torch like a club, aimed at about where a person's head might be.

It landed again on . . . *something.* A solid something under the fabric for the torch to bounce off of. Sparks flew everywhere.

No question someone was there, but even though his quarry was clearly standing within the radius of light cast by the fire, Robbie could hardly see the intruder at all.

Robbie punched the spot where he thought the face was. To his surprise, his fist connected; he heard and felt a metallic crunch. It marked the first time Robbie had ever punched a person—or whatever the intruder was—and decided based on how much it hurt his hand that he would try not to do this again.

For about two seconds after the blow, Robbie saw the creature's face.

It had a bulbous head that tapered to a pointed chin, with enormous black eyes and a tiny mouth. There was no visible nose; just a horizonal strip of silvery metal across the middle of the face where the nose ought to be.

It was an alien. There was simply no other explanation.

Robbie coldcocking it appeared to have come as a major surprise to it. It took three steps back, and Robbie couldn't see its face any longer.

"Geez, Robbie," it said, in a deep and somewhat familiar voice, "that *hurt*."

Then it made a gesture with its right hand and disappeared from the tunnel.

Robbie charged through the empty space, hoping the intruder had just receded into the shadows instead of vanishing outright. But it was gone.

"Tell me you saw that!" Robbie said, swinging his torch around like a baseball bat.

"Dude, he called you by name," Touré said.

"Yeah," Robbie said. "I heard that too. I think he's gone."

He looked at Touré, and Touré looked back at him, and then they both started laughing.

"I cannot believe this!" Touré said. "We're being stalked by an *alien!*"

"I know," Robbie said. "Now comes the hard part."

"Convincing the others?"

"No, not that," Touré said with a laugh. "Or, not yet. First, we have to figure out how to catch it."

THIRTEEN

Ananda

"SO, YOU DON'T KNOW WHAT IT IS," BETHANY SAID.

Ananda didn't need to see what the girl was looking at to understand the question. "I don't," she said. "I don't know what it is, and I don't know what it does. I have some ideas I'd like to test, but not until the weather turns."

"You think it doesn't like snow?"

"I don't believe it has an opinion on snow, but it's currently beneath a quantity of it, and I don't want to risk doing something to it by accident while cleaning it off."

"Do you think you'd hurt it?"

Ananda put down the notes. "Come here," she said. "Have a look at this."

Bethany came over, reluctantly—dragging herself along in a way so reminiscent of Jakob that Ananda felt like she was being jabbed with something sharp.

Ananda spread out a series of printouts showing reams of numbers, with almost no detail attached to the numbers that could explain what they were.

"What's this?" Bethany asked.

"You tell me. This came from the meteorological department."

They were standing in the same lab Ananda first camped out in, which was also the first one in the building to have heat and electricity. Since then, with the help of the others, they'd managed to power three floors and install hard barriers that kept the wolves out of the entire building.

This involved clearing the halls of the wolves in the first place, a task that was helped greatly by the generous use of Paul's very loud guns—but not Paul himself, who could barely stand when he first arrived. Win and Robbie didn't use the guns to shoot any of the wolves; just to frighten them off. It made for an afternoon of gunshots and shouting throughout the building, as if the place were under siege.

That had been a tumultuous week. First, Win and Touré had arrived, proving to Ananda that she was not the last person left on the planet—and also that horses, too, continued to exist. Then, after getting them situated—and after looking at Touré's leg and misapplying her PhD (which had nothing to do with medicine) to tell him she thought it looked fine—Ananda explained all that she'd learned about the apocalypse.

She enjoyed talking to Win, because she came off like a combination of time traveler and field expedition head. Ananda had remained in and around the MIT campus from the start, relying on scavenged reports—like the one Bethany was looking at—and what she could see from her window. She was also decently well versed in the various worst-case scenarios pertaining to climate change, knew what kind of disasters to expect if things remained unchanged for a century, and what to expect in under a century but *beyond* a certain average temperature. What she didn't know—what nobody could know, really—was what the world might look like if a hundred years passed but humanity went extinct before that century had elapsed.

Win's frontline reporting—on the weather, and the flooding downtown, and the countryside—was incredibly helpful. It allowed Ananda to hope that, at least for now, they were living in a world that had retained some measure of equilibrium.

Touré's experiences were less helpful, but he inadvertently proved his worth in a different way when, unannounced, he took off with Elton to search for his friends. He did leave a note, and in the end it all worked out, but Win had still been furious. She was certain, right up until he returned with Robbie, that Touré and the horse had inadvertently galloped into the Charles and drowned.

When Robbie arrived and explained he had three other people holed up in a home at the other end of Broadway, their first imperative became getting all of them to MIT, where there might be enough power to survive the coming winter.

The most wonderful surprise, though, was learning that Paul was one of them.

After they'd all been gathered together, the rest of that first month was spent working out logistics. They had to find bedrolls for everyone and arrange privacy where needed. Then there was a question of food: how much they had, how much more they needed, and where they were going to get it. An electric stove was retrieved from one of the kitchens and carried upstairs, and then hot water was available to all of them for the first time in a long time.

It was *glorious.*

The stove led to one or two mishaps, such as when Bethany and Carol tried to fry a slice of Noot bar to see if that made it more palatable somehow. It emphatically did not. It also emitted an odor that might have been toxic and definitely ruined the pan. Thankfully, they hardly had to eat Noot bars any longer, thanks to the arrival of their two hunters. (Ananda was pretty sure the source of protein in the bars was insects, so she certainly wasn't disappointed to have it minimized from her diet.)

Another two months later, they had a whole system in place for food, and living quarters, and now springtime was on its way.

"This column looks like dates," Bethany said, running her finger along the left side of the grid.

"Yes. Very good."

"But it goes past Judgment Day. 2055?"

"Correct. I tried to talk myself out of that very conclusion. But then I realized what this was. What else do you see?"

"Um . . . these look like temperatures?"

"Yes."

"Where is this, the Arctic?"

"It's global average temperature, only it's in Celsius. This is from a weather satellite. It was sending data down to one of the stack printers in the meteorological department. Take a look at what happened in 2044."

"I don't understand what I'm looking at."

Ananda took the sheet back.

"From here, to here, you can see the average global temperature went up two degrees. At the same time — you see this column here? It's showing carbon levels in the atmosphere — at the same time, it goes up as well. When it reaches 2044? It levels off."

Bethany looked at the numbers and shook her head. "I'm not seeing what you're seeing."

"The carbon footprint for the entire human race went to zero there. Or nearly zero. There was carbon in the bodies, so even when reduced to ashes —"

"Yeah, I don't want to talk about this anymore," Bethany said.

She put down the sheaf of papers and walked back to the other side of the room.

"I'm sorry," Ananda said. She wasn't positive what she was sorry for precisely, but she'd obviously done something wrong.

"It's cool," Bethany said.

"No, it probably isn't. You're just a—"

"Don't. Do not call me a child. Even if I'm the only one left on the planet, let's just not."

"All right," Ananda said.

Ananda sighed. She was never very good with adolescents. Even her own. And this didn't seem like the time to figure out how to get better at it, especially since she had exactly one adolescent— as Bethany said, in the world—to practice on.

Resolved to bridge the awkward silence she appeared to have created, Ananda walked across the room and took the photograph of the curious object down from the bulletin board.

"To answer your question from earlier," Ananda said, "no, I don't know what this is or what it does. But it's very interesting. Have you seen it up close?"

"No," Bethany said. "I don't even know where it is."

"I can show it to you. We don't even have to go near it if you don't want to. We can use the telescope. It's bright, most evenings."

"Because of the shimmer, yeah. That creeps me out too."

All of them had, at one time or another over the past few months, had close encounters with the traveling light show they called the shimmer. It seemed to appear and disappear at random, any time of day, for any length of time. It didn't care whether it was indoors or out, and had no personal preferences that they could discern about who it was visiting.

On more than one occasion, it appeared to be humanoid.

Ananda hadn't seen this herself, but both Robbie and Touré claimed to have jointly witnessed this, and Win had as well, on two separate occasions. Paul had too, but asserted that he thought he was looking at an angel (he didn't sound interested in relinquishing this opinion), which to Ananda sounded like a hallucination.

She didn't know what to make of these "humanoid" claims. If it was just a cloud of lights, hovering around the object, she might conclude—as she *had*, when she first witnessed it—that it was either emitted by or attracted to the white canister. The idea that some of the others were seeing a *person* implied an intelligence behind the lights. Not an intelligence that arrived in the form of a being with two arms, two legs, a head, and a torso; it could take any shape and *chose* that one. That could mean it was attempting to communicate.

It could also mean that the three or possibly four witnesses saw a shape that wasn't there.

That was the direction she should be leaning. It was one thing to argue that an unexplained phenomenon related to the unexplained object was manifesting around other planetary life-forms. That wasn't a leap, given the available facts. Asserting that the manifestation was an alien intelligence attempting to open lines of communication, on the other hand, was an extraordinary claim. It needed extraordinary evidence, and they just didn't have that.

"Well," Ananda said, "we don't have to see it to make this point. If you look at this picture, you'll notice differences between it and the object in the lot. Do you see these dents?"

Bethany looked at the photo. "On the top? Yeah."

"There are the vertical ones on the top, and there are pockmarks on the side as well. This was how the anomaly was found when they unearthed it."

"When was that? Do we know?"

"We don't. Robbie found this photo posted on a bulletin board in the oceanographic lab of all places. It's undated. We're still looking for the research. If it's even here. I've never been a part of a possible alien artifact investigation before, but I imagine a great deal of the work ends up classified."

"Sorry, did you say *alien?*"

Ananda sighed. "I said *possible.* My point about the marks on the top cap: They're not there now."

Bethany laughed and handed back the photo. "It got better, you're saying."

"I'm not sure what I'm saying, yet. I told you all that I saw that young man, right? Raymond, he said his name was."

"The vampire."

"Yes. I saw him here, by the device, hitting it. He made these marks."

"Wait, when did you see him hitting it?"

"A few months ago."

"This picture's from, what, seventy-five, eighty years ago? You're not making any sense."

"I agree. See this mark here? I made that one, with a piece of rebar. It's also not there now. I undid it when I hit the object."

"Well, sure, that sounds alien to me," Bethany said. "I don't get it. You can't undo a dent you made by hitting the dent."

She returned the photo to the bulletin board and stared at it for a few seconds. "There is one way," Ananda said.

Bethany stood motionless for a few seconds, staring at the photo as if it might reveal the answer through extended viewing.

"Nope," she said. "I'm stumped. What's the one way?"

Ananda smiled. "Think about it and come back when you've

figured it out. Maybe we'll have the same guess. Wouldn't that be something?"

Carol

It was beginning to look as if Carol would have to change her major.

This was based entirely on the selection of texts in Braille in the Hayden Library. They were mostly the newer books, which was fine; stale scientific texts weren't going to be all that helpful to anybody. Though a new definition of *stale* might be needed. They were all a solid fifty to seventy-five years old, but no new research had been taking place in the interim due to the cessation of humanity, so there was nothing more recent out there to replace them.

She had spent much of the prior week reading about cost-effective energy infrastructure scenarios for developing nations. It was dry reading to say the least. This week, she was trying to choose between biological engineering and the ethics of cloning, and something about neuroscience and dreams.

It wasn't a fantastic selection, but since she had no librarians to pester about a fiction shelf, it was all she was going to get until a larger resource could be identified. Boston had a library that was probably not underwater and hadn't been set on fire by anybody yet, so perhaps after the streets had been cleared she could check there. Harvard's libraries were likewise untapped, and there was a well-known school for the blind in Watertown that surely had a library of its own.

She could hope. The world had already been trending in the direction of audio recordings before everyone died, and now that electrical power was at a premium, Carol had no way to absorb all of that prerecorded knowledge.

This wasn't just a problem for her. The trend of digitizing everything meant there were fewer low-tech books to find, whether they were in Braille or not. There was also an enormous quantity of scientific discoveries archived on the MIT servers, entirely unobtainable by Ananda or anyone in the group, because somehow nobody considered a future without power.

Carol sighed and heard her sigh echo back. The library space sounded vast and was of course unheated. Nobody was around to say she couldn't take a book from the library and to the heated rooms half a campus away. She didn't, in part because she'd begun to enjoy the solitude of a library space, and in part because of the degree of independence her being there alone validated.

Learning the way to the library had taken a while to work out. She used Robbie's assistance the first few times, and Bethany's a few other times until she was confident about the possible routes. It helped enormously that the signs in the hallways all had Braille translations, so if on occasion she became lost she could reorient herself before long.

Being lost would be very bad for her. The campus was enormous; it might take the group *days* to find her.

She decided to skip past both the cloning book and the neuroscience book in favor of a volume on something called bioinformatics. It seemed perfectly daunting. She pulled it off the shelf.

Settling at one of the many long tables that took up the middle floor space of the library, Carol was a good distance from the door and in front of a window. She could feel the heat from the sun, which helped make the experience more comfortable, though she was dressed in anticipation of a cold room.

All aspects of their lives had been improved since the move from the dorm. Nearly every improvement had to do with the existence of electricity—a point not lost to her last week when reading about developing nations and access to energy. All seven seemed more capable of reasoned thought, because they were getting more sleep and were less concerned, in general, with whether or not they were going to survive until the next day.

It could have also given Touré and Robbie more opportunities to do what they wanted to do in the first place: head farther out of town to see if there were any other survivors. But Paul and Win *came* from out of town and could confirm there wasn't a large pool of living humans camping out on the other side of Route 128 or anywhere else that they'd seen. There was also Ananda's regular use of a shortwave radio, which went a long way toward proving the rest of the world was, if not dead, suffering from the same power shortage as they were locally.

With the question of survivors deemed unanswerable by current means, they were left with more time to do some of what Carol had been suggesting for a while—gathering a large collection of clothing.

There was now an entire room on their heated second floor that had nothing in it but clothes, in all shapes and sizes, for all seven of them. And so, Carol was sitting in the sun in the Hayden Library wearing a heavy men's parka, snow pants, leather combat boots that fit perfectly after three layers of socks, and a ball cap, reading Braille with fingerless wool knit gloves.

About an hour into it—the book was exactly as dense and dry as she'd expected—she heard the familiar pitter-pat of canine feet from the other end of the library.

"Over here, Nolan," she said, pulling out a piece of gristle from her pocket.

The coywolf walked over, panting and whining gently.

They had a system. When she was in the library alone, she left the door nearest the wolf den ajar. It was the only way he knew to get into the room to see her — there were several doors — so if it was closed, presumably he went on his way.

She put the gristle on the table and held out her hand, waiting. He greeted her by licking her fingers.

"Sit, Nolan," she said, holding up the treat. "Are you sitting?"

She really had no idea if he was, but liked to think so.

She gave him the treat. He ate it in one gulp and then curled up under the table.

It had not been her intention when first striking out on her own to conquer the library — and stave off the creeping death that was Total Boredom — to find Nolan and train him to act like the dog she pretended he was. *He'd* found *her*. All of them had been wandering the buildings for well over a month by then, so he must have already known — from her scent — where to look.

It was, of course, terrifying the first time he showed up, but only for a moment. He came alone — he always came alone — and never exhibited any aggressiveness toward her.

Carol didn't think he was *really* trained; she wasn't about to put a leash on him and bring him back to the quarters to meet the others. But having him there made it easier to get the reading done. If another wolf walked in, Nolan had her back.

Likewise, if anything or anyone else showed up.

After about an hour, Nolan sat up, then got to his feet and started to growl. He did this when an animal was out on the lawn on the other side of the window, but on this occasion he was facing the wrong way for that to be the case.

Carol caught a whiff of a familiar ammonia smell: the stranger was back again.

"Nolan doesn't like you," she said.

There was no answer, which wasn't new. Unlike their previous encounter in the dorm, the stranger didn't speak to her at all. He just stood in silence, keeping his reasons for doing so to himself.

He wasn't someone Carol *imagined,* certainly.

The coywolf settled into a low growl that she knew from experience would escalate shortly into barking.

"I don't like you either," she said. "Please go."

She heard a click and felt a rush of air, akin to what would happen had someone opened a door on the far end of the room. Nobody *had* opened a door, so this was something else.

Nolan whined, sniffed, and then curled up under the table again.

"Good boy," Carol said.

FOURTEEN

Bethany

THE FOLLOWING DAY MARKED A DRASTIC CHANGE IN THE weather.

According to Ananda, the angle of the sun indicated they were still in winter, but the temperature didn't agree. It was *hot*. Not *Let's figure out how to air-condition the building before we die* hot, but definitely *I didn't need a jacket to go outside* hot. It melted a lot of snow, and very quickly.

All of this was great news, because it was also the day Paul and Win were expected to return with fresh meat.

To celebrate the first occasion in which all seven of them were in the same place since the start of winter, the Apocalypse Seven planned a big party. That the weather appeared to be in a similarly celebratory mood meant they could expand that party to the only open, guaranteed land-animal-free space available: the roof.

This was Touré's suggestion. Bethany had to give him credit, because it was a good one.

She'd begun to appreciate that he maybe wasn't one hundred percent of a total asshat one hundred percent of the time. Her opinion was probably affected by the couple of weeks in which she thought he was dead—she surprised herself by tearing up when she first saw him alive, and on a *horse* somehow—and also by the change in circumstance.

He'd stopped calling her kid, too, and stopped treating her like one. Those were both big steps forward.

The party took an extra day to plan and execute. Thankfully, the weather didn't turn again in that time. For all any of them knew, warm weather meant another tornado was on the way.

But dammit if they weren't going to party first.

Robbie and Touré had a charcoal grill. They'd evidently been eyeing it for a while, as it had been a part of the window display at the hardware store only a couple of blocks away, which happened to be the same hardware store they'd looted for the axes.

They brought that up to the roof, then the charcoal and the lighter fluid. Win and Ananda scrounged up some chairs and a table, as well as some plates, forks, and knives.

Then Paul asked about something to drink other than water, and soon enough he and Bethany were making a beer run.

There was a liquor store on Massachusetts Ave.—it seemed to Bethany like *everything* was on Mass Ave., and maybe that was true—only a few blocks away. They took the same wheelbarrow previously used to ferry the unconscious Paul around and headed toward where the booze was.

"So how have you been?" he asked. They were walking down the middle of the street. Around them, the snow had turned into rivers of water, the trees were showing buds already, and in a few days, they'd probably hear birdsong again. It was nice.

"I'm fine," Bethany said. "How's the shoulder?"

"About as good as it's gonna get."

Paul stopped to take a look at the gun she had strapped to her hip. She'd spent two weeks making a holster out of old cloth for it.

It wasn't perfect—it was really just a pouch with a second strap for stabilization—but it worked well enough so she didn't have to carry around the gun in her hands. She could also store it in her bag, but didn't like how long it took to reach it when it was in there.

"Cute," he said. "You wear that everywhere?"

"Only when I leave the castle," she said.

He laughed. "The castle," he said. "I like that. Touré?"

"Of course."

"He's special, that one. So, is the safety on?"

"Of course it is. It bounces all over the place when I run. Maybe we can find a real holster."

"There's a sporting goods store downtown," he said. "Win loaded up her quiver there. Maybe next time we can find a holster for you."

"That'd be great."

Paul was also armed; he had a shotgun in a sling on his back. It looked a thousand times cooler than what Bethany was packing. She wondered if he'd let her try it someday.

"You been running around a lot out here?" he asked.

"A little. Why, are they worried about me?"

"They are. Don't take it personally. It's everyone's prerogative to worry about everyone else now. Don't think any of us have really come to grips with what's happened. It's too big. Much easier to concentrate on the little stuff, like *Where'd Bethany get to?*"

"Yeah," she said.

Bethany didn't know how well she was coping either, so she could hardly judge how everyone else went about it. And her trips away from the castle, sometimes overnight, clearly did alarm the others. Carol, in particular, had tried to talk to her about it on multiple occasions.

Bethany knew how it looked, but had no interest in explaining it to anybody — she'd been going back home ... and preferred to keep that information to herself.

The idea was to find out all she could about what had become of her family in the years since her disappearance. It was something none of the others could really do. Touré *maybe* could, but while he was raised in the same area, she didn't know if his parents still lived there by the time of the whateverpocalypse. He probably didn't know either, but he never showed an interest in checking.

The thing that stuck with Bethany the most was that her brother, Dustin, grew up, got married, moved to Tucson, and had a kid. Seeing his family portrait in her mom's bedroom was incredibly disturbing, because Dustin's son looked exactly like she remembered *him* looking last time she saw him.

On the same day she made that particular discovery, Bethany spent that night in her old bedroom, which was a phenomenally bad idea. She got almost no sleep and what little she did get was full of nightmares involving strange men in the shadows who smelled like pee.

Worst of all, when she woke up, the whateverpocalypse had still happened; it didn't all turn out to be a dream.

"I think that's the store," she said. She was in charge of the wheelbarrow because of Paul's various possibly permanent injuries. She steered toward it.

There was a metal gate pulled over the front door with a big padlock.

"Well, no wonder those two never tried to get in here," Paul said.

"I don't think alcohol was high on anyone's list of priorities."

Paul pulled down his shotgun, meaning to use it to open the door.

"Hold on, hold on," she said. She lifted the padlock and took a look. "Yeah, I got this."

"Ha. Just as well. I don't know if I have enough shot to put a dent in that lock."

"It's always brute force with you guys," she said, pulling out some bits of wire she'd been using to open doors. It had already turned into one of the more useful skills the team had, especially when a quarter of the doors in the castle came up locked. Robbie and Touré were talking about bringing her along to pick some of the ones they couldn't get open themselves. It would have been a whole lot easier if they just figured out how to pick a lock—it really wasn't difficult—but she didn't mind being needed.

Paul put away his gun and waited. "You had water," he said.

"What's that?"

"I said, 'You had water.' That's why nobody brought up alcohol."

"I guess."

She had a joke about Paul turning the tap water into wine so they could skip this expedition entirely, but she kept it to herself. She found Paul really interesting—of all of them, he had the best stories—but the God stuff made her uncomfortable.

"There it is," she said.

The lock popped open in her hands. She tossed it to the ground and pulled the gate back. The door on the other side was glass in a metal frame with another lock.

"Okay, you can break the glass if you want," she said.

"You can't pick that lock?" he asked.

"No, I can, I just don't want to be here all day."

He shrugged, and shattered the glass with the butt of the shotgun, then reached through and unlocked the door.

"Not sure you're even supposed to be in here, miss," he said. "You're a little young."

"I'm over a hundred years old, mister," she said. "Let's find some booze."

He laughed and held the door for her.

"After you."

Touré

1

Touré burned himself twice while trying to cook the venison steaks.

When they set up the grill, he was under the impression that someone who had manned a barbecue once in their lives might take the lead. Specifically, he'd expected Paul to step up, seeing as how he was the closest thing they had to a dad. (Ananda was the closest to a mom. Both appeared to be somewhere between their late thirties and mid-fifties, at least to Touré, who, again, was bad at guessing ages.)

But since it had been officially his idea, everyone stood aside and let him burn himself repeatedly. Never mind that the whole concept of a party came out of Touré and Robbie brainstorming the best way to ease the group into the idea that Robbie had recently punched an alien in the face. They couldn't very well share that thought process, and so apparently everyone went in assuming this was something Touré was familiar with in some concrete way.

He was not. When Touré tried to get the fire started, he ended up with flames that either shot up past his head or threatened to go out entirely. When he put the steaks on the grill, he didn't have any tongs, because he didn't know he'd need them, so he made do first with his hands and then a dinner fork. He eventually added a towel, so whenever a steak caught fire he had something to put it out with.

It wasn't going well. A couple of times he turned around to see half of the Apocalypse Seven with alarmed expressions on their faces and trying to hide it. He finally recognized that they were just trying to be polite.

"Guys, I do not know how to cook," he said. "If anyone here does, please step up."

"Oh, thank God," Win said. "We were about to have Roasted Touré for dinner."

"You're going to burn the meat," Paul said. "Step out of the way."

Other than that minor hiccup, it went really well. They all got their own bottle to drink—because they forgot cups but fortunately remembered a bottle opener—and ate too much.

The meat was delicious, but the highlight was definitely the surprise dessert Ananda unveiled: a gigantic can of peaches.

"I know this isn't much," she said, holding it up, "and we're going to have to address the balance in our diet soon. We have hardly any starches or greens. The Noot bars are somewhat balanced, but we'll need to find a long-term source of vitamin C . . ."

"Hey," Bethany said, "are you going to open that can or what?"

"Sorry, I'll save the speeches for later. Let's dig in, shall we?"

After the meal came a number of orders of business, which essentially just meant everyone took turns standing up and delivering a little speech.

Touré started by thanking everyone for coming and for stopping him from setting himself on fire, and then compared them to a Dungeons and Dragons party. The metaphor clearly made a lot of sense to him but probably not to anyone else.

He ceded the floor to Bethany, who surprised all of them by

talking eloquently about how everyone felt like family. Touré thought this sentiment was leavened at least partly by the wine bottle she was in the middle of finishing on her own, but it was still really nice.

Win was more businesslike. She gave a rundown on how the hunting was locally and discussed plans for an expedition back to the part of the state where she'd discovered Elton to see if there were any other horses out there. Considering how useful Elton had been, it made good sense, but Touré didn't think that was why she wanted to do it. She was trying to find Elton some company.

Paul followed up Win by thanking everybody for the party, describing what the outer reaches of their domain currently looked like, and saying a blessing. "I would have said grace before we started," he said, "but you all looked awfully hungry."

Next came Ananda . . . and a long lecture. She'd clearly been saving up a few revelations for when they were all together again, and she was going to lay them on everyone all at once. With drinks in their hands, no less. It had long been Touré's opinion that alcohol made everything Ananda had to say easier to deal with.

The presentation included data written on a whiteboard. Touré flashed back to every classroom experience he'd ever had and not in a good way.

Her talk began with the other ways in which the world ended.

"As we know, the planet reached one of the points of no return climate-wise around 2039," she said, pointing to one of the numbers on the whiteboard. "That was when we hit the plus-two degrees threshold. Does everyone know what that is?"

They did not, and thus began the lecture. When it was over, they learned that some of the things the world went through while they were away included famines, which led to wars, which led to refugees, which led to more famines. Touré lost focus several times—

again, just like those childhood classes, now with alcohol thrown in—but he did find it interesting that the invention of the Noot bar was likely in direct response to famine conditions. "Taste would have been a secondary consideration," she said.

There were also coastal floods—Carol was alarmed to learn her family's home in South Florida might be as underwater as the Boston piers—and a marked increase in extreme weather events.

"Extreme weather events like, say, tornadoes in Cambridge?" Robbie asked.

"That's a trivial example," she said, "but yes."

"It wasn't trivial when we were a few feet away from one."

The part that Ananda found interesting, in that way of hers that made her sound like a cyborg, was that five years later, the increase in atmospheric carbon levels stopped.

"As if everyone on the planet decided at the same time to stop contributing to global warming," she said. "Because . . . well, as you know, everyone appears to have died. The statistics bear out the year 2044 as being when that happened."

"Jesus," Win said.

It was all anyone had to say for a few seconds as the full magnitude of what Ananda was showing them really sank in.

"I'm sorry," Ananda said. "We did know this already."

"Nanda," Paul said. He was the only one who called her that. Nobody had asked why or if they should do it too. Touré thought he just started doing it on his own and Ananda hadn't figured out how to tell him to stop. "The problem we're all having, I think, is that it looks like you just proved what we hadn't been able to prove before now. *Everyone* died that year. *Everyone.*"

"Except for us," Carol said.

"Yes," Ananda said. "I guess that is what it means."

They all fell silent again. Ananda didn't look like she was sure whether or not to continue. Maybe she was mentally reviewing the rest of the presentation for other facts bound to upset non-cyborgs.

"Hey, guys," Touré said, holding up his bottle. It was an Italian red with a big price tag that tasted like every other wine he'd ever had. "To the human race!"

"To the human race," everyone said. They drank.

"All right," Ananda said, after a suitable pause. "Should I continue?"

"Go ahead," Win said. "We can always go out for more alcohol if this gets worse."

2

It didn't get worse, just more confusing.

Ananda shared the photograph Touré and Robbie found of the weird object everyone had spent the past couple of months pretending didn't exist—at least, that was how it felt to Touré. An object with no power running to or from it was producing a light show that followed them around; it should be dominating every one of their conversations until they figured out what it was and what it did. Instead, they'd ignored it and had more or less done the same with the shimmer.

After displaying the photograph, Ananda went on about how the marks on the top somehow got erased if you hit them very hard and asked for opinions on what that could mean.

"Let me see if I have this," Paul said, in his own deliberative style. "When was that picture taken?"

"We can't be sure," Ananda said. "Whenever the object was unearthed, which could theoretically be anywhere between 2020—because it wasn't here when I was—and 2044."

"Well, it wasn't 2020," he said. "Just look at the scene. You've got a hastily built fence, an army cordon that doesn't look like it's all that hard to go around, and only covers two directions. You've got a building they never finished taking down. Everything about it says they didn't have long to look at it before . . . well, you know."

"Whateverpocalypse," Touré said.

"Right," Paul said.

"You're skirting the point," Ananda said. "It's a photo taken before now showing evidence of damage that didn't occur until recently."

"Yeah, that doesn't make sense to me," Paul said.

"Oh, I understand!" Bethany said. "It's going in reverse!"

Ananda smiled. "Yes, cause and effect seem to be reversed, pertaining specifically to this object. Which effectively means that it's temporally inverted."

"Well . . ." Paul said. "That's . . . interesting. Dunno what it means." He looked around for some help.

"I'm gonna go on record as agreeing with Paul," Touré said. "That doesn't make a single bit of sense without using the word *magic*. And you probably don't want to do that."

"No, I don't," Ananda said.

"You said before that when you hit it, you healed it," Robbie said. "Now you're saying you're causing the damage after it was already . . . Yeah, no. I think Win's right, we're going to need another alcohol run for this."

"Cheers," Win said, holding up her own bottle. "You all sound like a college keg party at two in the morning. Oh, hey, am I the only one who gets that?"

"I never went to college," Paul said.

"We were just starting," Carol said, speaking for both herself and Robbie.

"I didn't go to the parties," Touré said.

Ananda laughed. "Neither did I," she said.

"You're all nerds," Win said, with a laugh.

"Hey!" Bethany said.

"Except for you. Sorry, Ananda, please continue. But if you start asking *How high is up?* or whatever, I'm not going to be able to control myself."

"How high is . . . ?"

"Sorry," Win said, "never mind. Keep talking."

"Uh, yes," Ananda said. "As I was saying, the evident cause-effect inversion is complicated. I've been afraid to draw any real conclusions from it, absent additional data. It's possible, in the twenty-four-year gap, that we developed technology that could make such a thing exist. Mind you, I don't know *what it's for,* and as long as that's the case, I can't know why it was important to build. But first, it would be good to know if its creation was within the bounds of the possible for the human race. My conclusion, however tentative, is that I don't think so."

She took a moment, perhaps to allow everyone to posit their own conclusions before rendering hers.

"I think," she said, "that this might be an alien object."

There was another long silence. It was considerably less ponderous than the first one.

It ended when Touré started laughing, then Robbie, and then the others fell in.

"I don't understand," Ananda said.

"Oh, hell," Touré said, "we all figured that was the case a long time ago."

"The shimmer," Win said.

"Yes," Robbie said. "So the device is probably alien; that's fine. What about the shimmer? Do you know anything about that yet?"

"No," Win said, pointing. "I mean, *there's the shimmer.*"

It was hovering off the edge of the roof.

Christmas tree lights in a washing machine, Touré thought.

He'd seen it three times already, possibly four, if the memory of what he saw during his fever was to be taken seriously. Often enough that he felt justified in observing that something seemed different about it this time. It was a weird idea, given this was just a cloud of lights.

But this time it looked *angry.*

From the edge of the roof, it swept forward and dive-bombed Ananda. She yelped in surprise. Then it went from surrounding her to examining everyone else: passing through Touré; hovering menacingly over Bethany, who looked ready to take out her gun and shoot it; bouncing between Win and Carol; knifing into Paul.

"What's it doing?" Carol asked, in response to the yelps and yips everyone around her was uttering.

"It's acting like it's pissed off at us," Touré said.

"Well, *that's* different," Carol said, at the same moment the shimmer traveled through her. That she didn't *know* it was passing through her was the best proof that any sensations they might think they were having because of an interaction with the light show was probably all in their heads.

The encounter ended with the shimmer spinning above them for several seconds before zipping off toward Boston.

"Well," Paul said, after a decent moment of silence, "I'd say producing that light show is one of the things that alien machine of yours is doing, Nanda. Maybe we should figure out why."

"Soon," Bethany said. "I didn't like that at all."

"I agree, of course," Ananda said. "It may take some time. I need access to the research conducted on it prior to the . . ."

She stared at Touré, as if saying, *Please don't make me say it.*

"The whateverpocalypse," he said.

"Yes, prior to that. It was studied in detail. Even if they only learned enough to conclude that evacuation was a wise decision, in 2044 they had access to technology I don't have and some technology I don't understand. I'm saying it may be a while before we have concrete answers."

Touré looked at Robbie, nodded back. It was time.

"We might have a shortcut," Robbie said.

"Oh?" Ananda said. "Did you find something?"

"Kind of."

"What we're thinking," Touré said, "is that the best way to find out what the alien device does is by asking an alien."

"Sure, dude," Bethany said. "Next time you see one, go ahead."

"I think I will, thanks."

Ananda flashed a somewhat condescending smile.

"You're talking about how the lights sometimes look human?" she asked. "Because there's a great deal of work in human pattern-recognition tendencies that could explain this."

"No, no, no," Robbie said. "That isn't what he meant."

He stood up next to the whiteboard like a kid taking over the class midlecture.

"We want to tell you guys something," he said, "if you're done, Ananda. For now. We can go back to you if you want after."

"Please," she said. "Go ahead."

She sat down. Her expression suggested it was *not* fine.

Robbie looked nervous. He took a sip from the can of beer he was working on, put it down, and did a little pacing.

"Well, go on," Paul said. "We're all friends here."

"Thanks. I'm not sure how to put this delicately, so I'm ... I'll just say it. I think—we think, Touré and I—the reason the seven of us didn't die with everyone else was because we were abducted by aliens. We also think—we *know*—we've been visited by those same aliens since then."

Ananda looked somewhat exasperated. "How could you possibly know that for a fact?" she asked.

"We know this," Robbie said, "because a couple of days ago I punched one in the face."

He was met with a lot of stunned silence.

"Way to sell it, Robert," Touré said.

"I think I need a bottle of stronger alcohol," Carol said, "before I'm ready to hear more."

FIFTEEN

Win

1

WIN DIDN'T KNOW ROBBIE THAT WELL.

He seemed like a pretty stable person and levelheaded enough to keep himself, a teen, and a blind woman alive despite not having any evident survival skills. That took at least a little wisdom and probably a generous dollop of luck. Waking up in the middle of a metropolis was one such example of that good fortune. If he'd opened his eyes to a farmhouse like she had, it would have gone differently for him.

The point was, he didn't seem like the kind of person who was susceptible to ridiculousness. Touré, perhaps, could encourage a wilder temperament in those around him, but she didn't think Touré was really like that either. She may have been the only one of them—Touré himself included—who thought his trips into fantasy were masquerading as insight none of the rest of them had access to.

No, this came from Robbie; Touré just bought into it first.

She had to admit, the abduction part . . . made some sense. Even Ananda agreed that it fit the evidence. She then pointed out that *taken to the North Pole by Santa* also fit the evidence, so maybe that wasn't as big a deal as they thought it was.

An obvious counterpoint to this argument was that while it may be true Santa could have abducted the seven of them instead of a space alien, Robbie didn't punch Santa in the face. Nobody made that argument, though, because it was clear Ananda simply didn't believe Robbie or Touré actually had had a physical altercation with their bogeyman.

Win wasn't sure if she was ready to believe it either.

The idea that they had all been abducted created a whole raft of new questions that none of them could possibly answer, such as (1) Why them? (2) Where were they taken? (3) What happened to their memories? (4) Why didn't they age? (5) Why were they put back again? . . . and so on. The problem was that there was no way to answer any of that without interrogating an actual alien. That should have been where the whole discussion ended, because any being who was capable of taking seven people—or eight, if the departed Raymond was properly included in their number—from the planet, years apart from one another, with nobody being the wiser . . . *that* being was going to be damn hard to catch.

But they still wanted to try.

"He came up behind us in the dungeon," Touré explained, shortly after Robbie connected his alien to the man Carol supposedly encountered in the dorm. "We'll have to go back down there and jump him when he does it again."

"All seven of us?" Paul asked. "Don't you think he'll notice we're all there?"

"We're *the idea guys,* not the tacticians," Touré said. "Maybe you and the goddess of the hunt here can stalk him."

"Not if he can just disappear," Paul said. "I have that right, don't I? He can disappear?"

"He did a thing," Robbie said, "with his arm, before he vanished."

"A thing with his arm," Paul repeated.

"Maybe he's waving his magic wand," Bethany suggested.

"No, he's employing some sort of technology," Carol said. "It makes a clicking sound."

"How do you know that?" Robbie asked.

"I heard it. If we can take that away from him, we may be able to punch him in the face a few more times."

"*When* did you hear it?" Robbie asked. "Not in the dorm. You would have said so."

"Not in the dorm," Carol said. She sighed, then, and shook her head. Win had seen her do this before. It usually meant Carol was debating something internally.

"Here?" Touré asked. "In the castle?"

"I don't want you to think I'm in danger," Carol said.

That was in response to Touré but directed at Robbie. Those two had an interesting relationship: very formal in many ways, but they took care of each other through tiny gestures of intimacy.

"He watches me regularly," Carol said. "I never said so because I didn't think you'd believe me."

The concern on Robbie's face was something to witness. He looked horrified at the prospect of Carol being harmed.

They've been through a lot together, Win thought.

Though Robbie's concern was displayed entirely visually, Carol somehow seemed to hear it. "I'm safe, Robbie," she said. "I have protection. The only reason I'm telling you this at all is that if he's real and you want to catch him, I can tell you where he'll be aside from the dungeon."

"In the library," Robbie said.

"Yes," Carol said. "But first, you're all going to have to introduce yourselves to Nolan."

2

A week later, Win was huddled between a stack of books and an empty bookshelf at the edge of the balcony floor of the Hayden Library.

She was under a blanket, which seemed weirdly juvenile to her. Sure, the library was cold, so the added warmth was welcome, but the idea that a blanket might make it so the monster couldn't see her was a notion she'd grown out of long ago.

She had a clear view of Carol and Nolan at a table near the window, thirty feet away.

Nolan was a damn *wolf*. As soon as Carol explained this, Win decided all four of them—Robbie, Carol, Touré, and Bethany—were entirely out of their minds and not to be trusted. Madness induced by overconsumption of Noot, perhaps. That they'd managed to survive on their own was a miracle.

Nolan was the reason it took so long to set this plan into motion. First, each of them had to meet with him someplace outside of the library. This was so the alien didn't see them meeting the wolf, which was just flat stupid, because they didn't know what he could and couldn't see and hear, regardless of what part of the castle they were in. For all they knew, he heard their conversation on the roof and the follow-up one in the living quarters when they'd come up with this very plan. Meeting the wolf in the library was surely not going to be the part where they blew the trap.

They did it anyway. Carol found a place down the hall from the library—she'd trained the creature to use a certain door—and waited for him to discover her. Then, one by one, Win, Paul, Robbie, and Touré came through a second door and introduced themselves.

Nolan seemed okay with Robbie. But he didn't like Paul—he appeared to remember their first encounter—and he would have probably torn out Touré's throat if Carol hadn't whacked him on the head with her cane.

He actively liked Win, which was strange; she had her hand on her knife the entire time and had thought very seriously about gutting him while the coywolf was licking her face. She thought it was a good thing Carol didn't befriend a boar instead, because that would have been a different story. Win didn't like the wolves, but she *really* didn't like boars.

Once that was done, they put the rest of the plan in motion. Win, Paul, Robbie, and Touré would sneak into the library in the morning—again, one at a time—and take up tactical positions where they would remain until the early afternoon, which was when Carol usually arrived.

It was a ridiculous plan, and it wasn't going to work. But with new snow outside and no need to go hunting or do much of anything else, they also had nothing better to do.

May as well humor them, Win thought.

Carol showed up on schedule, found her way to Nolan's door and cracked it open, then took her seat and started reading.

Win wondered what Carol's plan was if someone other than Nolan walked through that door. She decided Carol probably didn't have one, because the woman was evidently working out the kinks on a death wish.

Nolan did walk through the door as expected and nearly blew the game right away. About halfway to Carol, he stopped and sniffed the air, identifying at least one of the others.

"Hey, puppy," Carol said, waving a piece of meat in the air. This got him walking again. Crisis averted. Nolan curled up under the table like a good dog.

And so they waited.

After what had to be an hour (*fix the clocks* was high on Win's personal agenda for the springtime) she started to wonder at what point they should call this whole thing off. She was getting a cramp while waiting for the arrival of a figment of everyone's imagination, and needed there to be an all-clear, never-mind, ha-ha-just-kidding signal.

Does the alien even show up every day? she wondered. *Did anybody ask Carol this?*

Win had convinced herself that he wasn't going to this day, so when it finally happened, she thought her eyes were bugging out on her. The sun's angle through the window indicated late afternoon and elongated shadows. About ten feet from Carol, between the light from two windows, one of those shadows started growing independently . . . with nothing to cast it.

It grew, driving out the light instead of the other way around. This wasn't how shadows worked.

Then it gained some kind of form: a tall man in a black cloak.

I've seen you before, Win thought.

Nolan saw it and started growling. Carol couldn't see it, of course, but knew it was there all the same.

"You're back," Carol said.

The wolf barked but didn't advance. The bark caused the figure to raise its right arm.

Now.

Win loosed an arrow and at around the same time Paul, at the far end of the first floor, fired a shot with his rifle, both of them aiming for the right arm. Both appeared to find the mark.

"Ahh!" the alien shouted.

"*Get him, Nolan,*" Carol whispered.

Robbie and Touré jumped out from behind bookshelves a few

yards away and broke into a sprint. The wolf easily beat them
both.

Nolan launched himself at the alien, hit him right in the chest,
and knocked him onto his back.

Robbie dove to the floor to grab the device the figure had
dropped. Touré looked like he was trying to insert himself between
the intruder and Nolan before deciding this was an incredibly foolish thing to do.

"Get it off me, get it off me!" the alien cried out in a very nor-
mal-sounding voice. He was hand-checking the wolf, who was a
few seconds from making the alien impossible to interrogate, provided the intruder's throat was where everyone else's was.

"Nolan, down!" Carol said. She stood and tapped her cane on
the wolf's back to get his attention. It worked. He backed off the
alien and waited for a treat. Then Touré was on top of the intruder.
Paul, still nursing his knee, reached the scene last and pointed his
gun at the alien's head.

Win stayed where she was, with another arrow nocked.

"God, he *smells*," Touré said.

"Guys," the alien said, "we're all friends here."

"I don't think so," Paul said.

Touré backed away to give Paul and Win clean shots if necessary. The alien raised his hands.

"Look, I'm Noah, okay?" he said. "Call me Noah. And you're
Paul, and that's Touré, and Robbie, and Carol. Win's on the balcony. I know all of you, all right?"

"We don't know *you*," Paul said.

"No, I guess not. You wouldn't. Look, I can explain all of this. But
you gotta do me a favor first."

Paul looked at Robbie. "Can I shoot him?" he asked. "I feel like I
want to shoot him."

Robbie shrugged. "Yeah, maybe," Robbie said.

"Just keep me out of the light," Noah the alien said. "That's all."

"Are you gonna melt?" Touré asked.

"No, I'm not gonna *melt*, Touré. Come on. It can't be allowed to see me here. If it does, it's going to kill all of you, just like it did everyone else. Okay? So put me in a dark room somewhere and I'll tell you whatever you want to know."

"Get up," Paul said.

The alien got to his feet, albeit very slowly. He moved in a decidedly human way, although Win had to admit, she didn't know what an alien way to move around might look like.

Robbie stepped up, slowly, and pulled back Noah's hood.

Noah had a big, bulbous green head, black eyes, no nose, and a tiny mouth, just the way Robbie had described it. The raised hands consisted of elongated fingers—only three of them, and a thumb—with an extra knuckle.

"Well?" Carol said.

"It's an alien, all right," Paul said.

"What do you mean, it's going to kill all of us?" Robbie asked Noah.

I thought Noah was just part of your fever dream, Touré, Win thought.

"Dark room first," Noah said. "Someplace without windows."

Robbie

1

Finding a room away from any windows wasn't all that difficult.

There was the entire labyrinthine tunnel system, which appeared designed specifically so no MIT student ever had to contend with direct sunlight and fresh air, but it lacked room for a proper interrogation.

What they used instead was a lecture hall in the chemistry building. It was an area Robbie and Touré had already searched and was just an underground tunnel stop away. The wolves didn't know the building, because the tunnel was the best way to get to it without coming in through the outside and the wolves didn't use the tunnels. (Carol wanted to take Nolan with them, which would have meant introducing one of the pack to a tunnel. It took them a little while to convince her that was a bad idea and to send him back instead.)

It was a raked auditorium, with the chairs looking down on the lectern. That was where they put Noah. Since he'd insisted on there being no sunlight in the room, they were using torches to see by, which just made the alien seem that much creepier.

Touré fetched Bethany and Ananda, while Paul and Win debated tying Noah to a chair.

"We don't even have rope," Win was saying. "What are you going to use?"

"My belt is a rope," Paul said.

"Guys, you really don't have to, I can't go anywhere," Noah said. Then he coughed. "Believe you me, I would if I could."

He shook his right hand, where the arrow and/or bullet had struck him. He'd been wounded, but not seriously. When they picked him up off the ground, there was a small pool of yellow liquid left behind on the floor.

Bethany was right, Robbie thought. *He bleeds yellow. We'll have to apologize to her.*

The device Noah had dropped and Robbie had picked up was a small metal stick with a plunger button on the end. It looked like the back half of a large syringe or a bomb trigger in a movie.

Robbie said, "What's this do?"

"Push the button," Noah said. "Find out for yourself."

"Will it send you back to wherever you came from?"

Noah shrugged. He had almost nothing one might call shoulders, so this looked really odd.

"Will it send *me* to wherever you came from?" Robbie asked.

"Give it a try," Noah said.

"Don't," Carol said. She was sitting next to Robbie in the front row, as if patiently waiting for the lecture to start.

Noah laughed. His speaking voice managed to be simultaneously deep and nasally; his laugh was kind of a low chortle. It was the only sound he made that didn't come off as exactly human, like whatever translation program he was using couldn't interpolate laughter.

"I'm kidding, Robbie," he said. "Press the button or not, it won't do anything. It only works on me, and I have to be holding it. Please don't lose it, though."

Noah looked at Win and Paul. "So what's the consensus?" he asked. "You tying me down or not?"

Win turned to Robbie. "What do you think?" she asked. "He's your prisoner."

"Leave him be," Robbie said.

"Okey-doke," she said.

"I'll just keep my rifle trained on him, if that's okay with everyone," Paul said.

Ananda burst into the room then, trailed by Touré and a worried-looking Bethany. "Where is it?" Ananda asked. She headed straight for the stage. "Oh, my goodness," she said. "Look at you."

Paul and Win stepped back to give Ananda room for whatever perambulations were going to be a part of her process. They'd all seen her work before; she was a whirlwind pacer.

"Hi, Ananda," Noah said.

She gasped. "It speaks," she said.

"We told you he did," Touré said.

"Yes, well, you'll excuse me for mistaking *that* for exaggeration."
After circling Noah a few times, she stepped closer.

"May I?" she asked him, holding up a hand.

"Sure," Noah said, "whatever you gotta do."

She touched Noah's face and head, then stood behind him and
pulled gently on his skull.

He laughed. "It's attached," he said.

She moved next to him and touched his chest, on one side and
then the other. Then she felt along his back.

She leaned in close and sniffed the side of his face.

"You're wearing a device," she said. "It's providing ammonia to
you through the hole in your face. Can I call that a nose?"

"You can call it what you like," he said. "And you're right about
all of that. Prolonged exposure to oxygen will end up killing me, so
I'm sort of hoping you guys'll let me go after this."

"Well," Ananda said, stepping back and turning to address the
lecture hall. "He's impossible."

"How do you mean?" Win asked.

"He's a bipedal alien with rubbery skin who speaks the vernac-
ular flawlessly, and so he's clearly a regular man in a costume. Yet
he's breathing pure ammonia, has only five ribs per side, three fingers and a thumb per hand, and no beating heart where a human
being's beating heart would be."

"So he's an alien," Bethany said. She was sitting one row behind
Robbie, next to Touré. He noted that she had her gun in her lap.

"Yes," Ananda said. "Except it's ridiculous that an alien would
actually look like this. Imagine the vast number of evolutionary

pressures on this planet, over hundreds of thousands of years—millions, even—necessary to produce us, a bipedal apex species. He was standing? And walking?"

"Yep," Paul said.

"Then his musculature is such that it would allow him to survive in this gravity, at this atmospheric concentration, and *balance* on two legs. The number of variables is preposterous. He would have to have evolved on a planet the same size as ours, with an ammonia-rich atmosphere, and would have somehow had to win the same historical lottery we did, just to develop the intelligence necessary to understand speech. Aliens are not impossible. Aliens that look this much like *us* are the stuff of bad dreams suffered by people with overactive imaginations, and special-effects artists."

"Can I speak?" Noah asked.

"Go on," she said.

"You're right," he said. "She's right. It's *practically* impossible, which is just another way of saying highly unlikely. I mean, I don't know, maybe being a biped with opposable thumbs is a requirement for interstellar travel. But, look—I'm real, this is really me, and this is really me talking. I'm not saying I learned the *language*. I've got a really great translation package, that's all. But I get what you're saying, Ananda, I do. I'm a scientist too, and believe me, you guys weird me out just as much as I do you."

Ananda looked as if she had ten things to say all at once and yet couldn't figure out which to say first, and didn't know how to proceed from there. She shrugged and faced the room. "I cede the floor, but not the argument," she said. "Who wants to go first?"

At no time in his life did Robbie consider himself a leader. Even way back as far as grade school, he was the kid in the back who thought not socializing was less of a hassle than actually having friends. A group dynamic in which he was the one who made the decisions was just out of the question. Even in the dorm, when it was four—and then three—of them, he was always just one voter.

It made no sense, then, that when Ananda asked who was going to be leading the interrogation of the extraterrestrial in their midst, everyone turned to him.

But he wasn't going to let the opportunity to interrogate an alien pass him by.

"Yeah, all right," he said. "Let's start with an obvious one: Why did you abduct us?"

"No, that's the wrong question," Noah said. "You don't wanna ask me that first, Robbie."

Paul, off to one side of the stage, said, "Answer the man's question," in a low growl, over the top of his rifle.

"Rein it in, pastor. I'll answer—it's just not the best place to start."

"Okay," Robbie said. "What happened to the rest of the human race? Did you do that?"

"That's the question. And no, I did not! I love you guys. But I was there when it happened, and I tried to stop it. You've seen the sparkling, right? What do you call it? The shimmer? Good name, very spooky. *That's* the alien you're looking for."

"The lights are an alien intelligence?" Ananda asked.

"They are indeed. I know that bugs you, but it's true."

"And they're who you're hiding from?" Robbie asked. "Here in the dark?"

"Yeah, but not for my sake. For yours. Just *one* of them wiped out the entire human race, and as soon as it figures out how you guys survived, it's gonna take out the rest of you. It's not going to hurt me, but if it *sees* me, it'll put two and two together and work out that you were off-world when it happened. Once the mystery is solved, you're no longer interesting. Then it'll be *boom*, bye-bye to the rest of humanity."

Carol grabbed Robbie's hand and squeezed. He didn't know if that was because she believed what she'd just heard or the opposite.

"The entire human race . . ." Robbie said. "Just one of them did that?"

"What are they?" Bethany asked quietly. She was speaking to Robbie, not to Noah.

"Does anyone here know what a tachyon is?" Noah asked.

"Yes," Ananda said.

"Faster-than-light particles," Touré said. "But they're, like, made up."

"They're *hypothetical*, not *made up*," Ananda said. "There's a difference."

"But it's not a thing, right?" Touré asked. "Nothing goes faster than light. I thought we all learned that."

"You guys are cute," Noah said.

"Hey," Win said. "How about a little less condescension from the spaceman?"

"Sorry."

"It's not possible to take a slower-than-light particle and accelerate it past the speed of light," Ananda said. "There's no prohibition on particles that *exist* at that speed."

"There you go," Noah said. "Look, it's stupid complicated. If I tried to explain all of it to you, I'd be dead before I got to the important stuff. The speed of light is the speed of massless particles. Anything with a positive mass can't go faster. Particles on the other side . . . We'll call it negative mass. It's not really accurate, but it's close. Since human beings never got this far with the science, you don't have any words that really describe this properly."

"So the shimmer is another alien," Robbie said. "And it's made up of . . . what's the word?"

"Tachyons," Touré said.

"Yes and no," Noah said. "There are other particles on the other side of the light speed barrier. Tachyons are one, but there're others. Incredibly high-energy stuff. But yes, these creatures are made from those kinds of particles."

"But we can *see* it," Ananda said. "How can we see something that is gone before light reaches it?"

"Good, good. Smart. But you're *not* seeing it. What you're seeing is . . . like a contrail, sort of. The evidence that something *was* there. Tachyon-type faster-than-light particles don't interact with us usually. But like I said, they're *very* energetic; they can excite an electron on the way by. Again, I'm dumbing this down. Not because you guys are dumb; you're just missing about ten generations of physics."

"Is that how they killed everyone?" Robbie asked. "Exciting the particles, or . . . I guess I don't really know what we're talking about."

"Kind of. These are beings made of energy. Sometimes they radiate that energy. If you're near them when that happens, there isn't going to be very much of you left."

"Turning bones to powder?" Win asked.

"Among other things. And given how fast they move, they could sweep the whole globe in a matter of hours and nobody would be able to stop them. That's what happened before, and I'm sure that's what happened here, too."

"Before what?" Robbie asked.

"I told you, I'm a scientist. I've been studying this race of . . . we don't even have a name for them. Tachyonites. Let's call them that. I've been studying them for a while, and this isn't the first planet

I've seen one of them do this. Not *my* home planet, thankfully, but others. I always got there too late and had to piece it all together after the fact. They're traveling extinction engines. This time, I thought I might be early enough to help."

"The anomalous object," Ananda said. "You put that there."

"It's a prototype. It was supposed to prevent the mass extinction here. It didn't work, obviously, but I made some adjustments." He looked at Robbie. "Okay, ask me now."

"What? Oh. Why did you abduct us?"

"Every time a Tachyonite interacts with another life-form, it leaves behind a signature on the atomic level. It's not something anyone on this planet would have been able to notice; you have to be able to detect tachyons in the first place, and nobody on Earth figured out how to do that until, like, Earth year 2041. *Way* too late. All seven of you guys—eight, actually—had traces of that signature. Poor Raymond, by the way. That was rough. I tried to talk him down, but I think I just made it worse. He totally snapped. Good kid, too."

"I don't understand," Robbie said. He looked around the room to see if he was the only one. It was a tough room to read, though: Everyone was on some level of shocked and confused simply by default. "Are you saying we had encounters with the ... Tachyonites? Are you saying we met them before you abducted us?"

"This is where faster-than-light particles get interesting," Noah said. "They travel in an inverse direction through time. What I was detecting was traces of your interaction with them *now*. It faded, but when it faded, it was toward your past, not your future. And that's what tipped me off something was gonna happen."

"You took us from our homes," Paul said.

"Yeah, I did," Noah said. "Sorry. Like I said, I've seen what these aliens can do up close. I was here already, doing a biological study . . . like what you guys do. Oceanographers, essentially. Same deal. Been here for a couple hundred Earth years. Just collecting data. Raymond was the first one I detected the traces in. I hung on to him, stuck him in stasis, and went looking for anyone else. You seven were the only other ones I found."

"Did you . . . *probe* us?" Touré asked.

"Dude, grow up," Noah said. "Noninvasive tests, okay? I don't know anything about those guys complaining about anal probes and all that, but it wasn't me."

"What was stasis like?" Robbie asked.

"Uh, kind of like suspended animation, only not really. Temporally locked. If you're wondering if you're missing a hundred years of memories, you aren't. You're missing probably a few hours, tops."

"Suspended animation that killed our electronics?"

"Anything with batteries died over time, but not from the stasis. I had to remove them; they created interference."

"Hey, I have a question," Bethany said. "I have a question."

"Go ahead, Bethany," Noah said.

"Whoa, it knows my name," she muttered. "Okay, why'd you put us back in our own homes and all? Was that to trick us?"

"Because of Raymond," he said. "He was the first one I took, so he was the first one I put back, but he didn't take it well. I didn't even think about putting him back in his home, but in my defense, it wasn't there anymore. I thought if you guys started out somewhere familiar, you'd have a chance to, I don't know, ease your way into things. Better than he did, anyway. And it worked, right?"

"It was terrible," she said, quietly.

"I know. But it was gonna be terrible either way."

"What year is this?" Ananda asked.

"Oh, easy one. It's, um . . . it's 2127. March, I think. You want the exact day? I'd have to look it up for you."

"That's good enough," Robbie said. "You found traces of tachyons in us, kidnapped us, and then buried a machine in Cambridge. Why'd you do all that?"

"Why? I like you guys. As a species, I mean. When I picked up traces, I tried to understand the when and the where and all that, but I also knew that regardless of when and where, the whole human race was about to get wiped out and I wanted to stop it. My device is kind of like a roach motel for Tachyonites, or it was supposed to be. But like I said, it didn't work."

"It's a prison?" Carol asked.

"Should've been. I was trying to catch it before it did what it did. But I messed up."

"Everyone was trying to get away from it," Win said. "On the roads, everyone was leaving town. Was that your fault?"

"Yeah, sure, indirectly. I didn't mean for them to find it. I stuck it in the foundation of a building around 2022. In 2043, they decided they didn't want that building anymore, they found my tech, and it went south from there. All they were able to figure out was that it had something to do with tachyons, which it does. It's kinda like a Thermos, with a layer of tachyon-reactive . . . never mind. It's advanced. I'll give you the poop on it later, Ananda, if you guys survive this."

"'Survive'?" Robbie said.

"'If'?" Toure said.

"Yeah, like I said: It's still going to wipe you guys out soon, but let me finish. They unearthed my roach motel and, after doing a bunch of tests, figured out it was extraterrestrial and thought it might be a bomb. The attack came during the total evacuation of the area. I think that's probably a coincidence, but maybe not. I was too busy trying to understand why my trap didn't work. But the good news for you guys is, I think I got it right this time."

Paul laughed, then went and sat down in the first row. "I know what comes next," Paul said. "You're going to tell us we're bait, aren't you? To see if your toy works?"

"No, no, no. It's not like that at all."

"How is it, then?"

"For starters, if you don't do anything at all, it's *going* to kill you. You're not *bait*, because you're already in mortal danger. I'm offering a lifeline to you, the last of the human race."

He stopped, perhaps for dramatic effect. Noah might not be human, but he seemed to know a lot about theatricality.

"Has it started to get aggressive yet?" Noah asked. "The lights?"

He looked around the room. No one wanted to answer.

"It's okay, you don't have to say anything. I can tell by the way you're looking at each other, it *has*. Well, that's going to keep getting worse. What it's doing is conducting experiments to work out what makes you seven different. It'll eventually get tired of trying to solve that puzzle and just clean up after itself and move on. Then we both lose out. I miss out on an opportunity to gain valuable information about these creatures, and you miss out on living. Your other option, what I'm offering, pastor, is a chance to maybe not die."

"This device of yours," Ananda said, "does it kill them?"

"I don't know how to kill something like this. I can trap it, is all. The trap won't even hold it forever, but it'll hold it for long enough to get it off the planet and a very long way from here. Maybe I'll throw it into a sun, I don't know. I can buy you time and distance is what I'm saying. Can't guarantee it will last forever, not until we have a better idea of the Tachyonite's motivation. Figure that out and we can move the human race off the extinction list."

"Sounds great," Paul said. "I don't believe a word of it."

"Neither do I," Carol said.

"It's your choice," Noah said. "I'm just laying out the options.

And, I mean, I apologize about the whole abduction thing, but you have to realize that I saved your lives when I did that. Don't hold that part against me."

"Robbie?" Carol said. "What do you think?"

Robbie didn't know what he thought yet and hated that the others wanted to know. It was all a lot easier when this was just a crazy idea he'd had about an alien hiding in the shadows.

"You let us catch you," Robbie said to Noah. "You've been helping us all along. You gave Bethany a wheelbarrow and unlocked the door on the supermarket roof. Am I forgetting anything?"

"Elton?" Win said.

"No, the horse was just good luck," Noah said. "There's a few dozen of them running wild west of here if you're curious. But yes to everything else. If you want to know why I haven't just popped in and said hello, that's what I did with Raymond, and he did *not* handle it well. I tried to open up a dialogue with Carol, but I think we all know how that went. You guys had to work it out on your own. Hopefully, before the Tachyonite decided to get rid of you."

Robbie nodded. He looked around the room to see if anyone else had more to add, but they were all looking to him. Their leader, apparently.

"Okay," he said. "What do you want us to do?"

2

What Noah wanted them to do was simple enough: gather at his device, all seven of them, at a particular time.

It was a slightly problematic ask, only because they had no timepieces, and he couldn't give them more than *a certain occasion to be named later.*

"I'll know when," he said. "The problem is in the detection. I'm looking for that moment when the . . . What were those things, the, um, the jewelry? . . . *Mood rings.* It's like mood rings. I'll be able to detect when the creature's about to attack because its energy levels will crest. Again, I can't explain it any better without a ton of detail, and the truth is, I'm about a half an hour away from the oxygen eating through my skin here."

"How long will we have?" Ananda asked. "Once you've notified us."

"An hour, maybe two. Think of it like a grenade. The Tachyonite has to be near the device when it's about to blow. If one of you isn't near it, there's a risk the grenade will go off around that person first instead, and then we've lost our window, because it's only vulnerable to the trap right at that moment."

"This is happening soon?" Robbie asked.

"Not sure. Could be a week or a month. Maybe two. Look, I really have to go, man. Can I have my doodad?"

Robbie looked around the room for someone to decide this for him. Nobody did, so he stood up and handed it over.

"Thanks," he said.

He pulled something else out of his cloak and tossed it to Ananda.

"If that box gives you a solid red light, it's time to go," Noah said.

"What do the other lights mean?" she asked.

"Don't worry about those."

That just about guaranteed it would be all she was going to worry about, but maybe Noah knew that.

"You're not coming back when it's time?" Robbie asked.

"I will, but not until it's over. Like I said, if it sees me, you're done where you stand. Okay? See you guys on the other side."

He raised his injured right arm and pushed the button.

Noah's disappearing act was fascinating. It was as if he walked backwards into a darkened room until overtaken by that darkness, except that there was no room to back into, and the darkness came from within him.

They all stood there awhile, just staring at the spot he'd vacated.

"Yellow spots," Bethany said, pointing at the floor. "See?"

Noah had dripped some blood next to the chair.

"Saw that," Robbie said.

"Told you I winged him in the driveway."

"Yep."

Robbie sat back down next to Carol.

"So," he said, "are we going to do what he says?"

"I thought you already made that decision," Paul said. "I wouldn't have let him leave."

Robbie turned to Paul. "Nobody here was stopping you from making that decision," he said. "If you had something to share, there was time for it."

"Sure," Paul said.

"No, really," Robbie said. "I'm not the last word here. I think we should do it, but there are seven of us and nobody elected me. So I'm asking what you think. All of you."

None of them wanted to go first. It was an odd new dynamic for the Apocalypse Seven, Robbie thought. They never really had to vote on many things before this, because in the past there was always a clear expert on the subject—whatever the subject— among them, and everyone else was willing to defer. They didn't have a first-encounter-with-an-alien expert, though.

"Touré?" Robbie asked. "What do you think? Do we do what he said or not?"

"It's a lot to take in, dude," Touré said. "But I vote yes."

"Yeah, so do I," Bethany said. "Anything that stops those lights."

"Carol?" Robbie asked.

"I don't trust Noah," she said. "But if you do, I'll go along."

"I'm not sure I trust him either," Robbie said. "Win?"

"I don't know," she said. "Something smells funny."

"That's just how he smells," Touré said.

"Ha, not what I mean. You mentioned him, when you were feverish. Do you remember?"

Touré looked shocked. "No — did I?"

"Yeah, by name. You kept talking about having to get back to the gang, and Noah was one of the people you named. He said we were only missing a couple of hours from our memories, which I took to mean the time he abducted us and the time he put us back. I'm just wondering if it was more than that."

"Maybe Touré's fever helped him remember whatever Noah erased," Robbie said.

"I'm saying, it could have been *more*," Win said. "We have no way of knowing, not when we're dealing with someone who can vanish like he just did, someone who can alter our memories like he already admitted he was capable of."

"That's fair," Robbie said. "Does that mean you're not in?"

"No, I'm in, for now. I just feel like we're missing something."

"Okay. Ananda?"

"I'll do it," she said. "It's a risk of death versus a virtual guarantee of it. But I reserve the right to change my mind."

"Sure."

Robbie turned to the pastor, sitting in the first row.

"No," Paul said. "Absolutely not."

"This will only work if all of us participate," Ananda said. "You heard what he said."

"I did. The space alien said a lot of stuff. About the only thing I'm willing to believe is that he's really a space alien. For the rest of it, I'll hold out until a better explanation comes along."

"I understand it if this is troubling for you—" Robbie began.

Paul cut him off. "No, it's not that, kid. I know where you're going. You all think I'm just some Bible-thumping yahoo. Maybe that's what I am, but this isn't about that. I'm not going to debate divine intent or whether the thing that just vanished is a devil or whether space aliens have souls. It's not about any of that. This is about *free will*. I think I have it, and I think what I just heard said otherwise, and so I am exercising that free will by rejecting the premise."

"You're thinking we don't have a choice?" Robbie asked.

"No, you're not looking big enough. You want to tell me the shimmer is the afterimage of an alien who moves backwards through time . . . no. The Lord gave me free will, and that free will resulted in my being chosen to remain on this Earth for reasons only He understands. I accept that even if I don't understand it, because I am in control of my decisions. Now I'm hearing that the spaceman saved my life and dropped me into the future because he could detect some kind of trace evidence that I was *going to be* in the future. That's the description of a world where our fates are predetermined, and I can't abide that. So, no sir. You can count me out."

With that, Paul got up and left the auditorium.

They all sat in the near darkness in silence for a little while.

"I'll talk to him," Win said.

"No, I will," Ananda said.

"Give him some time," Robbie said. "Maybe he'll come around."

Ananda held up the box Noah gave her.

"We don't know how long we have," she said.

"I know. Give him some anyway. He's a reasonable person."

SIXTEEN

Robbie

1

SPRING ARRIVED A WEEK LATER.

With it, the spirits of the seven remaining members of the human race should have been lifted, as that was what springtime ordinarily did to members of the human race. It didn't work, though, because the shimmer was still turning up randomly . . . and it was getting worse.

Or it *seemed* like it was. Everyone reported seeing it more often and that it had been coming off as more aggressive than it had previously, but — and it was Ananda who pointed this out — it could be that they only felt that way now because the idea of malicious intent had been planted in their heads by Noah.

This observation was not helpful.

By the fourth week of spring, everyone was on edge. Light-show assaults were coming daily, and nobody was getting much sleep while waiting for the red light Noah had given them to come on, which it thus far stubbornly refused to do. (It had a blinking yellow, a solid green, and an intermittent orange light, none of which seemed to be detecting useful things.)

At the same time, the situation with Paul was becoming strained, though aside from the moment when he'd stormed out of the meeting, he was his usual pleasant and chatty self. Which was great—at first. He remained approachable, certainly, and so every one of them, at one time or another, did approach . . . and asked him to reconsider.

He debated Ananda for three hours on the nature of free will, and Win for two or more on the nature of the soul. With Bethany, it became a discussion about fear and how one should not let it govern one's actions—information Bethany only found useful in the abstract.

Carol's effort nearly worked, at least according to her. Robbie didn't entirely understand what her approach was—she'd cited Hume, Saint Augustine, and Descartes, but couldn't say how those citations coalesced into a cogent thesis—but when she was done she was certain he'd been convinced.

He was not.

Even Touré tried, despite having already gone on record with the admission that Paul made him nervous. They went back and forth for the better part of an afternoon on game theory and the prisoner's dilemma. It didn't change Paul's mind, but Touré nearly changed his.

Robbie waited until everyone else had taken a turn before trying himself, because he was really hoping one of the others had a key to unlocking Paul that Robbie already knew he did not.

2

Robbie found Paul sitting at a table in front of a taco place around the corner from the campus.

The pastor was drinking a beer and attempting to derive pleasure from a cigar that was so stale, it somehow even *sounded* stale every time he puffed on it. Despite his scarred face, he looked beatific, staring off into the middle distance.

Paul could be equal parts serene and terrifying at any moment. It was kind of amazing. Robbie envied the serenity part.

"Can I sit?" Robbie asked.

"Sure," Paul said. "Do you want a beer?"

"No, I'm good. I never really enjoyed beer."

"It's what you were drinking at the party," Paul said.

Robbie had a moment of disconnect, thinking at first that Paul was referring to the keg party Robbie had been at on the night of his abduction. But he was talking about the rooftop barbecue.

"Yeah, I keep thinking the next time I try it, I'll like it. Hasn't happened yet. Dunno why I'm still trying. Maybe if it was cold."

"Nah. The cold just means you're not tasting all of it. It's fine like this. How about a cigar?"

"No, definitely not," Robbie said.

"Fair enough. You know, I didn't really get around to appreciating this until now, but there's a lot of stuff just lying around here, owned by nobody in particular. Now that I'm not spending all my time worrying about how to make it to the next sunrise, it's sort of nice to indulge. Even if the cigars are stale and the beer's flat."

Robbie smiled. "Not a bad way to look at it, I guess," he said. "Sounds like something Touré might come up with."

"Well, he's flighty, but he's got the right attitude."

Robbie looked down the street, in the same direction as Paul. The view caught part of the river and the bridge spanning it. There were deer running all over the place, especially near the grassy area, under the tree cover right at the riverbank.

"I'm thinking the population crashed," Paul said, pointing up the road. "The deer, I mean to say. Not us. Well. Us, too. But one of the things I expected to see more of, in the future, was deer. Their population was exploding back before you and I left the region for a while. At least it was around my edge of the world. Only way to control it was by hunting them down to a level the forest could support. Without that, you figure all we'd see around here is deer."

"We have seen a lot of them."

"Should be a lot more, though. That's why I'm thinking their population must have crashed."

"Maybe I will have that beer," Robbie said.

Paul handed him one from under the table. "Here you go."

Robbie opened the can, which hissed gently. He took a quick sip and wondered if cigar smoke was the secret to enjoying it.

"What about predators?" Robbie asked, regarding the deer.

"Predators could help keep them down, sure," Paul said. "But —and again, I'm talking about a hundred years back—even with the coyotes and wolves and whatnot, even with an explosion in pack hunting, the deer were making baby deer faster than the four-legged hunters could keep up with. No, I think they ran out of food."

"Nothing stopping the plants from growing," Robbie said. "Isn't that what they eat?"

"Sure. But not every kind of plant; just certain kinds. I'm not a botanist, but I knew my share of farmers, and they'd talk your ear off about invasive species."

"You mean, like Noah?"

Paul laughed. "No, but that's funny. He's a different kind of invasive. I mean plants that don't belong to this region, brought here by people who should have known better. Plants that thrive in the new climate rules around here, that can overwhelm the native species, and that may not be edible for deer. You wouldn't even know it to look at it, especially around a city."

He leaned back and puffed on his cigar. The five deer Robbie could see from his chair got spooked by something upriver and ran off.

"So are you going to ask me?" Paul asked.

"Ask you what?"

"You know. Ask me to join your merry band of survivors. It's why you're here—let's not pretend otherwise."

"Oh, that," Robbie said. He took a sip of his own beer and continued to dislike it. "I don't know yet."

"Okay. Well, we can sit here all afternoon. Weather's nice."

Robbie was ad-libbing this whole conversation. He meant to have some talking points—either actually written down and in his hand, like this was a moderated debate, or memorized—but when he sat down to try to work them out, he came up with nothing.

"I actually had a bigger question for you," Robbie said.

"Shoot."

"I was wondering if you still had faith."

Paul nearly choked on his cigar. He coughed, took a sip of his beer to clear his throat, and shook his head.

"Sorry, that was unexpected," he said. "Do you mean that, or are you just trying to get a rise out of me?"

"Why would I try to get a rise out of you?" Robbie asked. "You're bigger than I am, and you're armed. If anything, I should be afraid of you."

"Ahh, come on. I'm not a scary person. I've just led a weathered existence. You really want to talk about God right now? Because the impression I've been getting from you and the rest of your team is that nobody wants a part of that."

"It's a bad time to believe in a higher power," Robbie said. "Look, I'm just trying to understand where you're coming from, your perspective. You're also the only preacher we have, so I figured maybe that's where I should start. But they're not my team. Nobody's in charge here; I think that's obvious by now."

Paul laughed. "Just because you don't want to be the leader doesn't mean you're *not*. Besides, who else is there? Nanda's too far in her own head, Touré doesn't seem to live in reality half the time, Carol's always gonna be more interested in problems than solutions . . . Who's that leave? Bethany? She's just a kid. Win maybe could do it. Not sure she has the temperament."

"How about you?" Robbie asked.

Paul nodded. "Yeah, I think our current predicament takes me pretty much out of the running," he said. "Not that I was ever really in. Look, better or worse, you've been the last word around here for a while. I know it doesn't seem that way to you, and I know you don't like it, but that's how it is. Congratulations."

"Well, I'm going to keep on pretending none of that's true," Robbie said. "At least until I can figure out how to prove you wrong."

"Pretty sure that's not the hill you want to die on in this conversation. You asked me about my faith."

"Yeah, I did."

Paul leaned back and puffed on his cigar for a bit. Robbie tried leaning back and pretending he was enjoying something as much as that cigar.

"I used to be a sinner," Paul said. "I mean, we're all sinners, but I was one of the better ones. I drank too much, smoked too many of the wrong things . . . got a girl pregnant, married her, and then abandoned her . . . you know. Just me being selfish. Maybe listening to the wrong body part too many times. Broke the law often enough to end up in prison for a few years, all before I was even thirty."

"What'd you do?"

"Lots of stuff, but the one the state was most interested in was that I shot a guy. It's a dumb story. I'll tell you if you want, but I promise you it's dumb. He didn't die, but he never walked right after. Attempted murder was the charge, and I did earn it. The Lord rescued me from that cell, though, and I mean that both ways. I converted in prison, so first He rescued me with His word and later with His actions."

"Are you saying God busted you out of prison?"

"I call it as I saw it. There was an open door, and I walked through," Paul said. "I never looked back. Truth, one reason for my living up on the mountain like I did was to stay off the grid. Figure I was still wanted for failing to serve my full term."

"I think you're in the clear now," Robbie said.

"Yeah, I think you're right. Thing is, when all this happened . . . when I was found unworthy, I was upset. But a part of me understood. I made choices, on my own, to do bad things to good people. Whatever penalty the Lord saw fit to try me with, I was willing to accept, because these were my decisions and I earned the consequences."

"And now?"

Paul smiled.

"Now I think the Rapture is more compelling than what that space alien had to say, which is pretty messed up. But I don't know. Could be this was the way it had to happen for His will to be expressed. But that seems awfully extreme, doesn't it?"

"It does seem like an overreaction, yes," Robbie said.

"So, to answer your question, I do still have my faith. It's shaky, but I still have it. But here's what I need you to understand, in case you get around to asking me what you came here to ask. Without free will, we aren't anything. We're neither sinners nor saints, and we're also not *people*. I would rather be damned to literal hell for my self-chosen sins than to be told they weren't choices at all. Destiny, fate, preordination—these are all excuses to explain away the choices we've made freely. Even when we're agents of the Lord's will, we are the authors of our own futures. Someone had to make a choice *somewhere*. Aside from the Almighty."

"Yeah," Robbie said. "I see it. I'm just not ready to say that the situation we've got going on right now runs contrary to all that. But we're in the right place for that kind of discussion, I guess."

"How so?"

"At a college, drinking beer, talking about the nature of free will. It's too early and we're not drunk enough, but other than that."

Paul laughed. "I think we need to get our hands on some weed, too, but I hear you. Bet there's a marijuana patch around here somewhere that's thriving."

They fell silent, and drank their beer for a little while. Paul continued to puff his cigar, which was somewhat annoying when the wind shifted and carried the smoke into Robbie's face. A fox scurried across Mass Ave., scattering a half-dozen bunnies that had been hidden a minute earlier, and another couple of deer returned to the banks of the Charles.

"Look," Robbie said, "talking about this stuff is fun. I really could do it all day. But this isn't an abstract idea. Noah said if we're not all there, we could *all* die. And that's it—that's the end of the human race. You have the free will to decide for yourself what you want to do, but this isn't a choice that's just *for* you. It's for all of us."

"Son, if that's what you think, you still don't understand what I've been saying. I'm saying, if the facts that have been presented to us run contrary to what I *know* to be the case, then those facts are wrong. I'm saying, this is a false decision and your buddy Noah isn't giving us the whole story."

"Paul, we need you aboard," Robbie said. "You're gambling with everyone's future. You must see that."

Paul took a sip, and a puff, and for a second, Robbie thought he had him.

"I'm sorry, Rob. I just can't do that."

3

That was the last time any of them tried to talk to Paul about his decision.

Everyone agreed that Robbie — for reasons that didn't make any *sense* to Robbie — was their last, best chance at swaying their resident itinerant preacher. If he couldn't do it, it couldn't be done.

That created some tension, which was essentially unavoidable given that they remained the last seven people on the planet; avoiding each other was simply not possible as long as they all relied on one another to survive.

To that end, Paul remained helpful, and useful, and plenty cheerful. He continued to hunt, and tend to Elton when Elton needed tending to and Win wasn't able. But Paul also spent less and less idle time with the others. He still slept in the same space with them sometimes, and still ate meals with them sometimes. Just not *every* time.

Meanwhile, the shimmer kept getting worse. One night, Bethany woke up to find herself being probed by the Tachyonite, screamed, and woke up everyone else. This prompted a meeting the following morning to discuss whether, should this happen again, it was the responsibility of whoever noticed it was happening to wake up everyone else. The discussion was pointless, because after that night none of them got any proper sleep anyway. This made all of them a lot more irritable, and some of that irritability was directed at Paul.

It was no coincidence that when spring turned to . . . if not summer, then a hotter spring, Paul was hardly spending any time in the castle. He'd take Elton out on long rides — Paul didn't say where to, and neither did Elton — ostensibly to hunt, although he didn't usually come back with any game. Some of these trips spanned three or four days.

Nobody openly speculated that maybe it would be better if Paul simply didn't come back one of these times, but that didn't mean nobody thought it.

Then came the day when their very hot late spring or early summer went from somewhat pleasant to possibly life-threatening.

SEVENTEEN

Ananda

"I'M SORRY, DID YOU JUST SAY *HURRICANE?*" TOURÉ ASKED.

They were in the part of the building Ananda had claimed as her research lab. It was mainly a bunch of desks with useless computers on them. About half the surfaces were covered with retrieved discoveries from other parts of the castle, and the other half with her handwritten calculations. Touré was there because he'd just delivered a new trove of documents.

"Yes, I did," Ananda said.

"Like, an actual hurricane?"

"A storm in which the wind blows very hard and lots of rain falls. I can't formalize the prediction without a satellite image, and we haven't been able to establish contact with the satellites yet, so I don't know if it's an *actual* hurricane. But something like it."

Their miniature solar power grid had been growing steadily since the weather turned. They were on three rooftops now and had begun to lay power cords to the castle's computer mainframe room in an effort to recover the local computer memory. It was a far cry from the Internet, but it would be a good beginning. Among other things, they could start to access data saved by the university before the great extinction.

They were also trying to get a satellite dish up and running. Ananda reasoned that the weather satellites overhead didn't rely on ground-based power to continue operating, so they were likely still up there, transmitting data that wasn't being received any longer. She hoped to change that.

In the meantime, what she did have was barometric pressure readings from different elevations throughout the campus.

Getting that done, and then finding a way to return to the locations to take regular readings, meant further reducing or isolating the castle's wolf population. Through a series of careful tactical maneuvers, they managed to reduce the percentage of the MIT campus in which one might come across a wolf by about ninety percent. It required closing off part of the Infinite Corridor on two sides—making sure everyone was clear on which doors they absolutely could either not open, or if they did open, not *leave* open—and persuading Carol to find another place to hang out with her pet wolf.

So far, it was working. Long term, Ananda hoped to drive the wolves out entirely, but that might involve a degree of violence the others weren't currently comfortable with.

"No way," Touré said. "Unless I'm counting wrong, it's only May. Hurricane season's not till the end of summer. And this is New England, not the Florida panhandle."

"We can't rely on what we think we know about the weather," Ananda said. "You know this already."

"Fine. Sure. When?"

"Soon," she said. "We may have only a few hours."

"So we have to get everyone inside," Touré said, "before the winds kick in."

"It's more than that. We'll need to close windows and doors, and the solar panels should come down. Just off the array, unless you think you can get them inside without burning yourselves. Use gloves. You and Robbie."

"We kind of need the power," he said.

"Those panels are currently irreplaceable, and I have no idea if they're heavy enough to withstand this wind. The array isn't bolted down, I can tell you that. I know because I put it up myself."

"All right."

Touré took off to find Robbie while Ananda headed down one flight to the living quarters. Paul was there and so was Win; both were pretending the other wasn't.

"We're getting a hurricane," Ananda said. "We need to secure everything. Win, we have open outer doors and windows all over the castle. You're fastest. Paul?"

Paul looked at Win. "Elton," he said.

"I should go out with you," she said.

"Can't be in two places at once," he said.

Win looked like she was in pain. "You're right. Find him. Please."

"You know I will."

"Do either of you know where Bethany and Carol are?" Ananda asked.

"Carol's with Nolan," Win said. "Not sure about Bethany. You want me to find her?"

"I'll go to Carol," Ananda said. "If you find Bethany, make sure she gets inside. We'll be losing power shortly."

Bethany

"You have to give him a treat the first few times," Carol said.

She and Bethany were on the lawn outside of the library with

Nolan, who was learning some new tricks. Carol only knew how to get him to sit, stay, and lie down. She wanted to see what else Nolan could learn, but she needed the assistance of someone with eyesight to accomplish that.

Bethany was available and willing. She was also a little terrified.

"What about *kill,* and *stop trying to kill*?" Bethany asked. "Have you tried teaching him that yet?"

Carol laughed. "I tried it on Noah. It worked, but the *don't kill* command required I hit Nolan on the back first. I don't know who else to practice on."

"Yeah, forget I asked," Bethany said. "Come on, Nolan, roll over."

It was easy to forget this was a wild animal who'd just as soon rip out their throats as not, especially once they started playing. Bethany was able to get him to flip onto his back for a treat, but he wouldn't flip over again on command and thus complete the roll-*over* portion of the trick. (He was also, evidently, not a *he.* Bethany didn't know if she should tell Carol this.)

"Roll over, Nolan," she said. "Here's the treat, come on."

A powerful gust blew across the lawn from the river, rustling the newly arrived leaves on the trees. It was enough to rock Bethany to the side. Nolan completed his roll then, but only to get his feet under him so as to look around and see what in the heck that was.

"Wow, that came out of nowhere," Bethany said.

"Are there clouds?" Carol asked.

There were. Newly arrived, from the west, looking like they were late for something.

"Yup."

Nolan turned, walked behind Carol, and started growling. Ananda was on the library steps.

"Hello!" Ananda shouted. "Is it safe to come over?"

Nolan barked.

"Nolan," Carol chided. "Be nice. Ananda is a friend."

Carol got up and put her hand on Nolan's head. "Run on home now," she said. She patted him twice on the rear. He whined. She did it again and off he went.

"He knows more tricks than *sit, stay,* and *lie down,*" Bethany said.

"That? That was just being polite. There's no trick to that."

"Come inside," Ananda said.

"Is there a storm coming?" Carol asked. She reached out for Bethany, who guided them to the steps.

"I'm afraid my forecasting skills are wanting, as it appears it may already be here," Ananda said.

"Hurricane?" Carol asked.

"Possibly," Ananda said. "How did you know?"

"Not my first," Carol said. "I can feel it in my ears."

"A hurricane?" Bethany asked. "How cool. I missed the tornado."

Carol laughed and patted her on the arm. "I hope you still think so after this one's over," she said.

Ananda led them back inside and made doubly sure the door was closed and bolted.

Win, looking red-faced from the exertion of sprinting down the halls, ran up just then. "Oh, good, you found them," she said. "I sealed up the Mass Ave. side. Should we worry about the wolf den?"

"Yes," Carol said.

"I don't know how," Ananda said. "Closing their outer door will just make them angry. They should know what to do in a storm on their own."

"All right," Win said, "I'm going to—"

Ananda grabbed her arm. "Wait," she said, with some measure of alarm.

Ananda pulled something from her pocket, looked down at it for several seconds, and then sighed grandly.

"Of course," she said. "Why *not* now?"

The device Noah gave her was vibrating gently in her hand. The light was solid red.

"Oh crap," Bethany said.

"Fantastic," Ananda said.

"What is it?" Carol asked. "Is it time?"

"It's time," Ananda said. "All right, new plan. Win, the boys are on the roof. Find them and meet us at the device. Hopefully this will be over before the full force of the storm hits."

"What about Paul?" Bethany asked.

"He's corralling Elton," Win said.

"I'll go get him," Bethany said. "Someone should, right?"

"Bethany, he doesn't want to do this," Carol said.

"He didn't before, but now it's happening. We have to tell him."

She looked to each of them for affirmation, but didn't see any. Bethany couldn't understand why. Sure, Paul was being stupid, but that was before. He'd change his mind when he had to. She was certain of it.

"He should know," Bethany added.

Ananda sighed.

"Try," she said. "But get to the site as soon as you can."

Robbie

"Wow, this looks like it's going to be bad," Touré said.

He was standing entirely too close to the edge of the roof for Robbie's personal comfort. "Hey, back up, man," Robbie said.

Just then, a strong gust caught the solar cell Touré was holding and carried him backwards a couple of feet.

"Noted," he said. "This came out of nowhere, huh?"

"I don't know. I haven't been through a lot of hurricanes."

Robbie unplugged the back of the second solar array, and—with heavy work gloves—began taking the panels down and putting them on the rooftop. The panels weren't as heavy as they looked and made excellent sails, but they were *hot*. They both had this down to a science, though; they'd already cleared one rooftop of solar panels, with only one more to follow.

"I mean," Robbie continued, "usually we know they're coming a few days in advance, so it's not dropping in on us from out of nowhere. Maybe hurricanes always go like this: It's really nice, and then it's not."

"That's *if* it's a hurricane. Ananda wasn't sure."

"Ananda doesn't say anything with certainty. It's part of her nature. You must have noticed that by now."

A new gust hit Robbie from an entirely different direction and carried with it a whiff of moisture.

"After this is over," Touré said, "step one is to figure out how to rivet the panel array to the roof so we don't have to do this again. Step two, figure out how to make a solar panel from scratch so we don't have to do this again."

Robbie laughed. "Deal," he said.

Win turned up in the doorway on the other side of the roof.

"Oh, here's some help," Touré said. "You need gloves!" he shouted to Win. "They're really hot."

"Hey!" Win said, waving.

"Hey, you here to help?" Robbie asked.

"No, we're out of time," she shouted. "World's ending—we have to get in position."

"Red light?" Touré asked.

"That's what I'm saying."

"Now?" Robbie said. "In the middle of a hurricane?"

"The end of the world doesn't get canceled by rain, Robbie," Win said. "C'mon. If we're still alive in a couple of hours, we'll take down the rest of the panels."

Bethany

Bethany ran through the castle and out the other side and onto Vassar, reasoning that the Vassar exit was the closest to the street, and thus the most likely one Paul would have used when coming from their rooms.

She remembered Ananda's description of her first few weeks alone in the castle, afraid to leave even to walk to the corner. It was the same fear that had kept them in the dorm so long: Animals were running wild all over the place, and nobody knew why. Bethany used to think that all of the people had been killed *by* the animals, which, in hindsight, was a much nicer conclusion.

Now there were hardly any animals walking around. That was partly because Win and Paul began hunting in their own neighborhood by day, to complement the wolves' hunting by night, but also because there was a hurricane coming and every sane creature had long since taken shelter.

She took a chance and turned left, heading for Mass Ave. Bethany hardly knew Elton at all, but it was a long straightaway; if she were a horse, she might find that appealing. She wasn't tracking Elton exactly—she was tracking the guy tracking Elton—but it still felt right.

At the corner, an aggravated raccoon hissed at her. She ignored it, turned—

And ran into a swarm of lights.

The shimmer had been getting angrier and angrier with each

passing encounter. She'd hated the shimmer even before Noah told them that it was something that wanted to hurt her. Once she did know it, the light show triggered a panic she couldn't really control.

What got her through it was that the red light wasn't on yet. As long as that remained true—if Noah was to be believed—the shimmer wasn't ready to kill her.

But now the light *was* on.

"Noooo!" she screamed.

She spun around to run away from the lights—as if they could be outrun—but only made it a couple of steps before her foot caught in a crack in the street. It stayed where it was while the rest of her kept going.

Pain shot up her right leg. She shrieked, landed hard on the pavement, and skidded a couple of feet before stopping.

"Ow, ow, ow," she cried, clutching her ankle, and rolling onto her back.

The shimmer was right above her now, and if it could be said to be glaring menacingly, then that was what it was doing.

"Not. Yet!" she said, through clenched teeth.

Then she drew the gun Paul had given her and shot at the lights. Predictably, it did exactly nothing, but she sure felt better. The shimmer continued to hover as if to convey its rage. Bethany was certain she was about to die.

"Hey! You okay, kid?"

Paul ran over, waving his way through the lights like he was swatting at a cloud of gnats. He knelt down next to Bethany and pushed aside the weapon before he got shot by mistake.

Elton, having been successfully retrieved, sauntered up behind him. He looked somewhere in the middle of confused and indifferent.

Either in direct response to Paul's arrival or just as a matter of coincidence, the shimmer evaporated rather than opting to murder them.

Did we scare it off? Bethany wondered.

Then she started crying, which was not at all cool. Of the few remaining role models she had to compare herself to, she thought Win was the best pick, and Win definitely would not have started crying under these circumstances.

"It's okay," Paul said. He sat down next to her and gave her a hug. "You're fine. It's scary, but you know, it's just a light show."

Win also wouldn't need a hug. Bethany did, though.

"It's *not*," she said, getting Paul's shoulder wet. "It's here to kill us. You heard."

"I know what we were told."

"No, but, Paul . . . you don't understand. It's happening *now*. The red light came on. I was looking for you so I could tell you."

"Oh."

He pulled back from the hug. Bethany wiped her eyes dry with the back of a scraped-up hand.

"I thought this was it," she said. "I thought we were too late and this was it."

"Well, it's not," he said. "You're fine. We're both fine."

"But it's about to be too late! We have to get to the site. You heard me, right? The red light came on."

"I did hear you," he said. "And I already told all of you I'm not participating in this."

He stood, brushed himself off, and took hold of Elton's lead rope.

"It'll be fine," he said. "I promise you that. Now, I have to get Elton inside before the weather turns. Already feels like rain."

"Paul," she said, tears welling up again. "Please."

He shook his head slowly.

"Bethany, I'm sorry, I really am. I just can't agree to this. But I wish you all the best of luck."

He turned and started down Mass Ave. The horse, seemingly aware of the oncoming weather conditions, looked eager to go.

"Paul!" she shouted.

He stopped, and looked back. "I told you . . ." he began.

"I can't move my foot," she said. "I think my ankle's broken."

"Then we'll have to get *you* inside," he said.

"That's not where I need to be."

He hesitated.

"*Please*, Paul."

He hung his head and sighed. His lips were moving; a quiet prayer, maybe.

"All right," he said. "I will bring you there. But I'm not staying."

Robbie

Robbie, Touré, and Win reached the construction site at around the same time it started raining. Ananda and Carol were already there.

They'd already cut away the fence meant to keep them out of the site and installed a wood ramp to climb down. This was done before they met Noah, so Ananda could study the device without risking a broken leg, but was very convenient on this occasion, at the front end of a hurricane.

"Where's Bethany?" Robbie asked. They almost had to shout to be heard over the wind.

"She went to find Paul," Ananda said.

"And you let her?"

"Couldn't stop her. She'll be here."

"I hope so."

Lightning bolts were dancing across the top of the sky. Robbie couldn't think of a worse place to be standing than in the middle of an open plot next to a possibly metal object.

"Great timing," he said.

"That's what I thought too," Ananda said.

The shimmer manifested over the device. Robbie at first thought he was looking at more distant lightning before his eyes adjusted and he realized what he was seeing.

"Here we go," Touré said.

"Bethany should be here by now," Robbie said. "Should we go find her?"

"There's no time," Carol said. "We have to trust she'll make it here."

Just then, Paul rode up on Elton with Bethany in the saddle in front of him.

"We're here!" she shouted.

"You're late," Robbie said.

"Yeah, I broke my ankle and had to hitch," Bethany said.

Paul hopped off Elton's back, then turned and helped Bethany down. Then he sat her next to the fence and waved to the others.

"Far as I go," he said. "Good luck to all of you."

"Wait, I have to get down there!" Bethany said, pointing to the other side of the fence.

"Yeah, all right, all right," Paul said.

He stepped away from Elton, knelt down, and scooped her up like she were a child. The opening in the fence was barely large enough for him to make it through, but he managed it.

As soon as he stepped off the wood ramp and touched the dirt on the inside of the fence, the overhead swarm's demeanor seemed to change.

The only way to describe it was *attack mode.*

It dove at Paul first, knifelike, shooting itself straight through the man's head. The pastor was uninjured by this, but was visibly startled. It was too late, by then, for him to go anywhere; he was part of this now whether he liked it or not. Robbie could see him coming to that conclusion in the subtle change of his expression.

The shimmer swung around and enveloped Carol next, and then Robbie. Then Bethany. She buried her face in Paul's chest.

"Stop it!" she screamed.

"Noah!" Robbie shouted, at the absent alien he hoped was listening. "Now would be a good time to get your machine going!"

Around and around the shimmer went, above Ananda and through Win, expanding and contracting. It was a cloud that surrounded them, and a blade that sliced through them. But even though its frantic motion now seemed coupled with the drastic winds and increasingly heavy rains, the shimmer still wasn't doing them any direct harm.

Suddenly, and with a loud clang, the round hat on top of Noah's device popped up a couple of inches—

And the swarm instantly calmed down.

"What's happening?" Carol asked. She was squeezing Robbie's hand tightly.

"I think Noah's roach motel has gone active," Robbie said.

A second swarm of lights manifested. Robbie's eyes might have been playing tricks on him, because while it seemed like what happened was that the single shimmer split in two, it also looked like the second swarm emerged from Noah's device. But that didn't make any sense. Both things couldn't be true.

A distinct pair now, the two shimmers took turns, stopping in front of each member of the Apocalypse Seven, coalescing into a humanoid shape of roughly the same height, and then moving on. It looked, weirdly, like it was taking portraits of each of them.

"Any idea what's happening?" Win asked.

"Not me," Touré said. "But they're not trying to kill us, so I'm cool with it."

And then the lights fizzled, as if the rain shorted them out and the winds carried them off.

Nobody could breathe for a bit. They just stood there, listening to the wind and feeling the rain on their faces, waiting for another shoe to drop.

Paul lowered Bethany to the ground; she sat down on the board and winced at an ankle that was already starting to swell.

"So?" Paul asked. "Is that it?"

Robbie let go of Carol's hand and circled the device, looking for evidence of renewed hostilities. There was nothing but the wind and the rain.

It's over, he thought.

"Guys, I think we did it," Robbie said. "I think we're safe."

"I think you're right!" Touré said.

Then everyone was hugging someone: Win and Touré and Ananda, Carol, and Robbie. Bethany hugged Paul's leg, while Paul looked like someone trying to fight back a grin.

A pinhole of shadow opened up next to the device, which grew into a human-sized bit of darkness. Noah stepped forth from it.

"It worked!" Noah said. "That's fantastic! Great job, everyone."

"Thanks, man!" Touré said.

"You too!" Robbie said. "Your device worked!" He stepped away from Carol and shook Noah's hand—it felt cold and rubbery—

before committing to a quick hug of the alien being who'd just saved their lives. "So what happens now?" Robbie asked.

"Now I think you guys better go inside before the storm gets any worse," Noah said. "Looks like a bad one. I'm going to take this and park it on the other side of the galaxy before the creature escapes."

"Yeah, do that," Robbie said. "Before it escapes. How long do you have?"

"What do you mean?" Noah asked.

"You said you don't think you can hold it forever," Robbie said. "I'm wondering how long you think it'll be. Like next week? Or a thousand years? How long are we talking about?"

"We have to plan ahead," Touré said. "For the next apocalypse."

"Oh, sure," Noah said. "I'm not positive. I just figured out how to get it to work right. A little while, but I have to run some integrity tests. Don't you guys worry either way. I'll take care of it."

Noah put his hand on the device's top cap. Then Paul stepped forward.

"No," Paul said.

He had his shotgun out.

"Paul, what are you doing?" Robbie said, instinctively stepping between Paul and Noah. "We won. It's over."

"No," Paul repeated. "Step out of the way, kid."

"Paul—"

"Rob, you have to step aside," Paul said. "I'm very serious."

Robbie took three steps to his left, exposing Noah to a shot he was certain Paul wouldn't take. This was too crazy, even for him.

"Paul, come on," Noah said. "I know we have some differences, but we won! You guys are good now."

"No, you're not done answering questions," Paul said.

"The sooner he gets that thing away from here, the better," Ananda said.

"Nanda, stay out of it."

"I really have to go," Noah said.

Noah raised his right arm, meaning to activate his teleportation device.

"Not yet," Paul said. Then he shot the extraterrestrial roach motel out of Noah's hands. It clattered to the ground a few feet away.

Noah jumped backwards.

"Are you crazy?" Noah shouted. "Do you have any idea how dangerous that is? If that exploded—"

"You're not going anywhere," Paul said, "until you answer Robbie's question truthfully. How long until it escapes?"

"Paul, he doesn't know," Ananda said.

"You're not using your head, Nanda. He knows. I do too, but I want to hear it from him. How long, Noah?"

"Look, I don't know—" Noah began.

"Eighty-three years," Paul said. "That's how long."

"That's really specific, dude," Touré said.

"Paul, you're not being reasonable," Noah said. "Let me get the trap out of here before you do real damage to it."

"Oh my god," Ananda gasped. "You're right."

"They live backwards, don't they?" Paul said. "I finally figured out what you were hiding. *They live backwards.* Eighty-three years in this creature's future is eighty-three years in our past. What happens in eighty-three years is, that creature you trapped in there breaks out of his prison and kills every man, woman, and child on the planet."

"While looking for us," Robbie said.

"And we weren't there, so it just kept on going," Paul said. "Tell me I'm wrong, Noah."

"Wait, no," Touré said. "No, no, no. Did we just kill everyone? *Just now?*"

"Wasn't us," Paul said. "It *had* to play out like this."

"He's right," Ananda said. "The human race died in our past. It had to happen the way it did. We had no agency."

"But *he* did," Paul said, gesturing at Noah with the barrel of his shotgun. "None of this happens without him."

"Guys," Noah said, raising his hands. "It's not really like that. Okay, okay, it sort of is, but do you have any idea how much energy those creatures produce? The thing on the ground is a power cell, and this is the best way to charge it."

"By entrapping a sentient being?" Ananda asked.

"It's the most efficient way, by far," Noah said. "Look, we use tachyonic energy for interstellar travel, and it's *hugely* valuable. This one battery holds enough to power a thousand ships for a hundred years."

"You're joking," Robbie said.

"I'm totally serious. Look, I'm sorry, I really am, but, I mean, look around. It's all about energy, right? You understand that."

"You went mining for energy," Carol said, quietly, "on our planet. By baiting a hyperenergetic being into a trap. He provides access to enormous amounts of energy in exchange for our extinction and you . . . you expect us to *understand?*"

"You're not extinct! I saved you guys!"

"Robbie," Paul said. "I'm going to shoot him. Do you have a problem with that?"

"I cannot stress to you," Noah said, "how important this energy source is."

"No problem," Robbie said. "Go ahead."

Win beat Paul to it. With a guttural scream, she charged Noah, smashed his head to the ground, and punched him in the face. She had her knife out and was ready to finish him off when Noah said the one thing that could possibly stay her hand.

"THERE ARE OTHERS!" he shouted.

Win screamed, plunged the knife into the dirt next to his head, and grabbed him by the throat. "Say that again?" she said, slapping him across the face.

"I said, there are others!"

"Win," Robbie said, "get off him."

She shot a look of pure murder over her shoulder, but did as he asked. She pulled the knife from the dirt, rolled off the alien, and stood. "We should still kill him," she said. "Right now. Gut him and see what his insides look like, up close."

"Just step back," Robbie said. "Paul's got him covered."

Noah climbed up to one knee. He looked annoyingly fragile.

"Thanks, Robbie," he said.

"*Don't*," Robbie said. "Now. Explain yourself. And make it good."

"I said, there are others," Noah said. "I didn't just save the seven of you. It's the truth. I have more."

"How many?"

"Um . . ." He looked like he was doing math in his bulbous head. "Three hundred and twelve."

"Where are they?" Robbie asked. "Did you put them back?"

"No, they're in stasis," Noah said. "Like you guys were. It was going to be a surprise! People selected for different genetic markers and professions. I pulled them out just before it all went down. Don't any of you understand? I *saved* the human race."

"Nope," Paul said, "not good enough. I'm going to kill him."

"Hang on, Paul," Robbie said. "Let me guess: If we don't let you go, they stay where they are?"

"I can't release them if I'm not there."

Robbie's eyes met with Paul's. It looked as if the only thing staying the preacher's wrath was Robbie's request that he not execute their visitor. A part of him wanted to let Paul do it and wash his hands of the whole mess. But he couldn't do that, not if Noah was telling the truth this time.

"We let you go," Robbie said, "and you do . . . what? Drop the other three hundred and twelve where you found them like you did to us?"

"I don't have to. Where do you want them?"

Robbie turned around. "Paul, if he makes a move for the roach motel, shoot him. Touré?"

He waved Touré over to him. Touré arrived to the huddle, reluctant, looking devastated.

"What do you think?" Robbie asked. "Should we believe him?"

Touré shook his head. "No, man," he said. "I'm done guessing about right and wrong now."

"Hey," Robbie said, trying for a laugh. "Come on. You're the guy who thought the apocalypse was cool. Give me an angle or a story. What's your spin?"

"Yeah, I don't know. I don't know."

"Nothing?" Robbie asked.

"We just murdered the human race, Robbie. I don't think I trust us to get this right."

"Yeah, okay. Thanks," Robbie said. "You're a big help."

"Sorry, but I'm done."

"We don't have a choice," Carol said, quietly.

"What's that?" Robbie asked.

"I said, we don't have a choice."

"We always have a choice, Carol," Robbie said.

He turned around to consider Noah again.

Robbie had never in his life wanted to see another living creature murdered before him, so what he was experiencing in that moment was completely new. More than that: He wanted to do it himself.

He didn't like the feeling.

"Ten a month," Robbie said to Noah. "That's what we want. Starting next week. Put them in the middle of Cambridge Common. Can you do that?"

"Absolutely," Noah said.

"Start with medical professionals."

"Of course."

"Robbie—" Paul said.

"Paul, we have nothing to lose that we haven't already lost," Robbie said. "If we let him go and he's lying, we lose. If you pull the trigger, we lose."

"I think we've already lost," Paul said. "You just don't know it yet."

"Goddammit," Win said. "No. He's *right*. I hate it, but he's right, Paul."

Paul looked down the barrel of the shotgun at Noah again, and everyone held their breath. Robbie prepared himself to be okay with whatever choice the preacher made.

"All right," Paul said, and lowered the gun. "Vengeance is the Lord's. Although I'd rather claim it for myself."

"Yeah, we all feel that way," Robbie said.

"NO!" Bethany shouted. She had her gun pointed at Noah, tears streaming down her face. "No, you can't!"

"Bethany—" Robbie began.

She pulled the trigger. Five times. But the gun didn't go off. "I'm empty," she cried. "Paul—"

"I think they're right," Paul said.

"No, you can't."

Carol found her way to Bethany, sat down, and gave the girl a shoulder to cry on.

"It's okay," Carol said, quietly.

Bethany sank her face into Carol's shirt.

"So, um, we have a deal?" Noah asked. He climbed to his feet and brushed himself off.

"Yes," Robbie said.

Noah extended his hand. "Shake on it?" he asked.

Robbie thought if he got that close to Noah, he'd end up doing the same thing as Win, only nobody would stop him.

"Just remember the deal," Robbie said.

"Cambridge Common," Noah said. "You have my word." He turned to Ananda. "And oh, hey, if you want, I can share some tech. There's enough spare energy in this to power this whole world, if you want it."

"Get away from us," she said. "You're not an advanced species. You're a monster."

"There are a lot of power-hungry civilizations who don't feel that way, Ananda," he said. "It's all a matter of perspective."

"Just go," Robbie said. "Get the hell out of here."

"All right," he said. Noah retrieved the machine from the other end of the lot. "Ten a month, starting a week from today," Noah said. "Be ready."

With that, he pressed the little button on his doodad and vanished into the shadows.

Then the rains grew heavy, the winds raged, and it was time for all of them to seek shelter.

EPILOGUE

Touré

IT WAS THE THIRD SATURDAY OF JULY, AND IT WAS A GORgeous day.

Touré sat on a bench in front of the low wood barrier that marked the edge of the Garden Street side of Cambridge Common. Slung between two trees a few yards to his right, there was a big white banner that read:

WELCOME TO 2129!

The first thing everyone did, without fail, was laugh at the sign. Then they'd look around and stop laughing. Reactions after that varied. A lot of them screamed. Some broke down and cried. A few fainted.

Not one of them got up, looked around, and said, *Oh, cool*. Touré was dying for that to happen, just once, because he knew whoever did that was going to be his best friend for life.

They always came through lying down, wearing whatever they'd been taken away in. Thus far, thankfully, it had always been outdoor clothing. No pajamas or lingerie or straight-up nudity.

That would have just made an awkward situation even worse than it already was.

The first ones through had it the toughest. None of the Apocalypse Seven had known what to expect, so after the initial shock and the screaming and crying, they didn't have anything else to tell the new arrivals aside from, *Sorry, but this is your life now.*

They'd gotten *marginally* better at it since. Adding ten people a month was a huge challenge at first, because it took everybody about three months to stop freaking out and start being productive assets to the society they were trying to rebuild. Now, two years into the process, that society gained ten more useful people every month.

These days, Touré had an entire welcoming party organized, with grief counselors, a minister (Paul, usually), and some physicians. There was also food and water, and a housing assignment for the first night.

Pretty smooth operation, he thought.

He saw Bethany on the other side of the field. She waved hello and headed over. "Hey, dummy," she greeted. "Looking sharp."

"You too, little girl," he said.

She stuck her tongue out, but smiled about it.

Bethany hardly walked with a limp anymore. The ankle didn't heal correctly, but they'd gotten an orthopedist in a few months earlier, and he had some suggestions for how to help. Touré didn't know how much of a physical change there had been, but she certainly seemed to be in better spirits about it.

They exchanged a quick hug. It was a far cry from back in the early days when they wanted to strangle each other. But a lot had happened since then.

Touré couldn't help but notice how much Bethany was turning into an actual young adult. This became especially obvious once

Noah's collection of humans went from seasoned medical professionals and tenured scientists to genetically promising twenty- and thirty-somethings, because that was when Bethany became a regular member of the welcoming committee. More to the point, a lot of those twenty- and thirty-somethings noticed her too. She noticed them right back, although when Bethany flirted, she tended to stick to the women.

"How close are we?" she asked.

"Another half hour, I think."

"Cool. I'm gonna talk up Rhoda. Back in a bit."

She headed over to Rhoda, one of the nurse practitioners. Touré was nearly positive her name wasn't really Rhoda, but that was what she was calling herself now. She'd shown up almost a year back speaking only Urdu. Like all of them, she'd come a long way in a year, but that was especially obvious for the folks who'd arrived not knowing any English.

Touré double-checked the time and laughed, because the watch on his wrist had the answer, and that was a remarkable thing. It had taken forever to get watches working and showing the correct date and time again.

Noah had provided them with a year and a month, but not a day. Ananda was able to figure out what a calendar for 2127 looked like, but couldn't narrow it down to a specific day until the equinox. That involved recording the time of the sunrise and sunset every day, which required the use of a timepiece.

They had access to all the wind-up watches they wanted, but they were useless if nobody knew what time to set them for. However, Ananda just needed to record how *long* the day was; as long as she was using the same watch for both the sunrise and the sunset, nothing else mattered.

Frustratingly for Touré, finding the day of the equinox wasn't as simple as marking down the first time the day was exactly twelve hours long; it turned out that wasn't how equinoxes really worked. *We don't measure sunrise from when the middle of the sun first appears,* Ananda said. Then she never elaborated, which was just annoying.

But anyway, it worked eventually. As soon as she figured out when the days had officially started getting shorter, she had the month, day, and year, and even the correct time, and they were set.

Some time over the course of these internal musings, Robbie showed up behind Touré's bench.

"How much longer?" Robbie asked.

Touré didn't know he was there, so he jumped up and yelped in surprise. "Hey! Dude! A little warning!"

"Sorry."

"Ah, forget it."

Touré embraced his friend. "How you doing, man?" he asked. "You never come out for these."

"I know," Robbie said. "It's been a while."

Robbie looked thin and ashen, which was actually an improvement. He had on sunglasses to hide the fact that he wasn't getting a lot of sleep, which was also a step up; he got no sleep at all, for long stretches, for the first year after Noah. Then he and Touré stopped hanging out altogether, and Touré lost track of Robbie's sleep cycle. Presumably, it had improved.

"Yeah, you can use the sun," Touré said. "Get you running around, get the blood moving. How's Carol?"

"She's okay. Busy. We haven't talked lately, but you know."

"Sure."

Robbie and Carol were either on-again, off-again, or were just so used to each other's company that they didn't know how to undo that more permanently. Nobody was sure, and nobody knew how to ask.

Carol was active, certainly. She'd been helping clear out the coywolves from the neighborhood by domesticating entire packs. Nobody was quite sure how she was doing it, but it worked; there hadn't been an attack in thirteen months.

The pigs in Boston were a much larger problem. Win took the lead with that one, and she wasn't making pets. There was a long way to go before the whole city was livable, but in the meantime, they had plenty of pork to go around.

Thankfully, there was other food now too. Post-Noah arrivals who knew what they were doing started growing vegetables and fruit. Touré stopped worrying that he was going to die from scurvy.

Robbie stepped around the bench and sat down with Touré, just staring at the middle of the park. It was a good choice, this location. Even in the middle of winter. Touré used to wonder if Robbie picked it because it was only a few yards where the three of them had first met. He never did get around to asking.

"What's on your mind, man?" Touré asked. "Or do you just want to greet the new crew?"

"No, no, I'm not staying," Robbie said. "Just popped in for a quick . . . It's been a while since we talked, you and I."

"Sure has!"

"So . . . yeah. I've been thinking a lot. About that day."

He didn't need to explain what day he was talking about.

"Sure," Touré said.

Truthfully, that particular day was never far from Touré's mind, either. It was probably the last thing he thought of when he went to bed at night, and the first thing to wake him up in the morning —and sometimes in the middle of the night—and he knew for a fact he wasn't the only one who went through this.

Robbie, though . . . it'd hit him hardest.

"What about that day?" Touré asked.

"I was remembering that there were two of them," Robbie said. "At the end. Do you remember?"

"The Tachyonites. Yeah."

"I talked to Ananda. She thinks they were attempting to communicate at first. At first for *them*. You have to think about it backwards, right? The last time we saw them was the first time they saw us. There were two of them, and they were curious. What we saw after . . . was just one of them then. Trying to free the other one."

"It really doesn't help to dwell on this," Touré said. "You know that."

"Yeah, I know," Robbie said. "But they weren't aggressive. You understand? *We* did that."

"It wasn't us."

"Right."

"No, man, I mean it," Touré said. "*It wasn't us.* You can't let yourself think that way."

Robbie nodded just long enough to sell the point that he was going to keep right on dwelling on this.

Maybe we'll get a psychiatrist in this next batch, Touré thought.

"What do you tell them?" Robbie asked.

"Who?"

"The new recruits. What do you tell them?"

"Are you talking about the patter?" Touré asked. "It's pretty standard. Stick around and you'll hear it live. Unless you want me to do it for you now."

"I want to know what you tell them about what happened."

"Oh, that. We all agreed—"

"I know what we agreed."

"We agreed on a version of the truth," Touré said. "I tell them we were taken off the planet by an extraterrestrial, then came a great plague, and now the danger's over and it's time to rebuild. I mean, it's close. Enough so they don't dig too much further."

There had been a number of doctors who came through, heard this, and wanted to know the details of the plague that never actually happened. They were told not to worry about it, but at least a few would probably keep looking for an explanation. It couldn't be helped, but it wouldn't matter, since they weren't going to find anything where they were looking.

"Is that *exactly* what you tell them?" Robbie asked. "In those words."

"Maybe not those words, exactly."

"Rescued," Robbie said. "You tell them we were rescued. Don't you?"

Touré sighed.

"These people are *scared*, Robbie. Their world just got upended, and ... they want to believe something good happened and that now they're okay. They need a good story; it gives them hope."

"We agreed to never tell them what we did, because they wouldn't understand," Robbie said. "That's fine. But *do not* make him a hero. Okay? Promise me."

"I don't think that's what I'm doing."

"That's exactly what you're doing."

"Okay," Touré said. "I promise."

"Thank you." Robbie stood. "I have a meeting with the council. Come by for dinner, you and Win."

"Love to."

They shook hands.

"See you around," Touré said.

"Yeah, see you."

Robbie walked off. He was intercepted by Bethany, who gave him a quick hug on his way by. Then she gave Touré a *What's his deal these days?* shrug, and went back to what she was doing.

"It wasn't your fault, Robbie," Touré said. "We all did it together."

Robbie couldn't hear him, but it wouldn't matter if he had, because Robbie wouldn't have listened anyway.

Touré sighed and checked his watch again.

It was time.

A dark patch opened in the middle of the lawn, expanding quickly to the size of a school bus. Several of the people near the tables, even people who had seen this all before, gasped at the sight.

Then the shadow bubble popped out of existence, leaving behind ten people. They were spread out on the grass, asleep, unaware that their entire life was about to get turned upside down.

Touré jumped to his feet and picked up his megaphone.

Let's get this show started, he thought.

"WELCOME, EVERYONE!" he said. "IT'S THE YEAR 2129, AND BOY DO I HAVE A STORY FOR YOU!"

ACKNOWLEDGMENTS

I had to lean on a number of people in order to get this story out of my head. Some provided expertise I didn't have, some acted as a sounding board and/or quietly put up with me, and a few did a little of both.

For the technical stuff: John Blackwell, who provided me with answers to my many astronomical questions; David Wallace-Wells, who does not know me, but who wrote the invaluable and terrifying *The Uninhabitable Earth;* and the Friends of the Blue Hills Reservation—specifically the ranger whose name I have tragically forgotten, but who was willing to answer a long list of rather outlandish questions during what was supposed to be a company outing.

For putting up with me: my coworkers Nikki Durand, Kevin Wong, Noam Katz, Shane Dwyer, and Hongshuang Li. Specifically, Kevin for mentioning the wild boars of Fukushima, Nikki for talking me out of a half-dozen titles, and Noam for confirming that MIT really does have a tunnel system. You guys let me rant on about the apocalypse on the company's time and nobody called HR or anything, so thank you.

Thanks to my editor, John Joseph Adams, for thinking "it looked like Robbie slept through the apocalypse" was a decent place to start, and Jaime Levine of HMH, for answering every random question with a sincere "Let's go find out."

And finally, thanks to my wife, Deb, who has spent years walking around Cambridge and Boston with me, little knowing that half the time, in my head, I was saying, *What if ALL these people were just . . . gone?* And just for putting up with me, in general.